From the Prairies With Hope

Jane L. Aberson

Edited by Robert E. VanderVennen
Introduced by Mark Boekelman

Canadian Plains Research Center
University of Regina
1991

Canadian Plains Research Center
University of Regina
Regina, Saskatchewan S4S 0A2
Canada

∞

Printed on acid-free paper

Canadian Cataloguing in Publication Data

Aberson, Jane L., 1900-

From the Prairies with hope

(Canadian plains studies, ISSN 0317-6290 ; 21)
Translation of: Van de canadeesche Velden.
Edited by Robert VanderVennen
ISBN 0-88977-064-6

1. Aberson, Jane, 1900-   – Correspondence.
2. Pioneers – Manitoba – Correspondence. 3. Dutch –
Manitoba – Correspondence. 4. Frontier and pioneer
life – Manitoba. I. VanderVennen, Robert.
II. University of Regina. Canadian Plains Research
Center. III. Title. IV. Series.

FC3375.1.A23A413 1991   971.27/02/092   C91-097129-3
F1063.A23A413 1991

Cover design: Brian Mlazgar/Agnes Bray
Cover photo: Jane L. Aberson, 1937

Printed and Bound in Canada by
Hignell Printing Limited, Winnipeg, Manitoba

Contents

Illustrations

(Between pages 94 and 95)

Bob and Jane Aberson, 1979

Sunday morning at the Dawson Place log cabin, 1926

The Aberson farm, 1927

The tobaggan to school

The tennis court serves as a hockey rink in winter

Log cabin in the Riding Mountains — cutting wood for the winter

The Aberson family, 1977 (left to right: Bob Jr., Wim, Jane, Bob Sr., Dirk)

Preface

About five years after our arrival in Canada in 1924 I started writing our impressions of the new world. By 1929 conditions had greatly changed all over the world. The Dutch had become greatly interested in emigration to Canada. I wrote letters in Dutch at regular intervals and had no difficulty in getting them published in the Netherlands. In fact, during the Depression I made several trips to the Netherlands to give talks about Canada sponsored by *Het Nieuwsblad van het Noorden* (*The Northern Daily*) and the organization Nederland-Canada. My aim was to give a firsthand account of the conditions as we saw them and to tell people what to expect in case they decided to make the move to Canada.

People in the Netherlands knew about our untypical background and that we had changed to a very different kind of life on the prairies, which made our Canadian experience all the more interesting to them.

In 1979 I decided to translate these letters and their stories. It proved quite an enterprise, but my husband Bob was willing to help me. Translation of my work seemed important to me because it would enable our three sons to read the letters in a language they understood well. They still can speak a bit of Dutch but have difficulty reading the language.

Another reason for translating the letters was that 1929 was now so far in the past — fifty years already — that a new generation had grown up in Canada that did not know anything about the conditions and the hardships people experienced during "the Dirty Thirties." The interest in multiculturalism we hear so much about today also influenced my decision to translate the letters.

I think it would be of interest to start with a short resumé about our life in the old country. We were brought up in carefree financial circumstances, which greatly influenced our outlook on life on this side of the ocean. What others might consider as a hardship we often saw as a big adventure, some tall tale to write home about. I will not say that we did not have difficult times, but the contrast and the adventure of life on the prairies made it an experience we would not like to have missed. We learned to love Canada and its people and have never been sorry we made the move.

Bob and I were high school sweethearts. We both lost our fathers in our teens, our mothers moved to the same city, we lived on the same street and we attended the same high school. After graduation

Bob undertook studies in trade and commerce. I tried different things and ended up in physical education. After Bob finished his studies he took a position with a large bank in Batavia (present-day Jakarta) on the island of Java in the Dutch East Indies. I stayed behind in the Netherlands.

Being engaged to be married but living on opposite sides of the globe is not very stimulating. It took two months to get an answer to a letter, and after a year we had had enough of it. Bob asked me to come over and get married. So I terminated my studies, took passage on a boat to the Orient and after a very adventurous journey I arrived in Calcutta, British India, where Bob had been transferred. We got married there with no relatives present. Nevertheless, people from seven different nationalities attended our wedding, and the native servants wore Dutch flags in their turbans in honour of the occasion. Now we started a life that in every way was totally different from the life we would lead later in Canada.

The young employees at the bank were very often transferred to learn all aspects of banking. Consequently we left Calcutta after half a year and were sent back on a freighter to Java. We were the only passengers on this ship and, moreover, I was the only woman aboard. When we crossed the equator I was the only one who had never crossed it before and the crew organized a big feast. We were given the cabin of one of the officers and we had our meals at the officers' table. It was a wonderful experience, especially since my father had been a commander on a warship in the Orient before he got married. I knew him only as burgomaster of a Dutch town, but I was brought up on tales of the sea and life on a ship. Now I found out a bit about what it must have been like.

We were transferred to Samarang, a city in central Java. It was beautiful there, but it did not take Bob long to find out that he had chosen the wrong profession. He simply detested office work and he shuddered at the idea that he would have to do this for the rest of his life. He started to read books about agriculture and became more and more interested in it. His contract with the bank ran for three years, and when his time was up we decided to return to the Netherlands and inquire about opportunities in farming.

However, when we broached this subject with our relatives, we met with great opposition. "Both of you are totally unsuited to this kind of work," they protested. They said to Bob, "Even if you have a very good set of muscles, developed by playing tennis and rowing boats, don't think for a moment that you are qualified to do the hard work required on a farm."

"And you," they said to me, "you have never had the slightest interest in housekeeping, you never cooked in your life, and you have been waited on hand and foot until now. You would be utterly useless on a farm."

Well, we were stubborn and did not want to give up. We got in touch with the Department of Emigration in The Hague and asked their opinion.

When we got to The Hague we saw a large billboard with a picture of a farm in Canada. It was a beautiful poster. A golden grain field waving in the breeze, a young farmer in a white shirt behind a beautiful set of horses, a young wife with a baby in her arms bringing a basket of goodies to the field. It was extremely tempting.

However, the reply to our inquiry from the Department of Emigration brought us down a notch. "We do not see anything feasible in your plans to start farming," they wrote us. "You do not have the background, the know-how and, most likely, not the stamina to become farmers. We advise you strongly to forget these plans and go back to the work for which you are trained."

Well, that made us think for a moment and, as a result, Bob started to apply again for an office job. But it was only a few years after World War I, and jobs were scarce. Nevertheless he succeeded in landing a job with a large shipping firm in Piraeus, Greece; but, the job fell through because the company was forced to close the office. After that he was accepted by a firm in the cotton trade in Alexandria, Egypt; but, the cotton trade collapsed and this office was also closed.

That settled it. Bob had had enough. His passport was still valid so he booked passage for himself on a ship and the destination was Canada. In the meantime I had become the mother of a little boy, Bob, Jr., which was the reason my husband thought it wiser to start out alone. If he succeeded in finding something to his liking, he planned to send for us.

I could write a book about his first experiences as a hired farm hand, which he realized was the only way he could learn the business from the bottom up. The letters I received during that first year were a mixture of sentiment about the beauty of the Canadian landscape and a nagging doubt about whether I would fit in. In addition his experience turned out to be very different from the picture we had seen on that poster in The Hague. I had better prepare myself to go back in history about a hundred years, he wrote me. Electricity and running water, which I had taken for granted all my life, were not to be found on most Canadian farms. I would have to get used to coal oil lamps and a pump outside — if I was lucky. Many had to haul water from a distance. It was very hot in the summer and very cold in the winter, but the weather was a lot more cheerful than the climate in the Netherlands.

Finally Bob wrote me that he had an opportunity to rent a small place, and he asked me if I was game to risk it. He expected me to come to Canada the beginning of August 1924, just about a year after his own arrival. He was now working on a nice large farm near Dauphin, Manitoba, and the lady of the house was willing to break me in, which meant that she would teach me how to cook and bake, and how to preserve fruit and can vegetables, and so on.

After spending about two months on the big farm, we moved to the small farm Bob had written me about. It proved to be a very isolated place, surrounded by dense bush. Our home was an old log cabin, but we fixed it up to be very cozy. There was a clearing of about thirty acres around the house and in that clearing Bob practiced farming. In the log cabin I learned to cook and bake, to wash clothes in an old washtub and to plant a garden. I also gave birth in the log cabin to our second son, Wim — a harrowing experience since we had no telephone and were far removed from neighbours. We survived it all, however, and my only regret was that our family lived so far away and could not see us.

I wrote long letters to my mother about all our experiences, and through these letters the thought was born to start writing stories about our Canadian life. These letters made the rounds of the family and were also read by an uncle of mine who was a language teacher in the Netherlands. He told my mother they were worth publishing, and that his judgement on this should be taken seriously.

However, I did not begin to write letters for publication right away. It seemed we were far too busy and had to learn so many new things. We soon began to realize that making a living in Canada on a small farm was far from easy. Prices were low, crops did not always come up to expectations, and many of the ventures we embarked on with livestock often proved disappointing. Suddenly the thought of making a few extra dollars writing about life in Canada looked very appealing. By this time I had really started to love the country, but I wanted to get even with that misleading picture we had seen on the poster in The Hague. Canada was a wonderful country and needed no extra embellishments. So I made up my mind to describe things in the way we saw them ourselves. This is all history now. Five years after I arrived in Canada I started to write letters home for publication, and I have learned a lot in those years.

Jane L. Aberson

Acknowledgements

This book has had a long period of gestation. It grew out of a research project initiated by the Multicultural History Society of Ontario to collect ethnocultural research material for deposit in the Archives of Ontario. In the course of his work as a researcher with the society, Mark Boekelman, a graduate student at the University of Toronto, discovered my letters which had been published in Dutch in the 1930s. He contacted me in Dauphin, Manitoba, in 1979 and with infectious enthusiasm insisted that I translate the letters into English for the benefit of future generations of Canadians. His interest led to a lengthy correspondence between us.

These letters were first introduced to an English-speaking audience by Dr. Boekelman in 1980 at a conference he organized at the University of Toronto on the history of Dutch immigration to North America. At that conference he gave a paper with the title "The Letters of Jane Aberson, Everyday Life on the Prairies during the Depression: How Immigration Turns Conservatives into Social Democrats." This appears in the proceedings of the conference, published in 1983 by the Multicultural History Society of Ontario as *Dutch Immigration to North America*, edited and introduced by Herman Ganzevoort and Mark Boekelman.

A major portion of my English text was edited to conform to English usage by Mark with the able assistance of Anne McCarthy, associate editor of the Multicultural History Society of Ontario. But the demands of Mark's career and family intervened, and the project ground to a halt for a time.

I acknowledge with thanks a publication grant-in-aid from the Department of the Secretary of State. I also gratefully acknowledge financial assistance provided from the Canadian Netherlands Heritage Fund of the Canadian Netherlands Business and Professional Association toward the preparation of this book for publication.

I am profoundly grateful to Dr. Robert VanderVennen, who used his professional skill and experience as a member of the editorial and production staff of the Institute for Christian Studies to see the work through to completion. I wish also to thank those whose comments on earlier versions of the text and of Mark's "Introduction" resulted in many improvements. They include Professor Jean R. Burnet and the late Professor Robert Harney of the

Multicultural History Society of Ontario, and Jerry Hallowel of the University of Toronto Press.

Finally, I acknowledge the contribution of Brian Mlazgar and Agnes Bray, of the Canadian Plains Research Center, for their assistance in designing and proofreading the book.

In the spirit of hope I wish to dedicate this book to all the people who have made it possible for the next generation to appreciate what life was like not so long ago, but under circumstances very different from those today.

Jane L.S. Aberson
Dauphin, Manitoba
July 1991

Introduction

by Mark Boekelman

Jane Aberson's newspaper articles document the everyday life of a Dutch immigrant family farming on the prairies six miles from Dauphin, Manitoba, during the Depression. They were published in Dutch from 1929 to 1966 as a special feature in *Het Nieuwsblad van het Noorden* (*The Northern Daily*), a regional large-circulation daily newspaper in the northern part of the Netherlands. The articles contain a continuous record, except for the war years, of the settlement experience of an immigrant family for thirty years. Those written between 1929 and 1936 were published in book form in two volumes entitled *Van de Canadeesche Velden.*[1]

At the age of eighty the author translated into English this particular set of articles covering the years 1929-36. The articles have been edited and abridged to remove detail that may have been essential for a Dutch readership but not for the Canadian public.

Kathleen Strange, writing for the *Family Herald and Weekly Star* in 1947, was the first to suggest that these articles deserved recognition in Canada. She wrote, "This talented farm woman may not be very well known in Canada as yet, but some day soon her stories will undoubtedly be translated into English and published here and it should be most interesting, and possibly very enlightening, to see how we Western Canadians appear through a Dutch woman's eyes!"[2]

Jane Aberson was featured in the Canada section of *Time* magazine in 1947 and recognized as a correspondent who had become "quite a propagandist for Canada" and "one of the most popular woman writers" in her part of the Netherlands, the province of Groningen.[3] In Canada, however, she never gained the recognition she experienced in her native land.

Jane Aberson was born Jane Uges in Stadskanaal, Groningen, in the municipality of Wildervank, on 7 April 1900. Her father was an officer with the Royal Dutch Navy and later became burgomaster of Wildervank. She was the oldest of three children. Her brother Hugo studied engineering at the University of Delft and became a director of the Netherlands Post and Telecommunications network (the PTT). Her younger brother Dirk pursued a career in business and married into a prominent New York family.

Jane met her future husband Bob while attending high school in the city of Groningen. She studied physical education and English after high school, but followed her fiance to Calcutta where they were married in 1921. Subsequently they moved to the Dutch East Indies (Indonesia), and returned to the Netherlands before coming to Canada, Bob in 1924 and Jane in 1925.

Bob Aberson was born in 1899 in Leeuwarden, the Netherlands, the son of the local postmaster of Gorredyk and Winsum. Bob became an accountant and consistently sought overseas employment. He worked for three years for the Nederlandse Handels Maatschappy (Dutch Trading Company) in India and in Indonesia. Returning to the Netherlands he worked for a local bank in The Hague (Muller and Company) where his request to be transferred to a foreign office was turned down.

In the 1920s the Canadian government was seeking prospective settlers throughout Europe to take up homesteads and populate the vast prairie provinces.[4] Advertising campaigns included newspaper advertising and large billboards. Bob Aberson decided to go to Canada to become a farmer after seeing a poster portraying a man in a white shirt and overalls, arms stretched wide, with the bold slogan, "Canada, My Land." Emigration authorities advised him against going to Canada to farm, pointing out that he had no background in farming. They advised him to continue his career at the bank.

Nevertheless he left his wife and child behind and with trepidation made the decision that changed his life — to emigrate and work as an inexperienced farm hand in Manitoba for one dollar a day. During his first winter in Canada, 1924-25, he attended agricultural college in Winnipeg, where he met the son of a farm family, the Durstons. They became Bob's first employer and later helped the Abersons establish themselves until they were able to purchase their own farm in 1928, where they lived into their old age.

During the first years, starting in 1925, Bob Aberson worked at the Durston farm several miles away and came home only on weekends, while Jane stayed behind with her son in an isolated log cabin. Their first crop failed, and the following year world markets collapsed, the great Depression started, and many farmers abandoned their farms and moved to the cities. Only the strong and stubborn and frugal stayed on the land, and it was not until twenty-five years later, after World War II, that the Abersons were able to make a reasonable living from their farm. Mr. Aberson credits his wife with their survival during those difficult years; he is quoted as saying, "Jane dared and showed initiative, courage and perseverance in the face of adversity."[5]

The editor of *Het Nieuwsblad van het Noorden* had asked Bob Aberson to consider writing a column about agricultural conditions in Canada, but instead it was his wife Jane who decided to try her hand at journalism to earn extra money. She became a "special correspondent" whom the paper asked to feature life on the Canadian prairies. The newspaper was the largest in northeastern Netherlands. Its readership was equally divided between rural and city people, with its urban readers concentrated in the major cities of Groningen, Emmen, Assen and Hoogeveen. Today its circulation is 140,000. Its present managing director is Mr. Hans Aberson, a nephew of Bob Aberson.

In 1929 Jane Aberson began what was to become a thirty-seven-year series with the simple words, "Now the winter has set in and the field work is done for at least six months, I will have time to tell you something about conditions here." In the years to come she became the mainstay of realistic advice for prospective Dutch immigrants.

Her column entitled "From the Canadian Prairies" appeared bi-monthly in her home town daily, with newspaper sales normally rising by 50,000 on the days her column appeared. In her articles she gave a personal account of her family's activities on the farm, living conditions in Canada and life in a small prairie community. The articles are characterized by their simplicity and direct approach towards the problems and events of everyday life. "From the Canadian Prairies" was rated the best feature of the paper and drew inquiries about Canada from readers throughout the Netherlands and as far away as Australia, Indonesia and Africa.

The theme of "mayor's daughter turned farmer's wife to change the wilderness into a model farm" caught the imagination of her readership and reinforced the Calvinist values of "struggle and victory" cherished by the northern Dutch. She dispensed a homespun philosophy to explain their success in the face of adversity — work as hard as you can but do it with optimism. She interpreted immigration as an epic venture — a "tall tale," literally true, worth sharing with friends in the old country whose lives seemed mundane and predictable.

Jane Aberson pictured life in Canada as difficult but interesting. She endured the disappointments and setbacks of Canadian farmers during the Depression without losing sight of the simple joys of family and community life. Mrs. Aberson's Canada demanded hard work merely to survive. She held that success in farming was not so much dependent on an agricultural background as on an attitude of indestructible optimism and enthusiasm. The most important lesson of her articles lies in the courage with which the difficulties and disappointments of one immigrant farmer's family were faced.[6]

In 1936, while convalescing in the Netherlands from cancer treatment she received in Winnipeg, Mrs. Aberson thought about ways of earning money to cover her expenses. She decided to give presentations about life in Canada based on photos she had sent her mother from Canada over the years, from which she made a series of slides.

"Mrs. Aberson-Uges speaks about Canada" was the simple text of the announcement in the Groningen daily paper. She spoke to sold-out crowds wherever she appeared, and her honoraria substantially improved the Abersons' financial situation. "We needed the money," she said quite frankly. "Things in Canada did not go that well." The local press reported that "she is overwhelmed with invitations to speak, and when she speaks in the city of Groningen there is not a place big enough to satisfy the demand for tickets, while at every repeat performance tickets are being fought over." She received more than a hundred invitations to speak about farm life on the Canadian prairies, and gave thirty-three presentations.

The publication of her articles in book form was prompted by the success of her lecture tour and coincided with her lengthy stay in the Netherlands. The first edition of 10,000 copies of her book was sold out in one month, and the second edition was sold out shortly after it appeared as well. Several months after her departure a second volume appeared.

We may wonder why such an enormous interest existed in both the articles and her presentations about Canada. As the author of a popular newspaper column, she had developed a devoted audience among both rural and urban Dutch in the northern part of the Netherlands. Mrs. Aberson's "tall tales" of struggle and victory satisfied a deep need for vicarious living. One letter to the editor expressed another side to the success of her tour — "The articles and slides gave an invaluable insight for aspiring colonists."

In 1948, eleven years after her visit to the Netherlands and after having lived and worked in Canada for twenty-three years, Mrs. Aberson returned to the Netherlands for a second time. The farm had by now been built up to 320 acres, including woodlots, and they had seventeen cows, 400 chickens and ten pigs. Her tour lasted for five months, and the proceeds enabled the Abersons to buy another farm. She gave eighty-one presentations at places which included major centres like Amsterdam, Rotterdam, The Hague, Utrecht and Groningen. She also visited with parents of war brides who had been the first Dutch immigrants to Canada after the war. Her popularity had increased from her first visit, and her first speaking engagement was sold out in ten minutes.

Dutch interest in Canada was at an all-time high in the aftermath of the liberation of the Netherlands by the Canadian Armed Forces. What impressed Jane the most in 1948 was the realization that so many of her countrymen were prepared to emigrate. She saw that especially the younger generation felt an overwhelming pessimism about the future. In response to the urgent desire of many Dutch to emigrate after the war, her second tour was more explicitly directed towards acquainting prospective emigrants to Canada with the conditions they would face. Upon her return to Canada she reported that Canadians were "immensely popular" in the Netherlands, and that the Dutch showed "a great understanding of Canada because they had met so many Canadian troops during the last war."[7]

Jane Aberson's second lecture tour about Canadian farm life brought her official recognition from Dutch authorities who saw emigration as a solution to the pressure on scarce resources during the period of postwar reconstruction. Canada restricted immigration immediately after the war to people who would settle on farms for at least one year. During the postwar years there was a major exodus of large rural families from the northern part of the Netherlands to take up farming in Canada. Mrs. Aberson's second lecture tour could not have been more timely. The lieutenant governor of the province of Groningen lauded her initiative and was "convinced that nothing strengthens the . . . bonds between Holland and Canada more than [her] lectures." He hoped that in the future Mrs. Aberson would be able to devote herself exclusively to the creation of "good will."[8]

Similarly the president of the Agricultural League, H.D. Louwes, in writing to the Canadian ambassador to the Netherlands, P. Dupuis, pointed out that "her articles have drawn an extraordinary interest and thousands of people . . . attended the lectures." In the aftermath of the war, when Dutch feelings of appreciation and affection towards Canada ran high, she was considered "an ambassadress in extraordinary service" laying the "foundations for the revival of . . . friendship between . . . two nations."[9]

In 1953, almost thirty years after she had left the Netherlands and five years after her second trip, Mrs. Aberson returned for a third time, this time in the company of her husband. Emigration to Canada had reached an all-time high. From January until Easter she gave sixty-one presentations to full houses, and again her amazing tales about Canada met with overwhelming interest. One of the tasks she faced during this tour was to squelch the notion that was widespread in the Netherlands at the time that the war brides had married into marginal elements of Canadian society, rather than men of respectable occupations and professions.

"Mrs. Aberson was and still is very well known," writes Mr. Hans Aberson from Groningen in a letter dated 22 January 1990. "Even after so many years — she wrote her last article in the early 1960s — older people still ask me if I am a relative of Mrs. Aberson."

Time magazine reported on 30 June 1947 that "her articles have not always been flattering to Canada." It was precisely this critical aspect of her writing that earned her a reputation as one of the few authoritative interpreters of Canadian farm life from the point of view of a Dutch immigrant. She recognized the traumatic fact that immigrants can never entirely forget their attachment to the old country. But she also highlighted the opportunities and adventures of beginning anew in a country 240 times the size of the Netherlands. As Kathleen Strange wrote, "There was always present between her lines what she once wrote: 'My husband has just turned on the radio, and we are entertained with stories about strikes, fights, dishonesty and famine in other countries. What a world! I am glad we are in Canada after all.' "[10]

Until their eighties Mr. and Mrs. Aberson still lived on the farm they bought in 1928. In 1973, when they were both in their seventies, the Abersons retired from farming and leased their land. In their eighties they moved from the farm to an apartment in Dauphin. All three sons have left the farm to pursue professional careers. Mrs. Aberson has outlived her husband, who died in March 1990, at the age of ninety.

It is telling that their success as farmers on the prairies owed much to the abilities of Mr. and Mrs. Aberson to use their professional skills to supplement their farm income. Bob had some income as an accountant and financial advisor and Jane was a journalist and lecturer as well as manager of the credit union which they founded and ran for many years from their home. Jane says, "We had a wonderful life on the farm, but we made our money with writing and with running a credit union."[11]

The articles of Jane Aberson are among the few instances of social-historical writing that do not reflect a British settler's point of view. The best-known contributions to the social-historical literature of Canadian immigration have been made by British immigrants and visitors writing about their experiences in Ontario and the west. These include Susanna Moodie's *Roughing It in the Bush*,

Anna Brownell Jameson's *Winter Studies and Summer Rambles in Canada*, Catharine Parr Traill's *The Backwoods of Canada*, and Georgina Binnie-Clark's *Wheat and Woman*.[12] Although these are valuable studies, they tend to perpetuate the myth of Canada as a homogeneous outpost of British civilization, and to contribute to the erroneous view held by new immigrants themselves that Canada's polyglot character emerged only after the mass influx of Europeans and Asians into Canada during the 1950s and 1960s.

The written social-historical record of continental European and Asian settlers in Canada is somewhat sparse, and the translation and publication of this literature is long overdue. Only recently have social historians and social scientists begun to deal with a variety of alternate Canadian sensibilities which harbour attitudes and values which are often at odds with the predominant ideological legacy of the Victorian era, that is, the Anglo-Canadian world view.

Dutch settlers in Canada have made a modest contribution to this alternate social-historical literature, chiefly in the form of letters back to the old country. In addition to the Aberson articles, the letters of Willem de Gelder, written between 1910 and 1913, and the letters of Frans van Waterstadt, written between April 1927 and April 1929,[13] are valuable sources for the study of Dutch immigration to Canada.

These Dutch letters are analagous to the Canadian immigrant letters written by British settlers. Like the English letters they were valuable in their own right as practical information for prospective immigrants from the Lowlands, but their detailed descriptions of the land and everyday life recapture for Canadians today the immigrant reactions to Canada of some who did not come from the British Isles.

In the United States there is a corresponding body of literature consisting of Dutch letters. Examples include *Letters from Amsterdam Emigrants*, edited by Johan Stellingwerff; the recent publication of *Write Back Soon*, translated and edited by Herbert Brinks; and, Gordon Oosterman's *To Find a Better Life*. Often these letters reveal the religious context of Dutch American ethnicity. Many other Dutch American works have not found an English language publisher but have been well received in the Netherlands.[14]

When Jane Aberson began writing articles for publication five years after her arrival in Canada, she intended to share the ups and downs of everyday life during the Depression with her readers in Groningen, the Netherlands, without thought of the socio-historical value her work might have one day, and without any thought that her writings might be published anywhere but in the daily paper back home. In addition to showing the need for courage in the struggle to survive, an analysis of her articles reveals three major themes: first, that downward social mobility fosters a tendency towards more liberal democratic social and political values; second, that ethnocultural diversity and the acceptance of other ethnic groups among immigrants was a way of life long before multiculturalism became government policy; and third, that social and cultural customs and traditions of the old country persist in spite of the pervasive influence of the North American way of life.

Politics and Social Class

As noted above, Jane Aberson did not fit into the common pattern of working class and farm labour Dutch emigration. Like Willem de Gelder she came from the upper class. Her social background was much like that of the British female chroniclers of pioneer conditions who had preceded her. Like them she was well educated for her time, a genteel woman more at home in the drawing room than on a Canadian farm that was still waiting to be carved out of the wilderness.

During her lecture tour Jane Aberson had been appropriately characterized as "a salon fähige [at ease in the drawing room] young lady rather than a pioneer farmer's wife."[15] Her great grandfather on her father's side was a judge in Winschoten. Her grandfather became the municipal secretary of the town of Stedum. Members of her mother's side of the family had been lumber merchants for generations. She wrote about herself, "In Holland we belonged to what they call the notabelen [notables]. It is the social class of doctors, lawyers, ministers, public officials and also the big industrialists."[16] In all respects the Abersons' background was at odds with a life in agriculture.

The Abersons were among a type of immigrant that could best be characterized as adventurers and idealists. Emigration represented for them the plans and dreams of a young couple to start a totally different kind of life.[17] The Abersons' relatives had been confounded by their plans to emigrate to Canada as pioneering farmers, to exchange a comfortable Dutch upper-class life, a carefree young adulthood, a well-paid position and standing in the community for a pioneer existence in a log cabin on a small farm in the bush. Her son Dirk Aberson (he was nicknamed Dick, which is the name used in the letters) writes about his parents' decision to emigrate in terms of loss on their part, and opportunity and gain for their children:

> My parents were both idealists and adventurers. Unfortunately, in order for them both to remain in the social structure to which they

were born, it would have been better if they had been realists and academics. Fortunately for myself and my brothers, adventure won out, and my parents set sail for Canada.[18]

The Abersons were not forced to leave their native land due to political or religious persecution, economic deprivation or a host of other reasons that are often associated with emigration patterns. Their romantic, idealistic nature comes through when years later Jane wrote that "those first years seem to me one long string of sunny days. Our lonesome primitive home at the foot of the mountains with nothing other than dense bush around us — how romantic it was! We felt like Adam and Eve must have felt in Paradise when we ran to our outside bath in the river.... Deer and elk sometimes stood like statues watching us at the edge of the bush...."[19]

With the advent of the Depression and the failure of their first year's crop, idealism and adventure were tempered by the harsh reality of living on the prairies, and the Abersons began to identify strongly with the plight of western Canadians, among whom were immigrants from many countries, particularly from Eastern Europe. At the Aberson farm people called who were literally starving. What the Depression meant for wheat farmers economically, with the drastic drop in market prices, Mrs. Aberson carefully recorded. She documented that even a good harvest meant big financial losses.

Immigration and settlement during the Depression affected Aberson's social consciousness, which she expressed as a commitment to social democratic reform and the cooperative movement. In the Netherlands she and her husband had held conservative political values as members of the upper class, but "their views . . . moved steadily in a more socialistic direction," reports their son Dirk. Dirk Aberson also notes in this connection, "By their own admission, they paid little attention to politics while growing up in Europe. The result of this awareness was that they both became involved in the co-operative movement. They supported the co-op grain elevator concept, the co-operative stores, and they organized and operated the Spruce Credit Union in Dauphin. This financial institution is still flourishing today. It was headquartered in our home and managed jointly by my parents well into the 1970s."[20] In 1976 its assets were $1.5 million.[21]

For thirty years Jane Aberson managed the credit union, retiring from it in 1973 at the age of 73. She took great satisfaction from being instrumental in pooling the limited financial resources of Dauphin farmers, and Bob Aberson was able to put to good use his early training as an accountant and his experience in banking.

Settling on the prairies rather than in eastern Canada meant that the Abersons were influenced by prairie populism and the radicalism of the 1930s. Jane Aberson was strongly influenced by such CCF founders as Stanley Knowles, J.S. Woodsworth and M.J. Coldwell.

During the Depression immigrants learned their political economy from what they saw around them. Jane Aberson saw desperate families starting the winter with barely enough food and clothing, and municipalities on the verge of bankruptcy because many farmers had not paid their taxes and their farms were being put up for tax sale.[22] Her accounts of young Canadian men who roamed the country from coast to coast in search of work and food became familiar to her Dutch readers.[23]

She shared the feeling of exploitation by the eastern establishment held by many western Canadians, but she was not sure that the new socialist party, the CCF, could bring much change.[24] Strong appeals were made over the radio and in the newspapers for people to assist all the victims of the Depression, and Jane Aberson supported the new party that proposed drastic changes to alleviate the hardship of farmers. She reported to her readers in the Netherlands, with gentle restraint, about the formation of Canada's socialist party, the CCF.[25]

Prairie radicalism, as the name Co-operative Commonwealth Federation indicates, came to be expressed in the cooperative movement which included grain elevators, department stores, insurance cooperatives and credit unions. Jane Aberson defended the cooperative initiatives and the subordination of individualism for the common good of all farmers. Critics of the cooperative movement charged that this cooperation implied the loss of freedom,[26] but she wrote that freedom is a relative idea and that in the absence of any participation in the decision-making process of the pricing of products by the producer such freedom is merely a deceptive ideology, particularly when a mortgage encumbers the producer's property in excess of market value.[27]

Mrs. Aberson's view of life was influenced by the social norms of her Dutch upbringing. Her reactions to the New World focussed to a large extent on the novelty of a more open and democratic and less class-ridden society which she found on the Canadian prairies. Georgina Binnie-Clark, who preceeded Jane Aberson, also noted the relative absence of class distinctions, describing her neighbours as hard working and "united in a solemn hatred of class distinction."[28]

Having been brought up "in very carefree circumstances" by parents whose social positions "put them in the top brackets of their communities," Mrs. Aberson wrote that her parents nevertheless were not considered "what we could call stuck-up over here."[29] In time she made the western Canadian lifestyle her own, but not before she had shared her initial Dutch reactions with her readers in the Netherlands. She wrote that she was amazed at how jovially the public and store personnel mingled, and how personally they greeted her when she shopped and even inquired about the health of her family.[30] She felt that western Canadians were not as stiff and formal as people in the Netherlands. She observed the different social customs with a keen Dutch eye, but implicitly favoured the more liberal and democratic ideas and attitudes she found in Canada, which were in marked contrast to the stratified social class divisions in the Netherlands in the 1920s. For example, in the Netherlands manual work had been associated exclusively with the lower classes. Dutch social protocol dictated that members of the middle and upper classes did not engage in manual labour.[31] So she was astonished when one harvest crew at their farm included local farmers, Ukrainians, Natives and even the local member of Parliament, who was simply called Bill by everyone.[32]

Jane Aberson was acutely aware of the transformation of social consciousness that had taken place in her since she had emigrated to Canada. In her articles she recalled a more self-indulgent lifestyle in the East Indies where she employed four servants, and in the Netherlands where she had one girl in her service.[33] At her parental home she was not taught to cook because there were servants to do such things.[34]

Jane Aberson by and large accepted the more egalitarian lifestyle of the prairies. However, she was also aware that in Canada egalitarianism was often superficial and restricted to everyday social interchange, while subtle and covert class distinction prevailed in clubs and societies. Comparing Canada and the Netherlands, she concluded that everything seemed much more free and easy than at home and that Dutch immigrants had better forget about the social distinctions they grew up with in the Netherlands.[35]

During the Depression the Abersons welcomed many young Dutchmen who had come to western Canada to build a future for themselves, but who instead had to face the grim reality of poverty. Young men from all parts of the Netherlands and from various social backgrounds sought a temporary refuge at the Aberson home. We know very little about them other than what Jane Aberson records. She wrote about both working-class emigrants in search of economic opportunity and middle- and upper-class youths who were unable to live up to the unrealistic expectations of their parents or to accept the social conventions of their society in the old country. For some of them emigration meant a sort of voluntary exile. Regardless of social background, occupation or skill, those who passed through Dauphin and were brought to the Aberson farm found it hard to get a start in Canada during the Depression, and economic conditions left many destitute.[36]

Multiculturalism

The articles of Jane Aberson reveal, in addition to the adjustment of political and social values, attitudes towards other ethnocultural groups. Manitoba, and particularly Dauphin, became a microcosm of a polyglot society with a power structure based on ethnicity.[37] Dauphin owed its growth to the coming of the railway to the district in 1896. The terminal became a new gateway to the north. The period 1887-97 saw the formative years of the province as "adapting institutions, of making the new land and the new peoples British and Canadian."[38]

The dominant group which exercised power in business and government in the area since 1880 hailed from British Ontario. In manners, speech and social outlook this group sought to enforce the assimilation of all who had preceded them, the French and Natives, and those who came after them: the Scottish, Irish, Welsh, English, followed by Scandinavian, Polish, Mennonite, German, Icelandic, and finally East European settlers.

The bourgeois values of the Victorian Ontario English were characterized by direct reserved manners and speech, self-control, disdain of showing emotions and feelings, emphasis on moral virtues, material success and ancestral roots. Ethnocentricity had been developed into its highest form by the Anglo-Ontarians, giving Manitoba its character. But by 1930 Manitoba had grown into a heterogeneous population of 700,000 consisting of a multitude of distinct ethnocultural communities.

East European settlers had been the last large group to settle on the prairies. They were often regarded as second-class citizens by the WASP element of society.[39] The Abersons lived in a virtually Anglo-Saxon enclave, but the larger district included settlers of many other national backgrounds, particularly East Europeans, or Galicians, as they were called.[40] The one-room school reflected the ethnocultural composition of Dauphin.[41]

Dirk Aberson, commenting on the attitude of his parents towards other ethnocultural groups, remarked that "it was their whole-hearted acceptance of these people that helped reshape the thinking of the less liberal-minded members of our community at that time."[42]

The Abersons accepted and practiced acceptance of people of other nationalities long before multiculturalism had become governmental policy. They lived predominantly among East Europeans in the larger community and had formed positive opinions about them which contrasted sharply with the low esteem in which Anglo-Saxon settlers held the East Europeans. About half the population of the greater Dauphin area was of Galician, Ukrainian, Russian, Ruthenian or Polish background, people who maintained their customs and language in the home. Mrs. Aberson noted the contempt with which these people were treated.[43]

The Abersons' high opinion of the East Europeans is consistent with the attitude of Willem de Gelder, who three decades earlier exhibited a positive attitude towards East European settlers. De Gelder's comparison of the East European and Anglo-Saxon settlers favoured the former in many ways.[44]

Jane Aberson's opinion was based on her observation of young men from Eastern Europe, and of Polish, Ukrainian and Russian peasants in their struggle for a better life. She recognized the promise the New World held out to the disinherited of the earth, and she marvelled at the personal transformation and the rapid social mobility of previously illiterate and destitute immigrants who had been less privileged than herself.[45]

A.R. Ford, writing in Woodsworth's *Strangers Within Our Gates*, describes the degree of prejudice that was tolerated at the turn of the century even among progressive Anglo-Canadians. While the English, Scotch and Dutch and other northern European settlers were described as "sturdy" and "progressive" and were attributed with all the virtues that one could possess, Eastern Europeans were held in such low esteem that the term Galician — used to refer to immigrants from the Austro-Hungarian Empire — was almost a term of reproach. The fact that they were also considered to be patient, ambitious and industrious, and that much of the rough work of nation building in western Canada was done by them, did not seem to weigh heavily in their favour. Southern and other East European and Asian ethnic groups also fared poorly in the estimation of Anglo-Canadians.[46] Prairie literature written by and about European immigrants reveals an awareness of this ethnic stratification, a pecking order that John Porter came to refer to as *The Vertical Mosaic*.[47]

By the time the Abersons settled on the prairies the northern European immigrant communities had just passed the stage in which they were considered foreigners by the Anglo-Canadians, and had in most cases become a respected part of Manitoba life. Their social and economic position *vis-à-vis* Anglo-Canadians had become much more secure and they represented a buffer zone between the Anglo-Canadians and the Galicians, who were still despised as foreigners. In her articles Mrs. Aberson captures the ethno-cultural divisions of prairie life with understanding.[48] Curiously, Dauphin's Main Street on Saturday night reminded her of the cosmopolitan city of Amsterdam.[49]

In the polyglot setting on the prairies during the 1930s the Chinese immigrant was central to the few social amenities small town life had to offer. Chinese restaurants were no less important than beer parlours, dance halls and the church. For her Dutch readers Mrs. Aberson described the Chinese cafés in Dauphin.[50]

Cultural Adjustment

Jane Aberson's immigrant reactions to North America related not only to political and sociological values, but also to the cultural customs and traditions of both the Old and the New World. In adapting to her new land she tried to recreate the world she had known in a different social context. All immigrants share this tendency to maintain ethnic customs and identity in the face of overwhelming social pressure to assimilate and adopt Canadian ways. In Mrs. Aberson's case these cultural adjustments were associated with recollections of Dutch gardens, the celebration of St. Nicholas Day, Christmas, Easter, familiar sports, eating and drinking habits, table manners and a host of other social graces that were practiced in the Netherlands in accordance with Dutch upper-class norms.

Entertainment and upper-class sports, like tennis, to which they were accustomed in the Netherlands, were non-existent in Dauphin during the Depression. The river proved either too dangerous or too shallow to swim, and there were neither golf courses nor tennis courts.

In pioneer communities the local preacher was frequently called upon to assume functions which today are dealt with, often less successfully, by governments. In addition the church was often the soil in which prairie radicalism was rooted. Community activity had its focus in the church. The ideology of cooperative ventures was not only expressed in politics but also in other activities. "Have contact with each other," "stick together," "have regular meetings," "form a group," "don't be divided" were common exhortations heard in church. The new Christianity of "community spirit and co-operation" since the turn of the century had grown into a powerful appeal "for democracy of religion, of culture, of politics and of industry."[51] Jane Aberson came to see that what farmers could not achieve individually they might be able to achieve together.[52]

Against this background Jane Aberson reported to her readers in Groningen that their minister had sparked a crusade to build a community tennis court on the Aberson farm with volunteer labour and with funds raised by the community itself. At the grassroots level the social gospel and the new Christianity often expressed itself in terms of the improvement of the quality of life, which translated into building social and recreational amenities.[53] Public concern for sports and recreation, in addition to voluntary community initiative, represented an important feature of Canadian life from the point of view of a Dutch immigrant.

Jane Aberson found drinking customs to be one particularly primitive aspect of Canadian life. The temperance movement in Canada had for generations given a one-sided interpretation to the consumption of alcoholic beverages. From the dominion-wide plebiscite in 1898 to the successful referendums of 1910, WASP Canadians had enforced their social norms with vigilance. But during the years from 1920 to 1926 the impact of a wave of immigrants with a cultural tradition that accepted, but rigidly circumscribed, the social use of alcohol was becoming felt. By 1927 Prohibition laws had been superseded by a system of government control still in effect today. However, even under the temperance and Prohibition acts "intoxicating beverages" were defined in such a way as to permit the sale of beer with a low alcohol content under strict government control.[54]

Upon coming to Canada Jane Aberson learned that the drinking of beer, wine and spirits was not associated — as it was in the Netherlands — with a tradition that looked on the proper use of alcohol as one of the civilized pleasures of life. Instead, drinking on the Canadian frontier was associated with illicit activity and moral degeneration. Her articles provide an interesting description of the social context of drinking in Europe and in North America.[55]

While Mrs. Aberson was offended on the one hand by the primitive North American drinking habits, she was impressed nevertheless with the social levelling and the egalitarian spirit in the rustic beer parlour, a distinct Canadian institution. In the Netherlands the drinking establishments were like neighbourhood pubs or cafés which catered to the specific social class of the area, encouraging the strict maintenance of social and class barriers. Not so in Canada, where men of all occupations mixed.[56]

While the men were drinking, the women and children, rather

than wait in the car outside, could go to a place of their own to rest and socialize. This was called the "Ladies Rest Room" provided by the United Farm Women of Manitoba.[57]

There were many other customs that Mrs. Aberson reacted to and compared with what she had been used to in the Netherlands. For instance, her opinion of the dance halls of the 1930s was not very high.[58]

Although on the whole she preferred her new way of life to the more restrictive lifestyle she had known in the Netherlands, she thought it a pity that the Dutch tradition of multilingualism, even among Dutch immigrants themselves, was quickly discarded along with their native tongue.[59]

Like many other immigrants the attachment to special holidays and cultural events — which gave a religious-cultural dimension to life in the old country — assumed a different meaning in the New World and often came into conflict with the ways they had known. Easter Monday was not celebrated in Canada at all, she noted with regret.[60] And in a small community the rites of passage were as inevitable as the changing seasons, and when death struck its impact seemed more severe far away from home.[61]

Cultural adjustment seemed most difficult during the Christmas season. While the host society exerted a certain pressure to conform to the popular culture of the New World, the old customs survived as a quasi-underground activity before a policy of multiculturalism had, to a degree, legitimized the cultural diversity of Canada's people. The articles reporting on the celebration of St. Nicholas Day, the highlight of Dutch popular culture, show a sense of underlying guilt associated with the awareness of being different and holding double loyalties. Christmas in Canada seemed more commercial and superficial, and the celebrations displayed a certain irreverence towards the birth of Jesus Christ. Adjustment to these cultural practices in Canada proved to be a painful process. To Jane Aberson Santa Claus seemed a poor match for St. Nicholas.[62]

Over the years that Jane Aberson wrote articles from the Canadian prairies a small colony of Dutch settlers had gradually formed in Dauphin. Some had come directly from the Netherlands, and others had come via Dutch colonies. Social contact with fellow Dutch immigrants was important during the first years. Loneliness in the new country was one of the many obstacles immigrants had to overcome. Looking back she realized the special significance of friendship with fellow countrymen. They represented a piece of the Netherlands, and more importantly they shared in the struggle to start a new life and they rejoiced together when their farming brought good prospects.[63]

For many years Jane Aberson shared her experience of prairie life with her readers in Groningen, and she received a great deal of satisfaction from it. She shared with them the plans and dreams of a young couple that had broken with tradition and started a totally different kind of life. There had been many doubts about their decision to emigrate, particularly in times of hardship when the crops had failed, prices had fallen or whenever disaster struck. She remarked that they had been spoiled in their youth, and expressed a great sense of admiration for the pioneers that had come before them. After twelve years on the Canadian prairies she realized that life in Canada had changed her, and when she was preparing to visit the Netherlands she wrote, "More than ever do I realize how much we have become part of this country and see how many good friends we have made."[64]

Jane Aberson realized that the inescapable burden of the immigrant is forever to be pulled between two worlds.[65] Of this her articles are an eloquent testimony.

NOTES

1. Jane Aberson-Uges, *Van de Canadeesche Velden* (Groningen: 1938), 2 vols. The title translates to "From the Canadian Prairies."
2. Kathleen Strange, "Interpreting Canadian Farm Life for the Dutch," *Family Herald and Weekly Star*, 10 September 1947, p. 35.
3. *Time* magazine, 30 June 1947, p. 16.
4. Herman Ganzevoort, *A Bittersweet Land: The Dutch Experience in Canada, 1890-1980* (Toronto: McClelland and Stewart, 1988), 35-59. This book provides an overview of the Dutch immigration experience in the 1930s.
5. *Nieuwsblad van het Noorden*, 29 December 1979.
6. *Dauphin Herald*, 27 October 1976.
7. Ibid.
8. E.C. Ebels to Jane Aberson, 11 March 1948 (no source cited).
9. H.D. Louwes to P. Dupuis (no date or source cited).
10. Kathleen Strange, "Interpreting Canadian Farm Life."
11. Jane Aberson to Mark Boekelman, 30 April 1981.
12. Susanna Moodie, *Roughing it in the Bush* (Toronto: McClelland and Stewart, 1962); Anna Brownell Jameson, *Winter Studies and Summer Rambles in Canada* (1938; Toronto: McClelland and Stewart, 1965); Catharine Parr Traill, *The Backwoods of Canada* (Toronto: McClelland and Stewart, 1968); Georgina Binnie-Clark, *Wheat and Women* (Toronto: University of Toronto Press, 1979).
13. Willem de Gelder, *A Dutch Homesteader on the Prairies*, trans. by

Herman Ganzevoort (Toronto: University of Toronto Press, 1973); Herman Ganzevoort, "Canada: The Last Illusion, Letters from an Immigrant: Frans Van Waeterstadt," *Canadian Ethnic Studies* 11, no. 1 (1979): 131-40; Mark Boekelman, "The Letters of Jane Aberson, Everyday Life on the Prairies During the Depression: How Immigration Turns Conservatives into Social Democrats," in Herman Ganzevoort and Mark Boekelman, eds., *Dutch Immigration to North America* (Toronto: Multicultural History Society of Ontario, 1983), 111-27.

14. Gordon Oosterman, et al., *To Find a Better Life: Aspects of Dutch Immigration to Canada and the United States, 1920-1970* (Grand Rapids: CRC Publications, 1975); J. Stellingwerff, ed., *Brieven van Amsterdamse Emigraten: onbekende brieven uit de prairie van Iowa, 1846-1873* (Amsterdam: n.d.); Herbert G. Brinks, ed., *Write Back Soon: Letters from Immigrants in America* (Grand Rapids: CRC Publications, 1986).

15. Jane Aberson's scrapbook of press clippings.

16. Jane Aberson to Mark Boekelman, 8 December 1979.

17. Jane Aberson-Uges, *Van de Canadeesche Velden*, vol. 1, February 1936. Hereafter cited as *VCV* and the date of the article referred to.

18. Dirk Aberson to Mark Boekelman, 14 September 1979.

19. *VCV*, February 1936.

20. Dirk Aberson to Mark Boekelman, 14 September 1979.

21. *Dauphin Herald*, 27 October 1976; *Credit Lines* 7, no. 12 (1 December 1973): 1.

22. *VCV*, November 1932.

23. *VCV*, September 1934.

24. *VCV*, October 1933.

25. Ibid.

26. *VCV*, March 1935.

27. Ibid.

28. Binnie-Clark, *Wheat and Women*, 64.

29. Jane Aberson to Mark Boekelman, 5 May 1980.

30. *VCV*, May 1933.

31. *VCV*, Introduction.

32. *VCV*, October 1931.

33. *VCV*, June 1933.

34. *Dauphin Herald*, 27 October 1976.

35. *VCV*, February 1934.

36. *VCV*, February 1933.

37. W.L. Morton, *Manitoba: A History* (1957; Toronto: University of Toronto Press, 1967), 266-68; Aberson articles, May 1933.

38. Morton, *Manitoba*, 266.

39. Ibid., 408-9.

40. *VCV*, May 1933.

41. Ibid.

42. Dirk Aberson to Mark Boekelman, 14 September 1979.

43. *VCV*, May 1933.

44. de Gelder, *A Dutch Homesteader on the Prairies*, 16.

45. *VCV*, October 1933.

46. A.R. Ford, in J.S. Woodsworth, *Strangers Within Our Gates* (1909; Toronto: University of Toronto Press, 1972), 109-14.

47. John Porter, *The Vertical Mosaic* (Toronto: University of Toronto Press, 1963). The literature that deals explicitly and implicitly with ethnic rivalry and prejudice includes Binnie-Clark, *Wheat and Women*; Marla Ostenso, *Wild Geese* (1925; Toronto: McClelland and Stewart, 1961); Laura Goodman Salverson, *The Viking Heart* (1923; Toronto: McClelland and Stewart, 1975); Ralph Conner, *The Foreigner: A Tale of Saskatchewan* (Toronto: The Westminster Co. Ltd., 1909); and Woodsworth, *Strangers Within Our Gates*. For early chronicles of farm life on the prairies see Frederick Phillip Grove, *Settlers of the Marsh* (1925; Toronto: McClelland and Stewart, 1966), and Robert J.C. Stead, *Grain* (1926; Toronto: McClelland and Stewart, 1963).

48. *VCV*, May 1933.

49. Ibid.

50. Ibid.

51. Goodman Salverson, *The Viking Heart*, 128-29.

52. *VCV*, July 1933.

53. Ibid.

54. Richard Allen, *The Social Passion* (Toronto: University of Toronto Press, 1973), 273-76.

55. *VCV*, May 1933, December 1935.

56. *VCV*, May 1933, February 1934.

57. *VCV*, May 1933.

58. Ibid.

59. *VCV*, December 1935.

60. *VCV*, January 1932.

61. *VCV*, May 1935.

62. *VCV*, December 1935.

63. *VCV*, June 1933.

64. *VCV*, August 1936.

65. Ibid.

1929-1930

Starting to Farm on the Prairies

November 1929

Now that winter has made its entry again and the field work is finished for at least six months, I'll have a chance during these long winter evenings to tell you something about this country and about the conditions here. It has been only five years since we ourselves were reading with the greatest interest the articles that were written in Dutch newspapers about Canada, the country we planned to adopt as our own.

My husband Bob, after working four months as hired help on a farm, spent his first winter as a student in the agricultural college in Winnipeg, where he studied the theory of farming. Here he met a farmer's son from Dauphin, a place about 200 miles northwest of Winnipeg. This young man offered him work and an opportunity to gain experience on his father's farm. That is how we landed in Dauphin, where we have stayed ever since. It is a mixed farming area and the main field crop is wheat, hard Canadian wheat, the best in the world.

While farmers in Holland always used fertilizer on their crops, it is not used at all here because the land is still relatively young and produces good crops without it. However, since weeds have become a nuisance, many farmers have started a crop rotating system. In a period of four years they will grow wheat in the first year, barley in the second, oats in the third, and in the fourth year the field is kept fallow. Fallowing not only keeps the weeds down but also preserves moisture for the coming year. This procedure is costly, though, because it gives no return at all on the land that is kept black (fallow). Some farmers grow oats instead, which they cut for feed in June or July and after that keep the land black until fall. They call that a green summer fallow.

Moreover, the cultivation of sweet clover, which can be sown with the grain, is becoming popular. Clover is a biannual plant which is grown along with the grain crop. The second year it grows at least a metre high and is cut for feed. After that, the land is kept black until the fall.

In contrast with the Netherlands, where straw is sold to the straw carton factories, in Canada straw has no value at all. After the grain

1

has been harvested, you can see quite a few piles of straw in each field. Most of the piles are burned right away, but two or three piles are saved to provide shelter for the horses and cows through the winter. Straw is also used for feed, but I do not think that animals grow very fat on it.

Perhaps there will be readers who will ask, "Are there any opportunities for young people to start farming in Canada?" With this in mind I would divide the prospective immigrants into two categories, those with some capital and those without any capital. Naturally it will be a lot easier for the "haves," but they must be very careful or they will soon go broke and belong to the other group. Therefore I would not advise anyone to buy a farm too soon. The best thing to do is to find work on a farm for at least a year to learn something of the customs and way of life, while in the meantime keeping your eyes and ears open.

At present there are many farmers willing to sell their land. The mortgage companies have many repossessed farms available which they are willing to sell for the price of the debt owing on them. The quality of the land is far from uniform. Even on a quarter section, which is 160 acres or 64 hectares, you can find a great variation. We bought our present farm after having lived two years in our log cabin in the bush. It was situated close to a river and we were very lucky because the soil is first class and produces beautiful crops. In contrast, on the other side of this river next to our own land, the soil was totally different and more suitable for pasture. It will pay to analyze the soil before deciding to buy.

If you decide to go into cattle, however, the poorer land will suffice. It can be used for hay and grazing, and naturally it is cheaper to buy. Most of the land west of us is still for sale and belongs to the municipality. All the farmers around us chase their cattle and horses onto it during the winter months, and catch them again in the spring. Naturally the animals have to be branded and, at regular intervals, the owners will ride on horseback over these prairies to see if all is well. It is a cheap way to raise horses and cows because it does not cost anything to feed them during the winter.

For a good quarter section you pay at present from $5,000 to $8,000, which is 12,500 to 20,000 guilders in Holland.

If a person is smart he should go to auctions and try to buy second-hand machinery and tools, as well as horses and cattle. There might be some items, however, like binders for cutting the crops, that would be better to buy new. Most men here are very handy and can repair things themselves, and perhaps a Dutch farm boy can do that, too. I would not know about that. But men like my husband, a city boy who seemed pretty smart to me in Holland, had a lot to learn.

One man is supposed to be able to work one quarter section of land by himself, and if he keeps livestock in addition, he has his hands full. During harvest time he needs extra help, of course, for setting up the sheaves. You need to have at least four horses to work a quarter section. I guess the expense involved in buying horses and second-hand machinery would be between $1,000 and $2,000.

Prices do vary. Four years ago a good team of horses could be bought for $200 to $300. At present you can buy the same for about $75 to $150 due to the scarcity of feed this year. We had a very dry summer, with only one good rain since seeding was finished, and as a result the crops were poor; only the summer fallow was good and the crops sown on newly broken-up land. Now it is freeze-up, which means that we get snow from now until April.

If a person has to start without money to back him up, life can be pretty tough. He has to work on a farm as a hired man. Wages for farm hands are, at present, $30 to $40 a month and, for a greenhorn, likely lower. They live on the farm and board is provided for them. Often during harvest time the employers pay a bit extra, but if no arrangement has been made, the farmer is not obliged to pay it. Quite a few young men go to Saskatchewan or Alberta in search of work. They claim the wages are a bit higher there. But if you want to settle in Manitoba, you might as well work in Manitoba, too.

After the harvest in September, the only thing left to do on the farm is plowing or cultivating all the stubble fields. As soon as the real frost comes, all field work is stopped. This generally takes place the first of November. Then the farmer pays the farm hand his wages and he has to leave. If he is a farmer with a lot of livestock, he might ask the hired man to stay, with room and board provided in exchange for his help, but there is a big chance that he will need to find work elsewhere. And that is not easy. There simply are no jobs available in the winter.

One alternative is the lumber camps, but that is a hard and rough life and not everybody is suited for it. The wages are meagre, too, and considering that you need good warm clothing and shoes for this work, it is understandable that you do not end the winter's work with a lot of money. So you might need to start from scratch again next spring.

If an immigrant finds it impossible to save enough money for a start, the only thing left for him to do is to take up a homestead. For this he has to become a British subject and to pay the sum of ten dollars for the land. He now becomes the owner of a quarter section of wild land, most likely far removed from the railroad and good roads. He also has to promise to spend six months of each of the first three years living on this homestead and making improvements on it. He must put up a house and a barn, barbed wire fences, and also break and make ready for plowing a certain acreage of land. If his place has big trees on it with large roots, he has a lot of work cut out for him.

Obviously this is not an easy way to start. For his remaining six months he must work to earn the money for the barbed wire and tools. He will also need a few horses to pull the tree roots out of the ground, and probably he will need to buy dynamite to blow up the stumps. One hundred sticks of dynamite cost about $15 and he might need quite a few for just one tree. And after all that, the real hard work still is to come — breaking the land, which is sometimes done with horses and sometimes with tractors. So you need to hire a man with a tractor, and that will cost you at least $5.00 or $6.00 an acre. If you do it yourself with horses you might have to hire a few extra horses if you only have four. In our neighbourhood decent homesteads are not available any more.

This, however, was the way many of the early settlers started their farms. In those years horses were not easy to get and often the work was done with oxen, which were not as easy to handle. If the oxen did not feel like working, nothing could move them. They would just lie down and the farmer might just as well lie down right beside them. A couple of times a year a trip to town had to be undertaken to buy supplies, with oxen pulling the wagon. As there were no decent roads yet, they sometimes got hopelessly stuck in the mud, and they often had to ford streams. On these infrequent trips to town, the farmer had to buy flour, salt, sugar and other staples in quantities of a hundred pounds or more. Coal oil is another item that should never be forgotten.

It is really not so very long ago that all this took place. The town of Dauphin is only thirty-five years old and the railroad has only been here since 1896. Now Dauphin has a nice main street where you will find most of the stores and restaurants; it has a few residential streets and a population of about 2,000. Quite a few farmers still remember the days when they were driving their teams over the very spot where you now find the Bank of Nova Scotia.

❅

Living Quarters in This Country

January 1930

The thermometer says -45°F. In Holland this would be -43°C. It is nine o'clock in the evening. My husband Bob, who has just finished the milking and other chores in the barn, has come in with his arms full of wood and he hopes to stem the cold with these heavy blocks. This cold and the misery you experience from it in many homes over here during these long, cold winter months gave me the idea to tell you something about our houses.

After you leave your native Holland and travel by train for the first time through this vast land, you will notice a big contrast between the beauty of the landscape and the unsightly houses you spot here and there. I thought at the time that they were deserted, probably condemned. I am wiser now, however, and have found that in Canada a house in the country is never condemned. A house might be ugly and never have seen a lick of paint, but most of them are inhabited.

This does not mean that there are not any nice homes in Canada. Especially in the towns and cities you can find attractive bungalows. In contrast with the Netherlands, where practically every house is built of brick, here a brick house is an exception. Almost all the houses are built of lumber, sometimes plastered with cement on the outside, but most often finished with wood siding. This is natural because Canada has vast forests and lumber is cheap. In the towns you can find comfortable houses not much different from what we are used to in Holland. One exception to this is that most of these houses have a full concrete basement underneath, and in that basement you will find a furnace for heating the house, either by water or hot air. In the wintertime these houses have double windows which keep the drafts out, and in summertime these are removed and screen windows are put in their place. Mosquitoes are a regular pest here in early summer, and flies are plentiful as well. Quite often the rooms in the nicer houses have beautiful hardwood floors, but in the majority of houses you do not find these luxuries.

Some of the early settlers started with sod houses. The sods were placed one on top of another, and when the walls were high enough, they put logs over them and more sods on top to form the roof. A few holes with glass in front were the windows. Generally the house had only one big room in which the whole family lived and slept.

I have never seen a sod house myself — I only hear the oldtimers talk about them. The farmer Bob worked for that first year, who now lives in a modern big house, started out that way.

What you still can find here, which is a step up the ladder, are the log cabins. Mostly these houses started with one good-sized room, but when the family got bigger and finances improved, they built additional rooms around it and sometimes on the top. Architecture was unimportant and these houses were not too convenient. I have heard them called "a growing pain."

About six miles from our farm I once visited a house which had only one room. In this house lived a father, a mother and quite a few children. The furniture consisted of a big kitchen range, a table, a few chairs and a few boxes. Homemade shelves served as storage room. There was one large bed in a corner, and we asked ourselves if the whole family had to be stacked like cordwood on top of this bed. But the mystery was soon solved when one of the children was told to go "upstairs" to get something. For this he had to go outside and climb a ladder that was placed against the wall. This scramble upstairs to the bedroom would not appeal to me on a cold night like this.

Besides log cabins there are also frame houses, and as we have had personal experiences with both, I'll tell you our own observations.

After spending close to two months in a nice big house on the farm where Bob was hired, I sure had a surprise when, for the first time, I saw this log cabin in the bush. As Bob was supposed to work on the big farm until freeze-up, I would live in the log cabin alone with Bobby, who was two and a half at the time. It was the end of September when I arrived, and I had never seen a more desolate place. The weeds which had grown wild around the cabin had grown as tall as a man and had started to dry up. The house itself looked to me as if it might collapse in a heavy wind. The main part of the house was a big room with three windows in it. A structure made from boards and with a sloping roof was built against it — this served as a kitchen, and there was a space alongside it that could be used as a bedroom.

The log cabin was quite small and proved to be far too cold in the winter. Upstairs, over the living room, were a little hallway and a bedroom, and the walls there were also made of planks. If someone had told me that six months later I would be describing this house as "not too bad at all," I would have laughed in his face.

I can still remember how Bob and I made jokes about the "airiness" of the building. With him standing outside and I in the room, we could shake hands through the walls because the filling between the logs had fallen out in different places.

The first few weeks I spent cleaning up the mess and placing different objects I had brought with me from Holland. Bob had bought some second-hand furniture, and with the rugs I had brought with me, it soon looked quite cozy. We draped the rough log walls with batik sarongs we had brought from the Dutch East Indies, and it really looked quite charming. One of the inconveniences that hit me right in the face was the fact that you had to go outside to a pump for every drop of water. This water was very hard. I could get soft water only from a small stream that flowed through the bush a few hundred yards from the cabin. At first I grumbled about all this lugging of water, but my opinions changed when I found out that on many other farms the families had to get their water in tanks, sometimes from miles away. This little stream was a godsend. We also used it to take our baths. The toilet was a small outhouse, all right in the summer but bbburrr! in the winter.

Another inconvenience was the total absence of drainage. Nowhere could you find a gutter or a drainpipe around the house, and to my surprise I discovered that you did not find any drainage around the nicer farmhouses either. The slop and dirty dishwater are just thrown out of the back door.

Farm Work in the Winter

February 1930

You are not far off to say that winter in Canada lasts at least six months. I mean by this statement the total stoppage of field work where we live. One year the frost might come a month earlier or later, and sometimes there might be some fluctuation with the time of starting the spring activities, but usually around the first of November, when heavy frost has set in, implements are put aside and farmers prepare for the winter activities. It goes without saying that one of their activities will be the care of the livestock, which have been moved to the barn by this time.

The first weeks after "freeze-up" most of the farmers take it easy, which they well deserve after the busy summer months and the harvest rush. They don't get up as early as farmers do in the old country. We get up between six and seven a.m., depending on the number of cows that have to be milked. In December and January the sun rises here around eight o'clock and sundown is around four o'clock in the afternoon. Because indoor lighting on the farm is still so primitive, it does not make much sense to spook around too early in the morning.

After the barn has been cleaned and the horses, cows, pigs and whatever else the farmer might have as livestock are fed and watered, the milking has to be done. Since we have no electricity, the milking is done by hand. There might be an odd farmer who has a motor-driven milking machine, but we do not have them around here. When the milking is finished the farmer goes with his full pails to the house, where his wife strains the milk into a separator bowl.

Many farm wives help with the milking themselves, but when I tried it was not a great success. One day when a cow tried to flatten me against the wall, Bob had enough of it and did not want to see me in the barn again. However, the separating of the milk is my job. Cream is separated from the skim milk. The skim milk is brought out to the pigs, and the cream is put into a crock until we have enough to take to the creamery in town. This is usually once a week, when we can do our shopping at the same time. During the winter months we often churn the cream ourselves, press the butter into one-pound blocks and sell it to the grocery store. With the proceeds we can buy our groceries.

During those first few weeks a lot of small jobs for which the farmers had no time in the summer months will be done, such as fixing fences, repairing machinery and making the house as warm as possible for the winter.

Pretty soon now the big bills start to arrive — taxes, rent, mortgage, threshing bill, or whatever you might owe — and as there generally is very little cash on the farm, the farmer puts a grain box on his sleigh and starts hauling the grain to the elevator in town. In every prairie town you will find one or more of these elevators. They look like rather dumpy church towers, and you can drive your sleigh or wagon through one side and out the other. The grain box is weighed and then mechanically put at an angle. The grain flows through a hole in the floor, and then, by a kind of Jacob's ladder, it is brought to the top of the elevator to be conveyed to the different bins. After that they weigh the empty box and you know by the difference in weight how much grain you sold. As you will notice, grain in Canada is shipped in bulk, not in sacks as is done in Holland.

You can sell your grain in different ways, either to a private elevator or to the provincial cooperative elevator, Manitoba Wheat Pool. The Wheat Pools at present handle about 52 percent of Canada's crop. It is a grain cooperative, the biggest in the world, I am told, and it has been in existence only six years. The grain that is handled by the Wheat Pool goes directly from the producer to the consumer and it is not subject to speculation on the grain exchange. The Wheat Pool sets its own price, maybe not the top price, but neither is it the bottom price. I would say it pays a fair average. When you deliver your grain you get partial payment, with the balance to be paid in three installments.

After most of the grain hauling is finished, another job looms up. At present we are right in the midst of it — getting our wood supply for the following winter out of the Riding Mountains. This means no more sleeping in. Often the men are already on the road by six o'clock, which means that the cleaning of barns, the milking and the feeding have been finished before they hit the road. They always have to wait with wood hauling until the roads are suitable for it. Because this is all done with sleighs there has to be enough snow. This winter we got our snow early, and now long caravans of sleighs pass our farm in the morning and return around six o'clock in the evening. It is such a cheerful sound, the tinkling of the sleighbells on the horses' harnesses in the crisp frosty air.

Some farmers who have no hired help have the job of cutting the trees done by another party. They have to pay $1.25 for a cord of wood, but they do the hauling themselves. If a farmer has sons or brothers who help him on the farm, he often does the hauling himself and leaves his chores for the evening. His brothers or sons do the actual woodcutting and live in a shanty in the bush. You see lots of these log shanties in the Riding Mountains.

To cut wood in the Riding Mountains you need a permit from the government. Long distances have to be covered before you reach the areas where cutting is allowed. We live about nine miles from the nearest camp, but many have to travel twenty miles and more. The wood we use for the heaters and the kitchen stove is hauled out in tree lengths of sixteen feet. It is piled up in the farmyard, and around the end of March a farmer with a circular saw does the rounds and cuts the trees into one-and-a-half foot lengths. After that the farmer himself has to split it. This is often a job which is done by a newly hired man, and Bob was at it for at least three weeks steady that first year.

A farmer here is often a jack of all trades. So you will find many a farmer in the wood business during the winter months. This will take care of all the spare time he might have, but it will also bring in some ready cash. He will sell his wood to the townspeople. For this purpose the wood is sawed up in four foot lengths and these have to be split in two, which is easy to do on a frosty day. After that he loads it on his sleigh. The price is $3.75 to $4.00 for one cord. Sometimes he leaves the wood on the farm to dry during the summer, and then he can sell it the following winter for $5.00 to $5.50 a cord.

There is still another occupation which will pay the farmers a few dollars. If there is money enough in the municipal treasury and the council has decided that a few roads should be gravelled again, every taxpayer in his own district can take part in this operation. For this they get paid 90¢ to $1.10 a yard (27 cubic feet). The work is not too pleasant. Because the ground is frozen solid several feet down, they have to use dynamite to blow it up before they can start shovelling the gravel into their sleighs. The average load will be between two and three yards, so they can make $2.50 to $3.00 a load. To make it worthwhile, you have to make several trips a day. This gravel business is heavy work for the horses as well, and if any part of the equipment or sleigh breaks, much of the profit is gone. This winter the municipality had no money available, so there were no jobs either.

Slowly we have entered the month of March, and even if the winter is not over by a long shot, the farmer starts to think about the work that will be waiting for him in the near future. Everybody starts to talk about seed grain and the cleaning of seed grain. This is done in a fanning mill, operated by hand or by a small gasoline motor. As the grain is often dirty and has to go through the mill quite a few times, a motor-driven mill saves considerable time. This grain cleaning is one of the jobs the newly-hired help is often used for.

After the grain is cleaned, attention is given to the horses. Some have spent the winter in the barn and are in much better condition than the ones that have lived outside. Those are caught and fed extra during the coming weeks. Now the machinery has to be looked over and repaired if necessary. Then it is a matter of waiting for warmer days and drying winds before the soil is in condition to be cultivated.

I will not end this tale without telling you that during this time the wife of the farmer has not been hibernating, either. "The farmer works from sun to sun, but the farmer's wife's work is never done!"

If I am well informed about this, the women on a Dutch farm really have nothing to do with the farm work at all. They look after their big homes with the help of one or two maids and that is that. Exceptions granted, the farm women here have only a hired girl during the busy *summer season, and quite a few never have help at all. Bread is generally baked at home and when, due to the excessive heat, cream for churning cannot be kept many days without spoiling, she herself has to take the cream by car or buggy to the creamery.*

Wintertime brings a lot of inconveniences for the farm wife. Just consider the laundry. Because no rain will fall for months on end, the soft water tank will be empty, and you have to melt snow first. A lot of snow makes only a little bit of water. Quite often you have your husband saw big blocks of ice out of the river which he can pile up behind the house to be used when needed. Often you will find an ice house on the farm, too — a plain wooden shanty in which big blocks of ice are kept between layers of sawdust. This is our summer ice which can be used in an icebox for refrigeration.

But even the handling of the clothes after they are washed causes difficulties because as soon as they are brought outside they freeze, along with your hands! Some people have a woodshed behind the house where they put up washlines. Then, if an unexpectedly strong wind starts up, which is quite often the case, at least the clothes won't all blow to pieces — which happened to me before I got wiser.

Poultry is the wife's department as well. When the husband is busy cleaning his grain, she looks after the incubators.

As soon as the soil is fit, out to the garden she goes and starts cleaning up, raking and seeding. Often she has her windowsills already full with cans and boxes in which young plants such as tomatoes, cabbages, cauliflower, and the like have been started and are waiting to be transplanted when the weather is fit. The garden gives her work to do the whole summer long. If it is not weeding, it is gathering produce and after that canning and preserving. As I already remarked, many farmers' wives and daughters help with the milking and feeding in the barn and, added to this, have all the other housework chores to do (not forgetting the raising of families). You will realize that they do not have much leisure time left.

The Country School

April 1930

While I am writing this the wind howls around the house and blows the snow horizontally past the windows. The thermometer tells me it is -18°F and it looks as if winter is starting instead of nearing the end.

11

However, we have already enjoyed unusually mild days with bright sunshine. It gives you the impression that spring is just around the corner. Bob opened the doors of the barn and henhouse so that horses, cows, sheep and pigs, chickens and turkeys could all enjoy these beautiful days. Suddenly it became very lively in the barnyard. There was neighing and lowing and bleating and grunting and cackling all over the place, and suddenly the chickens started to lay eggs. The snow, which had piled up high during the winter, started to slide down off the roofs and pile up around the house and the barn. The snow even started to melt and we saw the soil again. It's starting to get muddy during the day.

The pigs enjoyed themselves especially during these bright sunny days. One morning two of our three sows set out for the piles of straw in the field, and that same afternoon Bob came home with the joyful announcement that two litters of baby pigs were also enjoying the warm rays of the sun. The third sow decided to get her young ones into the barn, but she was not as lucky as her sisters were. She lay down on her litter and smothered them all.

The baby pigs were not the only new arrivals. We rejoiced in the birth of our son Dirk Hugo who, added to the two boys we already have, made us the proud parents of three boys. Dirk is a healthy lively baby, and it is a blessing that this land is big and that there is room for many. If a boy is willing, he won't have difficulties making a go of it in this country! He will not be faced with the difficulties Dutch boys have in finding a spot in an already overcrowded country.

On the other hand, a boy here will have to struggle with difficulties his contemporaries over there will have no idea about. Even though we have been in this country five years, our eyes were opened only recently to this. The reason was that our oldest boy, Bobby, reached the age of six last year, and so the time had arrived when he had to start school. I happened to come across an article in a Dutch paper not very long ago written by the well-known Professor Treub. In this article he pointed out the difference between today's young people and those of his time. Children are now often brought to school by nursemaids, while in his youth he and his brothers had to struggle long distances and in all kinds of weather over bad roads. It gave me real pleasure to read that, in his opinion, these difficulties were often good for children, and that surmounting these obstacles in their youth made them better prepared for the obstacles that they would no doubt meet later in life. Well, our three boys should do all right then. Our farm, which is really quite well situated in terms of distance from town (six miles) and is located on a good gravel road, is not as well situated in regard to school.

Rural Canada, if you look at a map, gives the impression of being divided into squares by a ruler. One square mile is called a section. The smallest farm unit is a quarter section, and thirty-six sections form a township. In each township you will generally find two schools. Our nearest school is two and a half miles away, which is not so bad in the summer, but quite a distance in the winter.

When Bobby started school in April last year, the frost had just started to melt and the road through the bush, as well as over the prairie, was impassible. The only solution was that his father take him on horseback every morning, and bring him home the same way every afternoon. Those trips over impassible roads to that isolated little schoolhouse in the country, where every morning a teacher and six pupils arrived from different directions, looked so adventurous to me that I wanted to see it, too. I asked a neighbouring girl, who lives half a mile away from our farm, to look after Wim and Dick, and I joined my husband in the democrat, a two-seated cart pulled by two horses.

On that early spring morning I got my first impression of going to a rural school in Canada. In three spots the road came so close to the river bank that I got nervous and closed my eyes so that I could not see that high bank so close up.

When we arrived on the open prairie we got the full icy wind right in our face, and with some alarm I visualized the long lonesome trips our little boy would have to make. Thirty or forty degrees below zero with an icy wind in the face — how could a little boy manage that? When at last we arrived at the little schoolhouse, a young boy on horseback arrived from the other direction. When he came to the schoolhouse he jumped from his horse, grabbed the animal by the head and led him to a small wooden barn, located behind the small one-room schoolhouse.

"That is Alfred," Bobby said. "He always lights the fire in the morning." Sure enough, after a few minutes Alfred appeared again, this time with his arms full of wood taken from the pile beside the schoolhouse. We all went inside. Blowing on his frozen fingers, he built up a fire from slats and paper in the big heater. In no time at all Alfred had the fire going.

I looked in surprise at his serious, mature face and compared him in my mind with a ten-year-old boy in Holland. When, however, the stove was burning brightly and needed no further immediate attention, his face relaxed and he turned to Bobby and started to talk with him about a rabbit skin which he had extracted from his pocket. We found out that the rabbit which had lived in this skin had been shot by Alfred. You see, a ten-year-old boy in Canada rides horseback, lights fires and handles guns.

Meanwhile two little girls had arrived who had been brought by an older brother on horseback. A few minutes later the woman teacher, accompanied by a little boy and a girl, arrived in a democrat. The teacher told me that the children's ages varied from six to thirteen years and that they all were in different grades.

After a few weeks, when the weather became milder and the roads dried up, Bobby started to walk to school. I went with him in the mornings through the bush, and in the afternoons would meet him again at the same spot. Later on, when summer activities demanded much of my time, I could not keep this up. We did not want to let him walk through the bush alone. In the summer, and especially when the wild berries are ripe, you can occasionally run into a bear, though that is certainly not a daily occurrence.

The best solution was for me to learn to drive the car which, until now, I had left to Bob. The road came so close to the river's edge that I refused to do it unless they moved the road. Bob got a few of the neighbours together and they gave him a hand cutting a number of trees to make a new road. It was not a first-class autobahn, you can readily understand. In fact it was so rough that on a certain day, when we hit a big stump in the road, our second son Wim, who was always in the back seat breathing down my neck, catapulted right over the backrest and landed in the front seat.

Young Canadians learn to cope with unusual difficulties at an early age. I suddenly remember one morning when we still lived in the log cabin in the bush. A neighbour, who had lost his wife, lived with his two young sons not more than two miles from our cabin. The boys were ten and twelve years old. One morning the boys came running into our yard all out of breath and asked me for a gun. When I hesitated a bit and asked them what they needed a gun for, they told me that they had spotted a bear and that their father had gone after it with an axe but he had asked them to go to our place and borrow a gun and then try to catch up with him. As soon as we had given them the gun they started to squabble about who had to go home and who would catch up with Dad. "Why does one of you have to go home?" I asked. "Well, it is baking day and we set a batch of bread this morning and in half an hour it has to go into the oven," was the reply.

14

1931

Working Through the Seasons

January 1931

It's a long time since I wrote last, which was April of last year. At that time we were surrounded by vast white fields, and it is the same now. But we had a very busy season in between, and that is the reason I could not find time for writing. When spring started I thought — no chance to find time for writing. But when the little chicks come out of the incubator, when the little turkeys have survived their first hazardous month, and when the seeds are sown in the garden, then some quiet evening I will sit down and write again.

Now I will tell you how suddenly seasons change here — such a contrast with the leisurely arrival of spring in Europe. How, in a very short time, suddenly all the white fields become spotty, and after that black. How every day the farmer starts to inspect his higher fields to find out if they will be dry enough to start with his fieldwork. How everybody heaves a sigh of relief when things really start to dry up and the dirty mess of the break-up disappears. And how then, suddenly, as if by appointment, all the farmers appear in their fields at the same time with their plows, their harrows and their cultivators.

My plans for writing never materialized. Once the work had started it got busier instead of easier. The garden needed weeding in the worst way, as we had put in such a big one this year. The summer clothes (put away in trunks) had to be aired, inspected and mended if necessary. The heavy winter clothing had to be brushed and cleaned and put away in mothballs so that it would be ready when needed next fall.

And then, of course, there was the spring cleaning. In that respect Canada is the same as Holland. The women here too become possessed by it in the spring. In reality it involves more work over here. At home my mother had domestic and outside help, such as hired painters and plasterers. Here you have to do it all yourself. So I wielded the broom and the mop, the paint brush and the hammer when needed, and I had no time for the pen. In the field I saw Bob sitting on some implement going up and down, up and down the field, the whole day long. I thought, "If all is sown, if the house is fresh and clean again, then both of us will have some time to ourselves."

But this hope never got out of the dreaming stage. The grain came

15

up. It grew higher and higher, and the higher it got, the higher our expectations. The crop looked really good. Then we got a prolonged dry spell, though last winter's heavy snowfall had given the grain a good start. But on account of the dry spell another job turned up, and there was no question of taking it easy or writing stories. After the children had been put to bed, we had to haul water from the river in pails and washtubs to prevent our newly planted garden from drying out completely. When that job was finished we were very hot, and my desire to write had considerably cooled.

Toward the end of June I thought we might have a few more leisurely weeks — seeding would be finished and haying not yet started, but Bob had other plans mapped out for those weeks. All of our buildings needed painting in the worst way. They not only looked bad, but they needed paint to prevent the wood from deteriorating too much. So paint we did. But I have to confess that we did not get the job finished. Windowsills and frames were left unfinished and have to wait until next year.

July and August were very dry and hot. The horses, their heads down, puttered slowly in front of the haystacks or went leisurely up and down on the summer fallow. Though we have not been pestered much by mosquitoes these last years, the bulldog flies were very bad. The horses kept throwing up their heads, kicking their heels and swinging their tails. The cows were bothered by them as well. Naturally this has a bad effect on milk production.

During those hot days I used to put little Dick in his gauze-covered pram under the trees near the river, and put Wim nearby with a few toys. The river was no danger to them because, save for a few potholes, it had gone completely dry. Then I would walk, pails in hand, to pick berries in the bush. Here you can find strawberries in the spring, saskatoons and raspberries in the summer and cranberries in the fall. In their wild state they are not as large as the cultivated ones, but their flavour is superior. Last year I put up 120 quarts of wild fruit and it tasted very good in the winter.

City people in Holland must envy us, having all this fruit just for the picking, but in reality we need to work hard for it. For these picking expeditions I used to put on a pair of Bob's overalls, buttoned up high to the neck, with an elastic band tied round the ankles to keep flies and mosquitoes away. Sometimes they even bite through all this. It was a very uncomfortable and hot garment but I could not do without it. Into the bush we went, but don't think this is a forest with nice trails and paths for walking. The bush is nothing more than a big wilderness of trees, scrub and weeds that grow as high as your head.

16

Sunflowers, which you will always find here on newly broken land, grew far above my head, and ferns grew practically as high as my head. In a forest like this you naturally will find a lot of trees fallen down from old age or felled by storms, fallen trees you cannot see because of all this wild undergrowth. You are stumbling, falling down and getting up again, crouching and climbing, and in between picking the berries.

The first few years it often happened that I would get hopelessly lost in the bush. I had to look at the sun, and from this try to get my directions again. But I would be scared to death and would stumble around in circles. Horrible pictures would flash through my mind, like Bob not knowing where I had disappeared to, and never thinking to search in the bush, and eventually finding the pails and a skeleton. So I stayed close to the edge of the bush, but the berries were not as plentiful there.

When at last I had picked all the berries I wanted, I now faced the canning, preserving and jam-making. This meant spending days over hot fires, which made the house unbearably hot in the daytime and hardly possible to cool off at night. The vegetables in the garden had to be picked, too. After that came shelling peas and threading beans in the evenings, and making more hot fires in the daytime to get them all sterilized in the sealed jars. When everything in the garden seemed to have ripened, the grain would be ripe too, and the busiest time of the whole year would be just around the corner.

The crop was good this year, and that means a lot. A man had to be hired for stooking (setting up the grain sheaves), and that meant a bigger household with an extra person to cook and wash for. Then came the busiest days of all, the days when the threshing machines were with us. Suddenly we had about twenty extra men for meals — four meals a day.

On threshing days we get up at four o'clock in the morning, when it is still pitch dark, and we go to bed at 11:30 at night, after all those stacks of dishes are washed again. For the farmer, after the hard work of threshing all day, it means spooking around the barn in the middle of the night milking and feeding his cows and looking after the other livestock. More than likely the poor animals will be a bit neglected. Only the real necessities are taken care of during these days. The men on the threshing gang don't put out their hands to help a bit. They are tired after a long working day and roll into bed as soon as supper is finished.

Our wheat crop this year was about forty bushels an acre, barley was fifty bushels, and oats around seventy. That was better than we have had for quite a few years. But the prices were a different story. Nobody really expected that the prices would go down still more. Lucky were the farmers who sold their grain straight from the threshing machine. Those same farmers looked a bit downcast when they were selling, because they thought the prices would go up later. But now they are smiling. When they sold, the price for wheat was 70¢ bushel, barley 28¢ and oats 24¢. If you consider that not long ago the prices were a $1.40, 60¢ and 50¢, respectively, you could not help but think they were poorly paid when they sold. Naturally the Wheat Pool finds it hard to survive. The banks are financing it using the grain as security, but since the prices have fallen so drastically this security is not sufficient any longer.

The farmers who are Wheat Pool members (their contract is for five years) did not receive anything other than the initial payment for their grain from last year, and this year they cannot expect any extra payments at all. That the present first payment is lower than the open market price is of course to be expected. Now instead of the farmers getting an extra payment for their 1929 crop, there is talk that they may have to make an additional payment themselves to make up the difference. Cattle and dairy produce bring abnormally low prices as well. Only a good milk cow still brings a fair price. Chickens and eggs are no longer paying propositions, and pigs that were sold at a decent price a while ago have now become very cheap, too. I read that there is a slump in agriculture in the Netherlands, too! We all seem to be in the same boat.

Woodcutting in the Riding Mountains

February 20, 1931

For a change we had a rather mild winter compared to other years. Quite a few people claim that they have seen crows already, and today Bobby came home all excited. He and his friends saw a lot of wild geese flying north again, and meadowlarks have been spotted close to the school. The teacher and pupils all ran outside to welcome them because this surely means that spring is not too far away. In fact, it seems to me that spring has really made its entrance already. All winter long the temperatures stayed around the freezing point, with just a few really cold days of -20° or -30°F. Now, however, it has really started to thaw, and after four days the snow has gradually disappeared and big puddles have appeared all over. Naturally the ground is still frozen so the melted water can't soak in. It is very icy and slippery outside. All day long members of the family have been coming to the house soaked wet to the skin, with mud all over. Mom has to be ready again with dry clothing and socks. We all changed our moccasins or fur-lined boots for high rubber boots. Later on, when the frost has left the ground, things will get worse, and quite often you have a hard time pulling your boots out of the mud.

However, we are all pleased with this mild weather. We do not need half the wood we used in other years to keep the house warm. The chickens never stopped laying eggs, and the cattle outside can find food much easier since the snow is not too high. They seem to prefer this to the dry straw piles.

The scarcity of snow has a darker side, though. Getting wood out of the forest is greatly hampered because sleighing is almost impossible. There are places where the road is totally bare already. Most of the farmers go out for wood in pairs, each with their own sleigh and their own team. If they get stuck, they double up and rescue each other. Three miles from our farm the road became totally impassible and they were forced to use the river instead. The river has a very high bank there, and it takes a lot of smart maneuvering to get a sleigh, piled high with wood, down that steep slope.

We are lucky because Bob started early in the season and already had brought his supply home. In fact the men with the circular saw have been here already and a big pile of sawn blocks lies in front of the barn. There will still be many days of work needed to split it all, but there is plenty of time for that before the actual farm work will start again.

Many of the farmers get their wood from the edge of the tree line and stack it there for the time being. Later on they can come with their wagons and bring it home. They do the same with lumber. Further up, where the needle trees are plentiful, about twenty-five miles from our farm, you can find a little sawmill. It really is hardly a mill but just a steam engine and a big circular saw. This mill is opened each winter for a few weeks. Many farmers go there to cut their logs into lumber. The boards are sawed into the lengths they order and then are brought home. While you would have to pay around $45 or $50 per thousand square feet in Dauphin for the lumber, you can get it here for about $10 per thousand.

This winter there were not as many farmers as usual cutting wood for sale in town. A few big trucks from town made use of the better roads, and we could see them pass the farm every day loaded high with cordwood. Now you find all kinds of people logging who never used to work in the bush. To help the unemployed, the town has opened up a lumber camp in the Riding Mountains. The camp consists of about two dozen log shanties in which these otherwise unemployed workers sleep, and a larger log building which is the cookhouse where they all eat. A cook is hired to cook the meals.

The town contracted for 4,000 cords of wood. The wages for the men are $1.25 a cord. From this they have to deduct 75¢ for their food, so not very much is left. However, this way they have room and board for the winter months, which means a lot to many of them. Because they are usually men who are inexperienced in wood-cutting, they often do not manage to cut more than a cord a day.

Joys and Hazards of Hunting

February 1931

The last few years much has been written in the newspaper about the Riding Mountains. They cover about 1,100 square miles and are really not much more than hills covered with dense bush and dotted with lakes and small streams. Until recently no decent road went through. They are just a wilderness. A law was passed, however, which made the area into a national park so that it will be preserved for coming generations. It is really very beautiful and the water in the rivers, creeks and lakes is crystal clear.

One of the lakes, only forty miles from our farm, is called Clear Lake, and will eventually be turned into a summer resort, I am sure. Already there are a few stores and garages, and they talk about tennis courts and a golf course. You can rent boats on the lake, and they are building a big dance hall. From this central area paths are being built through the bush, and for about $800 you can get a log cabin built.

One of the biggest attractions of the Riding Mountains is the wildlife which is still abundant there. This is one of the very few places on the North American continent where you can still find elk and moose in large numbers. Until recently these animals supplied meat on many tables. I do not know if it was ever permissible to shoot them, but it is a fact that the police were not too strict about it. A college friend of Bob's who had started farming near Prince Albert, Saskatchewan, wrote us that in his part of the country every farmer was allowed to shoot one elk or moose a year for his meat supply. I guess it must have been the same here at one time, but that is not allowed any longer. As long as we have lived here we have only seen the hunting season open one winter, and that was only for ten days, and even then there were restrictions. You were allowed to shoot only one male animal.

Bob and a few neighbours took part in the hunt that year and spent a few days and nights in the bush. With all the trees and the undergrowth it is not very easy, when the hunting fever possesses them, to differentiate between a male and a female. The animals are shy, too, and you have to shoot them from quite a distance. They arrived home with a female on their sleigh and felt lucky that they had not met a policeman or a game warden. Naturally, after having killed the animal, they did not feel like leaving it in the bush. The men divided the animal and it was hidden in a snowbank.

One bright sunny day two men on horseback rode into our yard and dismounted. One glance told me that one of them was wearing the uniform of the Royal Canadian Mounted Police. I realized right away that they would expect to be invited for dinner, which is quite usual if a person happens to pass by around dinnertime. Bob, who was busy cutting wood behind the house, shouted, "Better hide your roast," but I was afraid they already smelled it outside.

At my wits end I grabbed the fragrant pan in my hand and looked around in desperation. Where was I to hide it? One, two, three — I rushed upstairs and shoved the pan under a bed.

A few minutes later, with broad grins, the men entered the house, rubbing their cold hands. I thought, "I bet they think it smells really good here, and they are hungry. Won't they be surprised when they get eggs instead of meat?"

Not long after we started our dinner and were engaged in quite a lively conversation, the subject of hunting came up. "Did you go hunting, too, Mr. Aberson?" one of our guests asked.

"Yes," Bob answered, "I sure did not want to miss that."

"And did you have any luck?"

I started to blush guiltily. A pause, and then, "Yes, but it was the wrong kind of luck." Everybody looked a bit embarrassed, and then suddenly we all burst out laughing.

"Yes, that was a rather difficult stipulation," the Mountie said. "There must be quite a few more that had the wrong kind of luck. Well, I would say, you better enjoy it now that you have it!" And of course we did. But now we would think twice before breaking the law this way. Since the Riding Mountains have become a national park, the police are a lot stricter. You read in the paper all the time about fines for people who have broken the law.

We can hunt rabbits as much as we want, though. In Holland you needed a license for rabbits, too, if I remember well. Rabbits and jackrabbits (hares) seem to be considered inferior fare over here. When I lived all alone in the log cabin with little Bobby and the meat supply got low, I used to take the shotgun and shoot a few. They were easy to get because at night they would come out of the bush and sit all along the edge.

Every few years their numbers seemed to decrease, and I soon found out that this was due to a disease they contracted. When you skinned them you found lots of blisters on them. Then I did not fancy them anymore. After a few years their numbers increased again and the blisters disappeared. This year I am sure we will see hundreds of them again. At present they still have their white fur, and you can spot them very easily against the dark soil and the bush. This year they can't change their own colour fast enough to keep up with the quick melting of the snow. In a few weeks they will turn spotted, and during the summer they will be grey all over.

The first few years we lived here there were also many prairie wolves (coyotes) around, which make an awful noise. When you hear them howl you would think there were dozens around, but three or four generally are responsible for all the noise. When I was all alone with the baby in the log cabin they used to scare me to death, and I hated to go outside after dark to get water. Everybody told me that they are very shy and would never come near me. It is true that they never attack people. They live off all kinds of small animals, and if ever an elk or a moose dies in the bush, they will clean that up, too. People tell me that the coyotes have been scarce in the last few years because the rabbits are dwindling. As soon as the rabbits return the coyotes will, too.

Just now I remember something that happened a few years ago. My mother and Bob's sister were visiting us from Holland. In fact they spent a whole winter with us. Naturally they hoped to have tall tales to tell when they returned to Holland. Howling wolves around the house was something they hoped to hear, but this was a winter without many rabbits and with no wolves.

One morning, however, my mother came downstairs all excited. "I heard a wolf in the night and it was a mournful wail," she said. Next morning the same story, and this time sister Truus heard it too. Well, *we doubted it a bit, and we asked them to be sure to call us if they ever heard it again. And when the next morning at a quarter to four the train from Winnipeg blew its whistle in the frosty night, two excited voices came from the guest room. "Hear! Listen! Do you hear it now?"*

I don't need to say that they were quite disillusioned.

Winter Fun and the Poor Farm Economy

March 1931

March made its entry with sunny, frosty days. Quite a few people would have preferred a bit more snow so that getting the wood from the mountains would have been easier. But it is still easier to get around by sleigh than by wagon. The frozen ground is still hard so that the men can manage their wagons pretty well. Often in other years the wheels will be up to their hubs in mud. The gravel roads look now like they do in the summer, not a speck of snow left. The bush road and the prairie, which Bobby has to travel every day to school, were flooded during the latter part of February. The land is low there and swampy, and now he skates to school. Usually we do not have much opportunity to skate in the winter because the ice on the river is covered with far too much snow.

Because of those beautifully frozen stretches of ice this winter, and the full moon we are having at present, many of the neighbouring farm families get together in the evenings and amuse themselves for a while. These activities generally start pretty late in the evening because the farm chores have to be finished first. And then by sleigh, wagon or car, whatever is possible, they all come together accompanied, of course, by the children. To our Dutch eyes it seemed barbaric at first to see these youngsters get sleepy after a few hours and crawl under blankets in the sleighs or cars. But it does not seem to bother the people here very much. They are used to it. They were brought up the same way themselves and it is their only chance for a little diversion.

A few campfires are lit and the older ones gather around them. They watch their youngsters performing or they listen to tall tales from the old-timers who never seem to get tired of telling them. The boys and girls skate, organize hockey matches or go tobogganing down the hills, if there are any. The fun generally ends around one o'clock with a cup of hot tea, made over the campfire, and with sandwiches and cakes supplied by the ladies.

Economic conditions certainly are not improving. Grain prices still are terribly low. The price of pigs has not improved a bit, and you cannot expect more than $5.50 for a hundred pounds. It used to be $10 or $15. Because barley is so very low in price a lot of farmers started in the pig business again which, of course, lowered the hog prices for a little while. The government tried to help by subsidizing the purchase of pregnant pigs. After an initial payment to buy the pigs, farmers could pay off the balance in instalments. This all looks pretty nice on paper. Two years ago they did the same thing with sheep, but it did not work at all. By the time the lambs were ready for sale the prices dropped and produced no profit at all. Very likely the same will happen with pigs because there will be about half a million moze pigs on the market.

On all sides you hear talk of how to improve farm conditions. Practically every week we meet some place and listen to speeches given by government officials, agricultural societies, leaders of the Wheat Pool, etc. This week farmers are to vote on the Wheat Pool, a body of producers elected by the farmers who look after their own business, all of which is guided and protected by the law.

On the other hand, however, some farmers are starting another organization, the Manitoba Farmers Anti-Compulsory Pool League, to compete with the Wheat Pool. They want to defend the freedom of the Manitoba farmers. The battle is on, with each side fighting for the farmers' interests. It is now a question of who has the right idea. Personally I think farmers would achieve more if they could all pull together. It is no wonder that interest in a farming career is not very high with the younger generation. All they hear are lamentations about low prices and bad prospects.

However, a lot is done to foster interest in farming. At present the winter fair is on, which is held in Dauphin each year. It is sponsored by the Agricultural Society. People from the Department of Agriculture and from the University of Manitoba often give speeches and courses. Theory is alternated with practical lessons and competitions in the judging of grain, horses, cattle, pigs and poultry. Young people who belong to the boys' and girls' clubs take a very active part in this event. There will be judging of the livestock that these young people have raised and cared for by themselves. In the end these animals will be sold at public auction. There was also a meat judging contest for the farm ladies. And naturally the fair ends with a nice dinner and a dance.

✳

The Weather Plays Tricks

April 1931

In the end the old-timers proved to be right! When March started with beautiful frosty days, they shook their heads and recited the proverb, "When March comes in like a lamb, it goes out like a lion."

Nobody thought they would be right this year. Once in a while it would start to thaw with days warm and sunny. Then one afternoon, when Wim and I went to the henhouse to gather eggs, he suddenly shouted, "Look, Mammie, three suns in the sky!" Sure enough, he was right. It was that strange phenomenon that sometimes happens in the winter — the Sundogs they call it here. I have seen it only in Canada. On both sides of the sun, a bit removed from it, you see two other suns. The people here claim it is always followed by a very cold spell, and I believe they are right. So I said, "You know what? We will bring as much wood to the house as we can manage. Just in case it starts to get really cold again, and nobody feels like going outside to fill the woodboxes, we will be sitting pretty."

We were still at it when we heard Bobby yodelling in the bush on the other side of the river, and soon he and his three dogs, who always go to school with him, were running over the bridge.

"I saw snowbirds, Mamma," he shouted. They flew very low over the field. I am sure we will get snow again and we can play with our sleighs."

Around six o'clock the first big snowflakes started to come down. "Dutch snow," the boys shouted. "Do you think we will be able to make a snowman with it?" Here in Manitoba we are used to dry powdery snow which blows like sand in big clouds over the field and stings your face like needle pricks.

The cold was not a Dutch coldness. In the kitchen where two stoves were burning merrily it stayed icy cold because the wind hit the windows head-on. A big layer of ice covered them completely. At eleven o'clock we even needed to light the heater in the bedroom.

We did our best to stay comfortable with four stoves burning full blast in our small house. The old-timers had been right after all. Happily it did not last very long. After a few days the snow started to melt and suddenly, during the first week of April, we got the most beautiful warm spring days!

April on the Prairies

Easter is not celebrated here as fully as it is in Holland. In Holland everybody goes outside on Easter, whether for walks or for a drive, but here it is very dead and dull on the street in town. Only around eleven o'clock do you see people outside going to a church service.

This year Easter was not festive for us at all. A friend of ours had a horrible accident and on this Easter Sunday we attended his funeral.

That also seemed strange to us at first, that you could be buried or married on a Sunday. Another thing we find different here is that people go to a funeral in their ordinary clothes, not dressed all in black as we were used to at home. You can find the brightest hats and dresses at these funeral services, and I have never seen a veiled widow. Neither do you get an invitation to attend the funeral. You attend more as a spontaneous gesture.

Most often the funeral starts with a church service, and after that many will follow the hearse with their own cars to the cemetery. Our cemetery is situated about half a mile from town and if the deceased is a well-known person or an old-timer, it is not unusual at all to see sixty or more cars following the hearse. The coffin is carried from the church to the car and from the car to the cemetery by friends or neighbours, not by hired men as we are used to in Holland. This Easter day the roads were still in very bad condition, and all twenty-one of the cars got hopelessly stuck in the mud.

Monday morning we could amuse ourselves with visualizing how people in our old city of Groningen would walk in their new Easter outfits along the Heereweg and enjoy the beautiful spring day — if it was indeed beautiful and not rainy, as is so often the case there.

Here a different activity awaited us. The temperature rose so rapidly that around noon it was 72˚F in the shade. We had to hurry to do something with our meat, which started to thaw out in the woodshed. We spent the day cutting it up, salting a part of it, and putting as much as we could in jars for canning. We soon found out that we were not the only ones doing this. Ttttrrrr, ttrr, ttrr — one long and two short — our telephone rang.

"Hallo! How is everybody? What are you doing?"

"Salting and canning meat."

"The same here. With this temperature you can't wait a day longer.

If this weather keeps up, the men might be working on the fields in another week!"

"Sure enough. If we get a bit of wind with this it will dry the land in no time at all. So long for now."

The telephone is quite a thing in the country. I can't remember ever having heard about "party lines" in Holland, but that is what you have here on the farms. Instead of everybody having their own private phone, here a lot of people are served by one phone line, and to differentiate between them each family has its own different ring. You can dial one, two, three or four rings, or a combination. The rings can be short or long.

It took us a little time to get used to this system. No use telling secrets over the phone. They don't stay secrets. Anybody who might be interested only has to pick up the phone receiver and listen in. They claim that bachelors living alone often listen in because they hardly ever hear a human voice otherwise. Well, you can hardly blame the poor guys. Many farm women, too, make a lot of use of the telephone, not only for listening in but often for tying up the line for a very long time. You will hear them exchange recipes over the phone. They tell each other how busy they are because they have to do the laundry today and they are also baking bread. They are so very, very busy! It can happen that suddenly a male voice interrupts and says, "I'm sure, Mrs. X, that your bread is getting hot — I can smell it here. You better have a look and give me the line for a change."

Besides these functions, which in a way take the place of face-to-face gossip between neighbours, the benefit of a phone on a farm can hardly be overrated. So often horses or cows are missing, or you need to borrow a piece of machinery, or there is sickness or an accident and you need to make an emergency call. Farms are quite a distance apart here and the roads are often poor. Fortunately the phone rates were lowered a bit this year, or many might not have been able to afford the phone in these hard times.

We were lucky that the wind we were hoping for came and dried the land in a hurry. But as is so often the case, we had too much of a good thing. We found ourselves in a regular dust storm. In no time the fields were dry and then the soil started to blow away. Black clouds of dust blew across the road and through our house. It got so dark at four o'clock in the afternoon that I needed to light the lamps to finish the work I was doing. The sun was totally hidden behind the dust clouds. At last, close to midnight, the storm let up and left no other trace than a very dirty house. Fortunately I had not started my housecleaning yet.

27

In the meantime all the farmers were busy in their granaries. Everybody was busy cleaning grain. Instead of empty granaries except for seed grain for the coming year, as is the case in other years, everybody still has a lot of grain left. The reason is that the price has been so low, especially for barley, that it does not pay to sell it. Farmers who have barley will trade it for lumber or wood or whatever they can use. The old-fashioned barter trade has been revived again because there is very little money. For bartering the price of barley is taken at 20¢ bushel, while you can get only 12¢ at the elevator in town.

On Monday, April 13, all the farmers suddenly appeared in the fields with their cultivators and harrows. It was the same as a year ago, a very early start for field work. Everybody is working as hard as possible right now to get the wheat sown, because it is very important that the wheat gets in early due to our short summer season. We can still expect frost once in a while, yet generally it is not severe enough to do much damage to the grain. In fact, some farmers claim it makes the wheat stool out or sprout better. The sowing of barley and oats has to wait a while because it can't stand the frost as well.

But even if the future looks far from rosy the farmers can't do much else than stay optimistic and hope for the best. Who, after all, knows what the future will bring?

This year most farmers in our area are sowing their wheat in April, which is early for us. However, it is not very nice to be in the fields except for a few warm days when our temperature is 80°F. A strong chilly wind blows which causes occasional dust storms and loss of topsoil and of seed. As a result several farmers had to reseed their wheat. I enjoy seeing through the windows the rows of grain coming up nicely and, if nothing happens to it, the crop will be golden ripe in about a hundred days. Our growing season is remarkably short, and because so many things need to be done it seems shorter than it really is.

A House Party in Canada

Early May 1931

Opportunities for amusement in the country are very limited. In fact there is not much more entertainment than an odd movie in town or a house party. Sometimes a party is held in the schoolhouse, but that is only allowed on Friday nights. The townspeople skate, play hockey, tennis and the like, and there is a place a few miles out of town where they can play golf.

Quite a few districts have a community hall, a good-size wooden building consisting of one large hall and a lean-to kitchen where tea and coffee can be made on a cookstove. Chairs and benches are placed along the walls, and the hall often contains a piano or organ. The hall is used for dances and meetings, and on summer Sundays for church services.

Most parties, though, are held in homes. Called house parties, they were quite a novelty for us, for we never had this kind of party in Holland. I can just see the average Dutch housewife suddenly confronted with twenty or thirty people arriving at her home, and sometimes even far more. In a large farmhouse I have seen as many as a hundred guests.

I will never forget our own first house party here, and I'll tell you about it now.

We had lived only a few months in our log cabin on the first ridge of the Riding Mountains when one afternoon Florence, the daughter of the farmer whom Bob had first worked for and who owned the bush farm we now live on, arrived on horseback.

"We are coming here tonight for a house party," she said. "It is what we call a surprise party, but my mother said I better prepare you a bit because you are still so new here, so it won't be too much of a surprise for you."

I stood there flabbergasted. "How many people will be coming?" I asked. "Oh, I don't know that," she said. "That all depends. We did some phoning around to the neighbours, and with this nice weather quite a few might come. Don't they have surprise parties in Holland?"

I had never heard of it and asked Florence what to expect. "Do I give them tea or coffee, and do I have to bake cookies and cakes? I don't have too much on hand at present."

"No, no," Florence said. "There will be a lunch. The guests will look after everything, so don't worry." In Canada they call it lunch even if it is served at midnight.

After she had galloped at full speed out of the yard again I got busy sweeping the floor, dusting and arranging a few chairs around the table and trying to make our modest home as attractive as possible.

Around eight o'clock the first guests started to arrive. It was a bit cool now but still beautiful for October. The guests arrived mostly by democrat, buggy or wagon box, and an odd one by car. Not many farmers own cars.

In no time at all our little house was filled with people. The women and girls put boxes and tins filled with cakes and cookies on the kitchen table and disappeared upstairs to get rid of their hats and coats. I had not foreseen this invasion of our sleeping quarters and had in all innocence put Bobby to sleep there. Of course, he received them with glee and, as many of the guests had brought their children along, he quickly scrambled out of bed and joined the party.

In the meantime the men had not been sitting idle either. They took my nicely arranged chairs outside, brought in long planks and arranged those all around the room. I have been to house parties where it became so full and hot that they ended up carrying the heater, smoking away, out of the house and then closed off the stovepipe hole for the time being!

When most of our furniture had been put outside, everybody found a place to sit. About twenty women with their children were in the big living room and about the same number of men were crowded into the small kitchen. Bob and I were sitting a bit uneasy among them, not really knowing what was expected of us. Well, I guess nothing was expected. One of the younger men produced a gramophone and soon the Scottish reels and Irish jigs started up. Now the men started to crowd to the door of the living room, but they still did not venture further. This is the universal custom here. Men and women stay separated until later on in the evening when the company mixes up to have lunch.

After the gramophone music a young man stepped forward and sang a few Scottish songs. I heard later that he had made quite a name for himself and was a welcome entertainer at parties like this. The people do not seem to be very shy about performing. Anybody who can play an instrument or sing a song steps forward and contributes to the success of the party. A young Dutch friend of ours who has been in Canada a year and has hired himself out on a farm in the neighbourhood did his bit and did not have to take a back seat to the Canadian artists.

After a while I started to notice a bit of restlessness, especially among the younger people, and at last somebody walked up to Bob and asked him if they could dance. "By all means," he said, "at least if you can find a place for it." Well, there was no place, and on top of that the floor was not too strong. In fact Mr. Durston, the owner of the cabin, advised against it.

This, however, did not stop them. They spotted our woodshed behind the house and wondered if we would mind if they used that for dancing. We had no objection, but the woodshed was full of rubbish. It was the only place I had not managed to straighten out. But that meant nothing to them. In no time the men had emptied the building, shouted for a broom and started sweeping the floor. Clouds of dust flew out of the door and soon the fun could start. Stable lanterns had been hung from the rafters and they gave enough light.

"But what about music?" we asked. "That gramophone won't be loud enough." Three old farmers disappeared and turned up a few minutes later, each with a violin. They had been prepared for all emergencies. Because it was pretty chilly outside we all had to wear coats and sweaters, but that was no problem.

It was all so different from anything we had ever seen. The violin players held their instruments against their chests or across their knees and sawed and fiddled as loud as they could, especially if a quadrille was played. Then they would really get going, rocking back and forth with the music and stamping their feet at the same time. Another farmer called the figures with a loud voice, half singing, half shouting. The older generation also came to have a look, standing in the doorway watching the happy crowd. But it was a bit too cold for them so they soon disappeared again. We dancers were warm enough.

A while later I went back to the house and saw four older ladies bustling around in my kitchen, busy with cups and saucers (which they had brought), with sandwiches, cookies and cakes, cream and sugar. I felt like a stranger in my own house! They seemed to be able to find anything they needed. The tea was made in a washboiler, and I discovered that at a party like this the hostess is not supposed to supply anything herself.

When lunch was ready the dancers were called and in a short while all were back in the house again. Now the ice was broken and the young men joined the young girls in the living room, so it was soon crammed full. Pressed close together they were all sitting on the wooden planks around the room. A number of people, men as well as women, made the rounds with teacups, tea, milk and sugar, and trays full of sandwiches and other goodies. A few minutes later everyone sat with a boiling hot cup of tea in their hands and a lap full of sandwiches and cakes. They didn't wait until you finished what you were eating, but you got the whole lot at once.

When everybody had had enough cups of tea and refreshments, they all seemed to gather around a nice older lady. I was wondering what they were doing now. Then I saw the lady staring very intently into the teacups that were presented to her, and I noticed the young folks listening very attentively. The older ones offered their cups as well. I was now told that she could predict your future pretty accurately from your tea leaves. I am convinced that at least half of those present believed her!

When at last everyone knew enough about his or her future, the cups were gathered up again and a few ladies bustled to the kitchen and started washing them. The young folk, who by now were all thoroughly mixed, had a great time. A few of the older ladies had brought their knitting and crocheting and sat working and talking together. In the kitchen, crowded close together behind and around the big kitchen range, stood the older men talking farming.

When everything was cleaned up and packed away again the ladies went upstairs. Our bedroon sure looked funny to me. The big double bed was full of coats and hats, scarves and mittens and, in addition, it was full of sleeping children. As soon as the children had given signs of sleepiness they had been brought there by their mothers. My own little son had scorned his crib and slept peacefully among all those youngsters. Now they all were awakened, wrapped in shawls and coats, and with a lot of shouting and laughing all our guests got in their carts and cars and set out for home.

Spring is Here, Sort Of

Late May 1931

Now at last spring is really here! On the land we can clearly see the fresh green rows of grain, the grass looks lush and the fields are dotted with the bright yellow of the dandelions. We do not have the small daisy, the madeliefje, with which the meadows of Holland are dotted. The trees are starting to unfurl their leaves, and ferns and climbers seem to jump out of the ground. All the dead leaves, twigs and fallen trees disappear under the fresh green covering.

All through the bush you can spot the fruit trees with their white plumes of blossom. The garden seeds have started to sprout, and we have been able to eat our own asparagus since the middle of May. The rhubarb is rosy and tender, and you can almost watch it grow! Hens and chickens, turkeys and geese, pigs, lambs and calves, cows and horses all scuttle in the barnyard and in the meadow behind our barn.

It is hard to believe that it is only ten days since we had our last snowstorm. The first two weeks in May were so beautiful. Everybody felt that winter had left us and spring had made its entry. Already the sun gave such warmth, and the days were so much longer!

I got busy taking down all the heavy drapes to hang them on the wash line outside, along with the blankets and heavy winter clothing. After the dust storms we had in the spring they needed a good airing.

Toward the middle of May it became really hot. It was 85°F in the shade. Inside the house it became unbearable because I had been baking bread and the kitchen range was hot most of the time. When Bob came home for dinner the heat that met him nearly floored him. "Open your doors and windows," he shouted. "This is enough to suffocate you."

"You're right," I said, "but I am baking bread today and you know very well that it will spoil if I get a draft on it. Now you can see for yourself that it is high time to get the summer kitchen ready."

I had asked for this several times in the last two weeks, but so far without results. All I got was "You just wait, we will very likely get cold days again," or "I am far too busy now; later on when the seeding is done I'll give you a hand with it." But after his dinner in this suffocating kitchen no persuasion was needed any more. So it was done the next morning.

A few years ago we had moved an old granary behind the house. Bob broke about four planks out of the walls and made a kind of awning out of them. These he fastened with hinges to the walls again so we could open and close them as needed. He covered the open spaces with screening so that the wind can blow right through on a hot day, and installed a screen door as well. I find it an ideal place to do my cooking and canning in the hot summer months. We call it our camp.

To fix this camp for the summer calls for moving the big kitchen stove from the house to this building, which is quite a job. We were struggling with this heavy brute when the temperature was 90°F. Cleaning the chimney and the pipes could best be done all at the same time, we decided.

By five o'clock we were black as boots, but the stove was now in its summer spot and most of my kitchen gear and staples had been moved, too. Then we took a bath in the river. How lucky we are to have a river so close to the house. Washing in the river was the first thing that came into our heads once the dirty job was done. So we inaugurated our summer camp and our summer bathtub on the same day. Now every night Bobby and Wim, towels over their shoulders, have their dip before they crawl into bed.

After our dip in the river, refreshed and clean, we all crawled up the steep river bank. We saw the sheep and young lambs lying under the bridge, panting from the heat.

"Goodness, Bob," I shouted, "look at those poor beasts! How hot they must be in their woolly coats. They should be shorn right away."

"Sure enough," Bob said. "I'll do it as soon as all the seed is planted. I can't do it before then."

Well, two days later I would not have minded crawling into one of those woolly coats myself. The wind shifted suddenly to the north. Gone was the warm sun, gone the feeling of spring. Snowflakes were whirling past the windows again and an icy wind howled around the house! Green fields disappeared under a blanket of snow, and that was fortunate because the temperature went well below freezing. Plum blossoms were ruined by the frost, as well as some things in the garden. Wheat and barley can stand quite a bit of frost but oats freeze quickly.

In a way we were not too unhappy with the sudden change. The soil was very dry this spring. In recent weeks we had often heard people say that we needed rain or there wouldn't be much of a crop this year. Snow doesn't help half as much as a good soaking rain, and a lot of the snow was blown off the field by heavy winds, but this was better than nothing at all.

The snow stayed about three days, and then the temperature rose and we saw the green fields again. I took a lot of teasing from Bob and the boys. "Isn't it nice and cool cooking in your camp?" they laughed as they saw me huddled in a heavy coat with a scarf around my neck and a toque over my ears while carrying steaming dishes from the camp to the house.

The snow may have been good for the grain but it certainly was not very good for the young turkeys. We had twelve outside with a big turkey hen besides about two dozen in the henhouse under broody hens. The other turkeys were still sitting on their eggs, but so far we haven't been able to find them. The Sunday before it had started to snow we had been inspecting the growing crop with a few friends when we saw that big turkey hen with her dozen little ones in the field. That field is surrounded by bush and it was beautifully warm and sunny, an ideal place for them.

When the snow started to swirl around the house I suddenly remembered those turkeys, with grave misgivings. It was getting dark already and it would be useless to try to find them now. They might be miles from the spot we had seen them last. I have often been surprised how such small birds can cover so much ground in such a short time.

Early next morning Bob went out to hunt them. After about two hours he returned with five shivering little birds in his cap. All the others had died. We did not succeed in saving these five either.

We lost the two dozen in the hen house, too, but in a different way. One morning we found the door broken open by the pigs, and ten turkeys had disappeared. A miserable odor hung over the farmyard which even penetrated our house. A skunk had been around and had entered the open door and helped himself. We were very disappointed because we had high hopes of raising a nice flock of turkeys now that grain prices were still very low.

In the afternoon a neighbour dropped in looking even more downcast than we did. He grumbled that he got only 18¢ for a pound of butter, and complained that eggs, which were 9¢ to 14¢ a dozen a while ago, now sold for only 5¢ to 9¢ a dozen. How could you support a family on prices like that?

Heat and Drought, Dust and Grasshoppers

Early July 1931

When I first arrived in Canada I was surprised to see how country people were dressed here. The boys and men only get out of their overalls on special occasions. Even then, many keep a new pair for special events but turn up their trouser legs quite a bit to show they are wearing dress pants underneath. The overalls used for work often have plenty of spots and tears, and a button may be replaced by a nail which does the job. I won't say that every farmer dresses like that, but it is certainly not at all unusual. In Holland even the poorer people dressed in neatly mended clothes. Here it makes no difference if you are rich or poor, everyone dresses alike.

The women look very neat when they go out, and they make use of powder and lipstick like their city sisters. At home they wear cotton dresses even on the coldest winter days, often with a sweater to keep warm. Some are always neat, no matter what time of day you see them. Others are not as neat and sport tears or spots but never seem embarrassed about it.

The first few years when our family was still very small we often said, "I would rather die than look like that," but we soon found out that one person can do only so much work in one day. I hope we will never go down to the level of tears and spots, but we do go with bare legs in hot weather rather than wear stockings with holes in them. With the best will in the world I can't find time to mend them during the busy summertime.

The past month gave us a lot of work and a few disappointments. June 8 was the last day we were seeding and after that date we were looking for rain. June is supposed to be the month for rain, and we needed it badly this year. But every morning started with beautiful sunshine and it would get very hot during the afternoon. Every evening the people from town would drive out in their cars and enjoy a leisurely ride in the country, pass our farm and stop on the bridge. They would lean over the railing and watch the beautiful sunset we see so often in this country.

Under the bridge we would be working hard, filling barrels and washtubs with clear river water and moving them by horsedrawn wagon to the garden. The conversation would generally be about the dry spring and the crop prospects. Sometimes, very suddenly, the sky would cloud up, but always it raised false hopes as the clouds disappeared again.

Bob was very busy these days with shearing his sheep, plowing under some crops where too many weeds were coming up, and especially with fixing the fences. We do not have ditches around our farms like they have in Holland. Each quarter section has three rows of barbed wire around it, which means that for a quarter section of land we need three times two miles of barbed wire. This year he needed to put in a few new poles and stretch the slack wire.

Until this year we did not need a fence on the west because our western border is the river. But in the last few years a few horses and cows would wander across the river from the other side to eat our grain. So now there was no choice but to get busy and put up a decent fence on the west. This took quite a while because the river is very winding.

Then at last a very heavy thunderstorm broke the dry spell and brought the badly needed rain. It has saved the grain from drying out completely, but only the summer fallow looks very good. People returning from holidays in other parts of Manitoba and Saskatchewan tell us that conditions there are a lot worse. They have tales about areas that have totally dried out, where people have no vegetables in their gardens and no feed for their cattle. Most people do not have meadow land for pasture. They think it is more profitable to grow grain on all their land. So after the milking is finished they chase their cows out of the gate and onto the road.

In normal times the animals find plenty of feed there because, on both sides of the gravel road, there are stretches of about ten yards on which grass grows. But because grass is so scarce this year the cows wander farther and farther away. It is no fun after a day of hard work to have to go after your cows and find them miles away. Often the cows will wander to the "flats," the prairie land that belongs to the municipality. Sometimes you find them hidden in the bush. Sometimes you don't even find them before dark and need to search for them on horseback the next morning — since the prices of butter and cream are now so low it doesn't pay to waste gas to search by car. The price of butter is only 14¢ a pound.

Women have their hands full these summer days, too. Gardens, chickens and housework take every hour of the day. I can't manage a regular housecleaning this year, but instead I use each spare moment to tackle a cupboard or a room. But even if it was a slow process this year, I eventually finished. One evening I made the rounds of the whole house and thought, "Well, this is all I can do about it this year. More important work is waiting."

Two days after that I had a bad disappointment. Although we sometimes have bad dust storms, as I told you earlier, we don't expect them this late in the year because the land is green and the soil is mostly covered. But one afternoon a strong wind set up like I have never seen! The roof of our machine shed was thrown high in the air and smacked down again, quite a distance away. We were scared stiff that the barn and house roofs would follow. The sun disappeared behind a kind of yellow curtain. It was not so much our own dust but dust from Saskatchewan that was bothering us. It penetrated through every nook and cranny. The wind lasted through most of the night, dying down toward morning.

When we came downstairs in the morning we found everything covered with a thick layer of dirt. It had penetrated every cupboard and trunk in the house. Only the children had fun, scribbling and making pictures on everything. I walked disconsolately through the house and felt that I would not have the energy to start cleaning this mess up, after having just finished cleaning my whole house.

I lamented to Bob, "There is nothing more disappointing than to work your head off making a house presentable and then find it all undone in a single night!"

"Well," he answered, "I'll show you something a lot worse." He took all of us over the bridge to the edge of our farm. "Now look at the road and the land on the other side of the bridge," he said. Thousands — no, more like millions — of little grasshoppers were jumping over the bridge and road and through the shrubbery beside it.

The little bit of grass that had been there had already been eaten. Now they started on the young grain. We stood staring, powerless. Now a dirty house seemed small and unimportant. We had heard on the radio that grasshoppers had been spotted in different communities, but it had seemed quite a distance away. The government was providing free poison, but it is still expensive because it has to be mixed with large quantities of chopped grain and then spread over the ground. There is also the danger of poisoning your own livestock. So it is not used much around here. We had hoped that the river would protect us.

There is nothing you can do about it. Afterwards a litter of fourteen piglets was born, and a few lambs and a calf, which helped bring things back to a bit of balance.

✳

Welcome Visitors from Holland

September 1931

Day after day cars loaded high with camping gear taking people to Clear Lake came past our farm. I was envious and would think, "Those people leave all their worries behind and will have a real holiday now. When they come home they will feel refreshed and can start life anew."

But a farm family can never have a real holiday. We need to do the same things day in and day out. I remembered the long holidays we used to have at home, either visiting family or staying at the seashore. If only we could expect friends or family to visit us, at least that would be a welcome change. But that's not possible because they all live on the other side of the ocean. So I was feeling a bit sorry for myself.

But suddenly a letter arrived from Iowa, announcing the intended visit of a family who had come from the same part of Holland that we did. The man had been a foreman in a large lumber business owned by my mother's father. This man's mother as a girl had worked in the house for my grandmother, and after she left and was married my family kept in contact with her. We had heard that they had a hard time getting started in Iowa, but now were getting on very well.

One beautiful summer evening they arrived in their car, something they could never expect to own in the old country. Four of them came, the mother, their married daughter and her husband, and their twenty-five-year-old son. The father had stayed home to look after the farm.

What a joyous arrival! They spoke the Groningen provincial dialect from our home, something we had not heard for years, and that was music to our ears. They never spoke English themselves because there was quite a settlement of Dutch people where they lived. How much we had to show them! We never stopped talking.

Bob had started cutting his crop and naturally could not postpone his work. The two men went with him to the field and helped with stooking the grain. At home the women soon saw my overflowing workbasket and tackled the mending. We talked and talked.

I think they found it a bit hard to understand that we enjoyed our life in Canada. Such a simple house to live in, and needing to do all the hard work ourselves in contrast to Holland, where hired help did that kind of work for us. Whereas we saw the contrast with our former life of ease in Holland as an adventure, they saw it as a major step backward for us.

They also realized how young this country is compared to Iowa. They were surprised to see the simple, small houses in which most of our farmers live. They marvelled at the big piles of wood every farmer has behind his house, and the cattle roaming freely along the roadside. You'd never see that in the States.

But our district did look pretty good to them. When they walked over our farm they exclaimed, "Now, that looks like the farms in Holland! And in Iowa you can't find such heavy stands of wheat and barley. It is much too hot for it there." We learned that they live in the corn belt where hogs are fed the corn.

They stayed only four days, and early one morning left again. We felt that we were losing a bit of Holland. "We will come again," they said, "and you should try to visit us in Iowa some day."

When they left we were too busy to feel lonesome. Threshing season had started. Very soon we learned that the next day we could expect the threshers. We had a lot of work to do to prepare for them.

Bob and the hired man disappeared into the granary and were busy for hours dividing it into four compartments. I bundled the boys into the car and quickly drove for town, figuring out as I drove which supplies I would need. We would have about ten extra men to cook for, a smaller crew than in the past.

We were busy until late at night. Bob and the hired man filled the woodbox and got me a big washtub full of potatoes from the garden. I lowered twenty pounds of meat into the well to keep it cool, and was still busy making cakes and pies at eleven o'clock that night. We went to bed tired but in good spirits. With good luck we might finish harvesting three days from now. That would be the earliest we had ever finished.

Around four o'clock in the morning we awoke with a start. A pouring rain had started outside. In no time at all the garden was flooded, and the rain kept up the whole day. This was very bad news for us. The threshing would be postponed for a week or more and the quality of the grain would be hurt, and therefore bring a lower price.

But things turned out not as bad as we had feared. The air stayed cool and there was a nice little breeze. But it was a full week before the grain was dry enough to harvest. In my next letter I will tell you about the busy and exciting threshing days on the farm.

Threshing Days

October 1931

Threshing days are very different on the Canadian prairies than they are in Holland. We do not first carry all the cut grain into the barn and then thresh it inside or very close to the barn, as is done in Holland. Here all the threshing takes place out in the field where the grain is grown.

Our barns are much smaller than barns in Holland. The barn floor is mostly taken up with stalls for the horses, cows and pigs. There is no drainage in these barns. They need to be cleaned by hand and are often quite sloppy and dirty. On many farms you sink ankle deep in mud and manure, and if it gets too bad planks are put down. We are lucky that our barn at least has a cement floor.

The loft above the stalls is the place for hay and the sheaves of grain that are used for feed. Most of the sheaves are left out in the field to dry and the farmer hopes to get the threshing outfit as early as possible so his grain will be threshed as soon as it is dry enough.

Here in Manitoba most threshing is done with a machine that has a tractor on a steam engine to power it. We don't have any of the combines you read about that cut the grain and thresh it out at the same time. One of the reasons is that our farmers cut their grain before it is completely ripe and then they set the sheaves up in what are called stooks so they can ripen and dry out fast. The stooks are put up with the butt down and the waving heads up. When Bob did it the first time he did just the opposite, which seems to be the way most greenhorns do it the first time.

Lately we see the odd combine which uses a different system. With what is called a swather a mower cuts the grain and dumps it in long ribbons on the field where it will dry out. If you leave the heads of grain to dry on the stem before the grain is cut there is a chance that the kernels will dry out. Also the grain suffers more from strong winds if it is left standing. When the cut swath is dry a combine will rake up the grain and thresh it. The threshed kernels are dumped into a truck in the field whenever the combine's grain hopper is full. Although this is very efficient, the heads are cut with only a short piece of straw, while the rest of the straw is left on the field and burned. Our farmers use all the straw for feed and shelter.

This year our threshing gang consisted mostly of farmers' sons. But generally a threshing gang is very mixed company. Last year we had two farmers, five farmers' sons, two Natives, five Ukrainians, and four college students trying to make a few extra dollars to pay for their studies. To top it off we also had our own member of Parliament, who is a farmer all right, but he spends most of his time as our legislator in Ottawa. There are no formalities here as we are so used to in Holland, and he was just called Bill by everyone.

The big day is announced by the arrival of the caboose, the trailer in which this mixed company sleeps at night. It is lined with bunks just as you will find on a ship, but it is not exactly as shipshape. The caboose is driven to the next farm by the farmer who just had his own threshing finished. That is the tradition.

Following the caboose in the procession come the stook wagons, bumping and rattling. These wagons have hayracks on which the sheaves are loaded in the field. There will be from four to eight wagons. Behind them, snorting and puffing, comes the steam engine or the tractor, followed by the threshing machine itself and a tank wagon for water.

The crew of a steam-engine gang is the following: an engineer, a man to run the separator, a fireman (who needs to fork in the straw), a tank man for hauling water, six to eight men on the stook wagons, and three to four pitchers who pitch the sheaves onto the wagons. And of course you have the farmer with his hired help and a few neighbours to help with shovelling the grain.

If you have a tractor instead of a steam engine the fireman and the tank man are eliminated. One person will run both the tractor and the separator. There won't be more than six stook wagons.

The farmer points out where he wants the threshing machine placed. We sometimes have the outfit right in front of the barn so that the straw will blow straight into the hayloft; but the wind has to come from the right direction for this to work. While some of the men are busy setting up the threshing machine, the stook teams are already in the field loading up the sheaves. By the time the whistle blows the first loaded stook teams have arrived at the machine. If the outfit is large they will fork grain in from both sides. For the whole long day, until late in the evening, the empty wagons lumber back to the field to return at a slower pace with full loads.

Back and forth the grain wagons ride from the threshing machine to the granary. Some farmers have a lot of small granaries that can be moved, and they place them so that the grain will blow directly into the granary. We have only the one big granary with removable partitions. All the grain has to be brought to it and shovelled in by hand. Forking up sheaves the whole day is not an easy job, but shovelling grain the whole day is worse. That is the farmer's job.

This year many of the farmers rented trucks to take the grain directly to the elevator in town. The reason is that last year grain prices were much higher right after threshing. This year a fall in prices after the harvest is expected again. A farmer who works a whole quarter section by himself can't take the grain to the elevator right away because he first needs to finish his fall plowing and other work on the land. Farmers figure they will get a better price by trucking the grain in right away. Besides it saves a lot of work.

But there was a still more urgent reason. The owners of threshing outfits wanted to be paid in cash for their work this year because they have not been given credit for gas and oil expenses. The hired help, too, expect to be paid in cash as soon as their work is finished. The grain trucks charge ½¢ a bushel a mile for hauling the grain.

In normal times this is all reasonable enough; but now the price of wheat is only 40¢ a bushel for number one grade wheat. It is not often you produce that grade. Later the price went down to 35¢. The prices of grain are set daily at the grain exchange in Winnipeg. Their price is *what you receive no matter to which elevator you bring your grain. The freight charge, which in Dauphin is 17¢ a bushel, is deducted from the price.*

The elevators here do the grading of the grain. If you are not satisfied with their decision you can send a sample to Winnipeg and have it graded there. Grain is totally handled in bulk, that is, we do not use sacks as they do in Europe.

Prices do not cover costs this year. Rain has lowered the quality by one grade, which makes a difference of 4¢ a bushel. Threshing costs us 6¢ a bushel this year. When you then deduct the cost of bindertwine and the hired help, you find that the farmer has nothing left, only debts.

Women's Work at Threshing Time

Late October 1931

Having told you of the man's work at threshing time, I will now tell you of the work women do during threshing, which is not insignificant.

It is quite usual on Canadian farms to see a table overloaded with all kinds of delicacies, served in very simple surroundings. But Bob and I stick to our Dutch customs. We eat a lot less meat and more vegetables than people do here. For us cake and cookies are not daily fare but are considered treats. But as soon as we have hired help or visitors we copy the Canadian way, and at threshing time, of course, we need to follow Canadian customs.

Instead of making threshing meals simple but good they are regular feasts. As a newcomer I do not have the nerve to do it differently. For the men who are threshing the food is the highlight of the day. There are tales galore about threshing gangs that threatened to strike because they were not satisfied with the food.

The first few years I dreaded these days. Sometimes I could get help from a very young girl, but more often I had to handle it alone. Bread, cakes, cookies, tarts, etc., must all be homemade. You can buy these in a bakery in town, of course, but the homemade baked goods are far better. In this respect the bake shops in Holland have much nicer things for sale than you can buy here.

On threshing days our alarm clock rings at half past three. This is quite unusual for us because normally we get up at five o'clock in the summer and an hour later in the winter. So we are pretty drowsy when we start to light the coal oil lamps. Outside in the caboose there is no sign of life where the men are still sleeping. It does not take them more than half an hour to feed and harness their horses.

The house looks strange as we walk around in it. All unnecessary furniture has been carried outside. The table covers practically the whole length of the room, and boards on both sides of it serve as seats. Each person has a dinner plate and a porridge bowl. Next to each plate is a fruit dish, knife, fork and spoon. My head starts to reel already. As soon as the water boils I need to cook the rolled oats in it, and while this is boiling I must slice the cold potatoes left over from last night. I will need two frying pans because the workers like lots of potatoes. When the potatoes are done I empty them into a few bowls because now I need the frying pans for bacon and eggs. I run back and forth between table and stove because I need to slice the bread. I hope four loaves will be enough. And now the cake — two platters of cake need to be served for breakfast. Who ever heard of cake for breakfast? Two quart jars with canned fruit need to be opened and put into bowls. Did I forget anything now? Oh, sure enough! They have to have pickles. Without pickles it would not be a Canadian meal. Canadians serve pickles even with tea.

Right on the dot of five o'clock the whole caravan comes shuffling in. Some of the men are quite jovial and wish me a good morning, but others don't say anything. I don't notice that anyway — I only see that long table with the confusion of plates and bowls and platters full of food. Moreover I have my hands full filling all the teacups and handing filled porridge bowls to the men.

"More tea, please?" one jiggles his teacup. "More potatoes, missus," says another one. Quickly I fill the bowls again. "Is everybody here?" I ask. Two more men are coming, I am told, and the fireman is to have his breakfast at the threshing machine. While they are finishing their meal I pack the fireman's breakfast in a little box. With a sigh of relief I see them get up and leave the house.

Outside in the field the sun has risen and they are busy getting the engine of the threshing machine started. Exactly at six o'clock the whistle blows. They have started, and after a minute I see the dust from the threshing fly up again.

Relief until eleven o'clock! Then they will come in for their dinner. First I must wash all those dirty dishes, and then wake up the children. Better make the school lunch before I wake them. Afterwards, while the stack of dirty dishes slowly goes down and the stack of clean ones grows, I look out over the field again and see it bathed *in brilliant sunshine. What a privileged country with so much sunshine! The men are making good headway in the field. Most of the wheat stooks have already disappeared.*

These are wonderful days, really, the crown on a whole year's work, even if there is a bit too much work to do. A grain wagon comes into the barnyard again. I wave my dish towel and Bob waves back. We have had good crops the last few years, and that always makes these days exhilarating. The black spook of very low prices is pushed aside for the moment. That disenchantment will come back later.

When all the dishes are cleaned and piled up at the end of the table, I put down three smaller plates. Now I have the joy to top all joys — to sit on those wooden benches myself and eat from that immense table.

"Mammie, can we eat the same things the threshers have had? Please, please?" Bobby is a bit put out that he has to go to school while his little brothers will have all the fun today. There are so many cakes and cookies around, you can be sure they will have their share of them, not to forget the fun of riding with Daddy on the grain wagon. A few extras in Bobby's lunchbox will cheer him up a bit.

It is now eight o'clock, nice and early. I am sure I will be ready in plenty of time. Better start peeling that big pail of potatoes, then get a bunch of vegetables from the garden and wash them. Soon it will be time to put the meat in the oven. Later I will need the oven again to bake the pies. I better start setting the table again, put more sugar in the bowls and fill the salt and pepper shakers. Will there be enough bread for today? They eat bread here at every meal, which is why it disappears so fast. I am sure I can manage today, but tomorow I will need to bake a new batch. I had better set the yeast at four o'clock. I write that on the blackboard, otherwise I am sure to forget it.

Now it is half-past nine already. I better start making the pies. Pie is practically the only dessert served here. Pudding will be served the odd time, but pie is definitely the favourite. It is pie on Sunday and pie during the week. Pull out a piece of dough, line an enamel plate with it, fill it up with some kind of fruit, and then put another slab of dough on top. Make a nice design on it with a knife point so the air can escape while it bakes. After half an hour I have six pies standing in a row. The pies go in the oven at ten o'clock to be ready by eleven. While all this is cooking I quickly whip up a cake. That will need to be ready for the lunch in the afternoon.

Now the men come in for dinner and the breakfast story is repeated. The men come in, eat and leave me with a big mess. I need to watch the clock. Lunch must be served in the field at four o'clock, and that is a lot of work. Dishwashing will take more than an hour with all those greasy pots and pans. I have to rush, rush. Put Dickey in bed first for his nap, otherwise he will be trouble later on. He is a bit unwilling to leave the woodpile. Obviously the boys have had a great time there. By two o'clock the table is all cleared and the clean dishes neatly stacked at the end again.

Better make a batch of biscuits. I will need about thirty, but they do not take much time to make. When they are in the oven I can start making sandwiches. Making up four loaves of bread into sandwiches is a lot of work. I must not forget to ice the cake I baked this morning. If only my mother could see what a housekeeper I've turned into!

It is quarter after three already and soon time to boil the tea water. Start packing the lunch. This time I put the cups in a separate box, because I broke too many last time. The ride to the workers is over a rough stubble field. At quarter to four all is ready and I carry the box of goodies to the car. In front, on the floor next to my feet, is the scalding hot tea in a big kettle with a potato pricked on the spout so the tea will not splash on my feet as I cross the stubble field.

Distribution of the lunch takes place from the running board of the car. The men come in little groups and squat down around us. Sometimes they stop the threshing machine for a short while, but quite often they keep right on threshing with the men taking turns running it. In the beginning I used to send the lunch to the field and stayed home myself. But soon I heard complaints that some men did not have enough because some gluttons ate double portions. Now a watchful eye keeps them in line. I find this half hour in the fresh air very pleasant and relaxing.

Now the bustle for supper starts. It is the same as before. This meal does not differ at all from the noon meal except that pie will be substituted for cake and fruit. Meat, potatoes, vegetables, pickles, bread, etc. Around seven o'clock I put the two little ones to bed. Bobby can stay up for another hour to watch the proceedings and eat with all these men at the big table.

The first of the men start to come in for supper at about eight o'clock. I have set the table already, and wish they would hurry a bit. I am very tired now and I still have a lot of work ahead. But in the evening the men are not in a hurry. For them the only work remaining is feeding and bedding the horses, and then to bed for them. If only they would hurry a bit. All those dishes to wash yet, and to think that I need to get up again at 3:30 tomorrow morning. It makes me shudder.

The grain shovellers are tired, too. I can see it in their faces. Bob gets up from the table because he still needs to feed his animals and milk his cows. Slowly the others start to leave. Like a machine I keep on working, tired from head to toe. Not until eleven o'clock am I finished, with the table set for the next morning.

And so it goes. Every fall these days are repeated. Then the day comes that the threshing outfit departs, leaving in its wake the empty fields and an untidy house. Bob sits in front driving the caboose, and behind him the whole retinue goes out just as we saw them arrive. I am just as glad to see them go as I was to see them come.

When tranquility has returned we estimate our profit and loss for the year. "If only we would get a decent price," sighed Bob when we had climbed into the granary together to view our grain. I grabbed a few handfuls and threw some grain outside. From all sides cackling birds came rushing toward us, 200 chickens, 70 turkeys and 17 geese. I looked at them with pride. They represented my contribution to this year's proceeds, but even their market value is very low.

We finished by taking a stroll through the garden. The tomatoes were hanging in heavy clusters on the vines and quite a few have started to colour. The corn was also ripening, as the tassels were getting dark. Corn is a vegetable that we did not know about in Holland, but here it is very popular. The only trouble with growing corn is that the growing season here is a bit short. Quite often the corn freezes before it is ripe.

Then there are cabbage, cauliflower, beans, peas, carrots, beets, lettuce, cucumbers, and all sorts of greens — you find them all here. We looked them all over, and even if some had been damaged a bit by the dry season, most of them looked very good.

"Well," we said to each other, "we will not starve this winter, whatever the prices may be. A cellar full of our own produce, vegetables as well as poultry and other meat, is at least something to show for a busy summer!"

At nightfall I put three remarkably quiet little boys to bed. "We have a tummy ache," they said. Later on when I found their pockets full of nuts, raisins and cookie crumbs, and the spot behind the woodpile full of apple cores, it was no mystery any longer why that woodpile had been so attractive, and why there were tummy aches.

❊

Hunting Prairie Chickens

November 1931

One evening Bob read in the paper that the hunting season for prairie chickens and partridges would be opened the 16th of October. That happens to be his birthday, and I had been thinking for days on end how to make that day festive, something that everyone would enjoy.

Birthdays that fall in the summer or spring generally pass without much notice because there is no time for celebration. We only have something special for dinner and a birthday cake, that is about all. Somehow it did not appeal to me to spend a day cooking and baking indoors when outside it was such glorious weather.

Then I got an idea. The field work was practically over, so let's take the whole day off, take the car to the flats, take a lunch with us and go hunting!

Everyone said it was a great idea, except for Bobby who was irritated because naturally he had to go to school. But his dad assured him that the car would be at the school at four o'clock so that he could still have a few hours of fun with us. He was assured that besides the shotguns we would also bring the small rifle for him to shoot with. Then he was satisfied.

It turned out to be a wonderful day. In the morning we roamed over these flat prairies, dotted here and there with some scrub growth which gives it a parklike appearance. At noon we found a wonderful sheltered spot for a campfire and made our lunch. Then we put the two little ones in the car to have their nap, which gave Bob and me a chance to roam around and look for birds. I can't say that we saw much wildlife, and not being a very ardent hunter I personally couldn't have cared less, but I was glad that Bob had a chance to shoot a few prairie chickens and a partridge, which he brought down very smartly.

We almost got a jack rabbit, too — what we call a hare in Holland — but it happened that both our guns were empty at the time. I gave a cry of joy to see him standing there so perky on his hind legs. In my heart I was glad he got away, seeing him bound off into some bushes.

Promptly at four o'clock we arrived at the school. Bobby came running to meet us.

"Did you shoot anything?" was his first question.

"Only three so far," Bob told him.

"Did mama shoot any of them?" he asked with a very doubtful look.

"No, mama did not shoot anything," I had to confess.

"I bet you close your eyes when you shoot because you are scared of the bang," the naughty rascal said.

Well, mama had enough of the hunting now and preferred to sit in the shade of the car and read a book, watching the little ones at the same time. Daddy and his oldest son had a chance to disappear for a few hours. When the western sky was a rosy red and the sun had disappeared over the horizon they returned with four partridges.

Happy and satisfied about our nice holiday, we returned home where the evening chores were waiting as usual.

Winter Clothes and Native Moccasins

December 1931

By now all our farming implements have been inspected and put away for the winter. While Bob put on the storm windows and the storm doors, and put manure around the house to keep out drafts, I was busy with my steamer trunks in which we keep our winter clothes. The whole family was calling for gloves and mittens, for scarves and toques, for moccasins, sweaters and what not. There was measuring, fitting and cries of "This is too small for me," and "That is far too large," and "I can find only one of these," and "That one has a hole in it."

At last I covered my ears and said, "Each find something that will do for today, and I will get busy and sort it all out when you have left me alone for awhile. Go and play, or work, or whatever you want to do."

When they had finally left me alone the sorting started. Shoes always are a big problem. The men often wear high felt socks with low rubbers over them. Everyone who has to walk a lot in dry snow wears moccasins. If you go out in the sleigh and have to sit long stretches at a time you wear heavy felt boots with heavy felt soles. If you have to be really dressed up you wear your ordinary leather shoes with galoshes over them and have cold feet all the time. All these shoes, with the exception of the dressy leather ones, need felt soles in them. And it is better to wear more than one pair of socks. We also wear mittens double, wool ones underneath and leather ones over these.

As for coats, the warmest and most suitable to wear is fur, of course. But that is only for those who can afford it, which is to say not many of us on the farm at present. The fur coats that some farmers wear are remnants of a glorious past. They have lost a lot of their fur, and the rips and tears that they have suffered through the years are obviously home mended. We ourselves wear ordinary cloth coats lined with flannel or silk and interlined with chamois. You feel like a stuffed sausage in them, but they are warm and the next best thing to fur.

It took me quite a while to sort out our winter clothes, and it was quite a shopping list of footwear that I presented to Bob that evening. I had already calculated how many of my turkeys had to be sold to buy the moccasins alone.

That same evening a group of Natives camped at the edge of the river near our house. Nearly every fall they pass by our place on their trip to town to do their winter shopping and collect the money the government grants them. As you probably have heard, most Natives live on reserves. There is a reserve close to Clear Lake, and when the Natives go to Dauphin they have to pass our place. The Native father sauntered into our yard and asked in broken English if he could buy some oats for his horses. When Bob disappeared with him into the granary I suddenly remembered that the Native women make moccasins themselves and sell them to the stores in town. It did not take me long to put on my coat and head for the river. In the distance I saw their campfire shining through the trees, and when I came near I saw them hunched in the shelter of their grain box.

The grain box was covered with an old blanket and on the straw underneath, covered with some rags, I saw two children. An old woman and a boy about twelve years old sat close to the fire. We could not talk because they did not speak English, but with sign language I got across that I was interested in buying moccasins. A nod of the head confirmed that she knew what I wanted, and after diving into the wagon box, she returned with several pairs of moccasins. They were very pretty, decorated with colourful Native embroidery and bead work.

A few minutes later the men reappeared with bags of grain on their shoulders. Just as people did in olden times, we bartered for the price and felt on both sides that we had made good deals. This year I got prettier and cheaper moccasins than ever before.

❋

Nice Weather Lures the Bachelors

December 1931

The most beautiful winter weather and the bright moonshine prompted the bachelors in our neighbourhood to come out of their lonesome quarters. When the evenings are cold or stormy they do not have the urge to get out and are in bed by nine o'clock. But now the weather is so mild that an evening walk is attractive to them. They must have visions of a cozy living room, a radio to listen to and people to talk with.

When I see the bachelors sitting cozily in front of our fire, barn odours radiating from their clothes, telling a story that we have heard before, then I think about how much a bachelor really misses in life. To sit there, day in and day out, all alone on his farm, doing his chores and coming home weary and tired, needing to start making his supper, washing and mending his own clothes, and straightening out his house now and again — it certainly is not much of a life for a man. It is probably not too bad in the daytime, working around the barn with his horses and cattle, but when evening comes and he goes inside his lonesome abode with nobody to talk with or listen to, I can very easily understand that he wants to escape that for human company once in a while.

Bob will start turning the knobs on his radio and the Irish jigs and Scottish reels begin resounding in our room. I cannot say that this is our preferred kind of music, but to many people here it is tops and they never seem to tire of listening to it. Often they start humming and stamping their feet with enjoyment.

After that the farm talk starts, of course. Grain prices have gone down again, and are just as low now as they were right after threshing. Pigs sell for only $3.00 a hundred pounds, sheep $2.00, butter 13¢ a pound and turkeys $1.50 each. These conversations do not make us very cheerful, and everyone wonders where it will all end.

Slaughtering the Turkeys

December 1931

We started the month of December with slaughtering our turkeys. We had moved our heater from the kitchen to the garage because the slaughtering would take place there, and naturally the place had to be heated. From nine o'clock in the morning until five in the evening Bob and two neighbours were busy killing the poor birds by sticking a razor-sharp knife into the brain. Most of the feathers were pulled out in the garage and then the poor bleeding creatures were brought into the kitchen where two neighbour women were helping me.

We had to wash the bloody heads and the inside of their beaks, and then pluck out all the small feathers that were left. We washed their feet and trussed them up exactly as the market demanded. The birds had not been fed for the last thirty hours of their lives, and then their insides do not have to be removed. They seem to keep longer that way.

We soon found that we women in the house had to do most of the work, with the men ending up helping us for two hours in the evening. Because my first brood of turkeys had died in the spring, this second brood was a bit young, so they were full of pin feathers which were hard to remove. If you leave any pin feathers in the birds the market docks you heavily for it.

Around five o'clock Bobby came home from school along with the neighbours' children. I still feel slightly sick when I think back on that evening. The children were playing and romping all over the house. Blood and feathers were sticking to everything in the kitchen, and naturally were trailed into all the other rooms. In the middle of all that unspeakable mess I had to prepare a meal for all these people. We could not even sit down for our supper because the tables, chairs and benches were all occupied by the dead turkeys. We had to treat them with the utmost care if we did not want the price docked because of bruises.

Around ten o'clock our kind helpers went home and I dragged myself upstairs to the bedroom. Without looking around me, my face dark as a thunder cloud, I muttered that never in my life did I want to do a dirty job like that again for a few measly dollars. Bob, who certainly had just as miserable a day, was wise — he didn't say a thing.

When I woke up the next morning I heard him busy in the kitchen and then, a few minutes later, he ran up the stairs.

"Today three nice things are going to happen," he said. "First, we can get the money for the turkeys. Second, the mailman comes this morning, and third, I can call for the parcel from Holland which the customs office told us about over the phone."

I was not so dumb that I could not see through his optimism. I asked timidly, "Is it really as bad as that downstairs?"

"Well, try not to look around too much," was his reply. "In a few days you will have forgotten all about it."

We ate our breakfast in the middle of a horrible mess, with the dead turkeys all around us as silent witnesses. After a few minutes we saw the mailman's car at the end of our mile. Twice a week the mail is delivered to the farms. Each farm has a stand with a mailbox on it at the farm gate, and there is always a moment of suspense — will there be letters from home?

Good luck was on our side this morning, and while Bob was reading a letter from home, I was bent over a letter which made me blush. When Bob looked at me a few minutes later he said, "What are you reading there? You look positively guilty."

I sure did feel guilty. To receive a letter from a perfect stranger commenting on one of the stories I had sent to the paper, praising us for adjusting so cheerfully to the changed circumstances in which we now found ourselves was more than I could take without being thoroughly ashamed of my attitude toward those turkeys. I had failed miserably these last few days and now I realized it only too well. It was Bob who deserved all this praise, but even if I did not feel completely worthy, it did give me the lift I needed at that moment.

So an hour later when Bob drove the car to the back door and I helped him load the turkeys, I could wave goodbye to him with a cheerful grin on my face and assure him that I would manage perfectly today. Bucketsful of soapsuds, brooms and brushes worked marvels. I kept muttering to myself, "What a stupid fool you really are. To be so upset about one messy, hard day of work." Everything got a really good scrubbing just before Christmas. I would have wanted an extra clean-up before Christmas anyway. "Maybe I'll find a few minutes to polish the silver, too," I thought.

Preparing for Christmas

December 1931

Two evenings later, December 5 (St. Nicholas Day), we were sitting in the living room, which still smelled of wax. Everything gleamed and glittered from the recent polishing. We sat around the big table and played ganze-bord with the boys, the old Dutch game that our parents also played with us when we were children.

After St. Nicholas Day a few busy weeks followed. But it was a different kind of bustle with preparations for Christmas. All country schools give a party around Christmas at which the pupils give recitations, take part in stage plays, sing songs, and dance. The schools try to hold the celebrations on different nights, so from December 15 to 24 there seem to be school parties every night. Many of our neighbours visit three or more of these parties, but we attended only our own district and the one next to it.

The children have been practicing for these performances almost the whole month of December. I think that in December not much thought is really given to the regular school curriculum. For the teacher, I am sure, these events are important, too. Her rating as a teacher is greatly influenced by the kind of Christmas concert she produces. Because our district school is rather small (only six pupils at present), the parents are often asked to contribute in the form of a song, a recital on the school organ, or a little play. Quite often we have to leave home in the evening after the chores are done to practice the play we are to produce. A neighbour's girl is asked to babysit those evenings.

Besides these activities there are others which take place at Christmas. "Daddy, don't put off too long getting the Christmas tree from the mountains. We want a good-sized one this winter." And, "Mammy, did you make your Christmas cake yet? You know that for good luck we get to have a lick out of the pan." "What will we have this year for Christmas dinner? A goose or a turkey?" We decided that this year we will have a goose, but it has to be a big one because we invited quite a crowd. We have had enough of turkeys to last us for awhile.

This year we will have an all-Dutch crowd. Three miles from our farm live four Dutch boys, farmer's sons from the province of Groningen. They came here one year after we had arrived. We see them quite often on Sundays and holidays. Because we all come from the same country and have so much to get used to here, we can understand each other in a special way, even if we did not know each other in the old country. So when the Canadians have their family gatherings at Christmas time, in our own home we will have nine Dutchmen, big and small, around our table.

1932

Christmas on the Farm

January 1932

Every year I am stunned again by the intense low temperatures we have here. In the morning I literally burn my fingers at the aluminum milk boiler. Those ice cold utensils give the same feeling and result as burning. It happens over and over again that I grab a doorknob with a slightly damp hand and, sure enough, I am stuck to it. This keeps on happening until finally the heat of the stoves penetrates the house and warms the metal objects.

On these cold mornings our two older boys are bundled into their coats, toques, scarves, socks and mittens, and then bundled into the sleigh. We need to take them and fetch them back from school each day because it is far too cold for them to face the wind for the distance of more than two miles. Dicky is still upstairs in his crib and I am left alone at the messy breakfast table contemplating all the work that has to be done today.

Each year there is more to do than the year before. There are more cows in the barn, which means churning more often. It used to be that seven loaves of bread would do us for a week (and I quite often bought them in town because it did not seem worthwhile to bother baking them myself), but now I have to bake ten loaves twice a week. Making school lunches takes quite a bit of time, and there are also more clothes to wash and mend.

December has been a month of preparation and festivities. St. Nicholas Day has passed. We continually had to tell stories about what it used to be like in Holland. With full enthusiasm we sang the old Dutch songs. Still a true believer, Wim sighed, "My, I wish St. Nicholas would come to us here in Canada, too. Do you think it is too far for him to come over here after he has been in Holland?"

"Of course," Bobby said. "You know very well that it takes two weeks to travel from Holland to Canada. He will be here right around Christmas time. And then he will come in a sleigh with reindeer in front. Let's sing 'Jingle Bells' now." And they kept on singing until they dropped off to sleep.

The streets in town look very festive. Little spruce trees are planted in the snow on both sides of Main Street, and coloured lights are put on them. It will look lovely in the evening with all those little Christmas trees. The stores all have their usual decorations up, and they glitter and sparkle with tinsel. It is unusually busy in the streets these days, with the crowds of people, the crunching and squeaking of the snow and the jingling of the sleigh bells all helping to create a real Christmas spirit.

On mail delivery days we start to notice special things on the farm when winter arrives. In the winter the mail is delivered by sleigh, while in the summer the twice-a-week delivery comes by car. During these very cold days the mailman has a totally closed-in sleigh, just like a little hut on runners. He even has a little stove in it. It is a comical sight. You see a tiny square house, with a stovepipe on top belching smoke, pulled by two horses with their jolly jingling bells heralding their coming. The mailman is a dour old Scot who used to be cross sometimes, but is now a good friend. If he needs us at the mailbox he blows his whistle ahead of time and then we run to meet him, full of expectation.

The mood of the mailman is strongly influenced by the condition of the road, for which I cannot blame him. If the snow has blown during the night he is most likely the first one to break the trail. Each farmer is expected to shovel the snow away from his own mailbox so that the mailman can reach it without having to get out of his sleigh.

I ponder a bit to find a spot to hide a parcel from little prying eyes, if the mailman brings one. Better use the top shelf of the pantry.

Our days are filled with other preparations. If I have not done it yet, I'll now polish all the silver, brass and pewter. We do have quite a lot. Maybe I should have left it at home. Who ever heard of using sterling silver in a farm kitchen, but since we have it I might as well use it. Our family silver, much of it with initials and dates on it, is something nice to leave to the boys when they are grown up. But maybe they will not even care for it.

Then there is all the brass we brought from India. I am afraid that a Dutch housewife would shake her head if she saw my things. At home we used to have one day a week for polishing silver — but my mother did not need to do it herself — so everything always looked spick-and-span. Mine does not because I only clean it once a year, around Christmas time. I need to do it myself, and it takes almost the whole day. But when it is finished it gives me a big thrill. I feel as if I just received it as a new present. It gleams and shines unusually bright, from all corners of the room. I had better clean the fine crystal and the old china, too, whatever is left of it — on the trip to Canada a lot was broken.

The curtains are washed and starched, and the house looks as if I had just finished spring cleaning. One afternoon I made a big Christmas cake. Most women make this cake a few months before they intend to eat it. It improves with age. Since I have my doubts that this cake would ever reach a venerable age in our house, I usually make it the week before Christmas and freeze it solid for a few days. When it thaws out it seems to mellow, too. As soon as I start to make the Christmas cake, the kitchen becomes a very attractive place for the children, as well as for their father. They hope a few raisins or nuts will be distributed, and it always ends with a lick of the pan for each, for good luck. We have to bake speculaas and after that make fondant, a special St. Nicholas treat. When I am finished, everything is stored in tins and put out of sight.

On the morning before Christmas day they all pile into the sleigh to hunt for a Christmas tree. There are not too many trees close by. In the mountains you will find them by the thousands, but that is too far away for a sleighride. However, so far we have always been lucky and found a nice tree, and we did this year, too. At home I hunt for the asparagus branches I had dried and hidden in the fall. With their berries they take the place of holly, which we do not have in Dauphin. The buffet and the table are adorned with starched, clean lace doilies, and in the corner of the living room the Christmas tree stands in all its glory. In a box upstairs I find the silver tinsel, the beads and the coloured balls and ornaments safely packed away.

The boys all come into the house now, with sparkling eyes and rosy cheeks, stamping their cold feet, but carrying the Christmas tree. They cut off the lower branches and put them in vases with red berries. We stick green branches over the door, on the window sills and around a few pictures. Suddenly the room smells wonderful, like Christmas. Before they go to bed the boys help to decorate the tree and hang up their stockings. Wim wants one of Daddy's stockings — he thinks his own is too small.

Then on Christmas morning, when all is still pitch dark and cold, excited voices come from the room next to ours. "Can we go downstairs and find out if Santa Claus has been there? Please, when are you going to light the stove?"

Well, no chance for more snoozing. Shivering in the cold with icy fingers we start making the fires again and boil the kettles. As soon as a bit of heat seeps upstairs there is no controlling them anymore. They come tumbling downstairs in their pyjamas, making a beeline for the tree and the presents. On a white sheet they find their gifts brought in the night by Santa. "And now say 'Thank you, Santa

Claus,'" Bobby admonishes them with a wink in our direction, and they shout it at the top of their lungs.

After breakfast there are lots of willing hands to dry the dishes or turn the cream separator. "Is there a lot to do, Mam, or are you nearly finished? When do you think they will come?"

"They" are the four Dutch bachelors who celebrate Christmas with us every year. I tell them "Well, better start looking around three o'clock. I am sure you will see them coming around that time."

But before three o'clock comes there is still lots for me to do. The goose has to be filled with the stuffing I prepared the previous day, and then put into the oven. Potatoes need to be peeled and a cold salad made.

Suddenly I think, "What an abundance, really. Even if prices for our products are low, how much we have for ourselves — butter, cream, eggs (even if only four hens are laying at present) and homemade ice cream." I enjoy that just as much as the children who are all crowding around me.

Finally the nicely decorated Christmas cake stands right in the middle of the table, and the red paper bells hang just above. Around noon we have a little lunch of milk chocolate and sandwiches. "I won't eat much," Bobby says wisely. "If I do, I can't eat much of all the nice things that come later."

After lunch the boys settle down to play with their new toys, and Bob and I read the magazines and papers which are full of Christmas stories and pictures. Around three o'clock we start glancing outside. These is nothing yet to be seen on that lonesome long white road. Not a single sleigh passes on Christmas day.

Then a team of horses appears over the ridge (a slight rise in our field, which on the road is about a half mile from our gate) pulling a grain box on sleigh runners, the usual vehicle for transportation in the winter. In it four men are standing up. Bob and the boys grab their coats, mittens, toques and overshoes and rush outside. A moment later I hear the jingling of the harness bells, the stamping of the horses and the happy shouts of "Merry Christmas."

With loud voices and happy faces they all come inside, and the room gets cold for a moment with the fresh, cold air they bring with them. The children have disappeared into the kitchen, each with a little parcel in his hand. By mistake Santa Claus had visited the bachelors' house, too, and had left a gift for each of our boys.

I am presented with a big pan containing a homemade cake made by Dirk, the brother who does most of the cooking. I am just as pleased with the cake as he is himself, because each year this cake seems to get better and more beautiful. I have reason to be proud of my pupils. When I started to explain to them how such a cake was made, I myself was not very proficient in the art.

The Christmas tree and the presents have to be admired before we all find a place around the fire and the men each light a Dutch cigar from one of the Dutch gift parcels. Then we must taste the homemade chokecherry wine. Sometimes it turns out beautifully, and sometimes it does not.

The time has come to put the finishing touches to the table. I have plenty of help. One starts slicing the big goose and scooping out the stuffing on a dish. Another is draining the potatoes. Someone else offers to slice the bread and fill the butter dishes. After that we all sit around the big table, just as we have done each of the five preceeding years. Even if I am always the only woman at these celebrations, our guests all certainly appreciate everything that is served because they have done their own cooking for so many years now.

Seeing us all at a table like this, you would think that there is no cloud in the sky, that farmers seem to be quite prosperous. But in reality the times are hard. There is a lot of laughter, making of toasts and klinking our glasses which lasts for hours on end.

Finally we all need to go back to work. We split up into two groups. One party goes to the barn to help Bob with the chores, while the other party stays in the house to help me wash and dry the dishes and straighten things out again. After that we all gather in the living room and light the candles on the Christmas tree. On the radio Christmas songs from far-off lands reach us. Once in a while we sing a Dutch song together.

The boys have become very quiet. Dicky has actually fallen asleep, and in a little while I take the drowsy group upstairs and put them to bed.

When I come downstairs again into the room perfumed by spruce boughs and cigar smoke, bathed in the light of many candles, and I see all these men peacefully smoking their cigars, it makes me think about the Christmas days of my childhood in Holland in the big old house with the very high ceilings. Christmas in Holland is essentially a religious day in which you go to church but receive no gifts. The first Christmas of my married life was spent in Calcutta, British India. It was an English Christmas and quite formal. The men were dressed in black ties and the ladies in evening gowns, but in the tropics it did not seem like Christmas at all to me.

I remember a Christmas on a lonely rubber plantation in Java, the Dutch East Indies, where we were staying with relatives, and it was even more isolated than here. Till late in the night we sat outside, under the palm trees. It was very quiet and beautiful, but we did not have a feeling of Christmas there either.

The next year found us in Holland again, in the midst of family and friends. That had been wonderful. It was the last Christmas we had at home, because the next winter we were in a log cabin in the Riding Mountains in Canada.

That Christmas we had a young Englishman, a former roommate of Bob's, with us. Both of them had worked in banks and wanted to change to farming, and both had been attending the agricultural college in Winnipeg at the same time. The Englishman had not actually started farming, and I do not know what he expected to find on a farm. He had brought his formal clothes along, and when we found this out we dived into our steamer trunk and produced a tuxedo and an evening gown, last used on our Atlantic crossing. We really never expected to have a chance to wear these clothes again, but it was great fun to wear them in our rustic surroundings.

There was one more Christmas that will always stand out in our memory. A few years ago, in 1929, when my mother and Bob's sister were both visiting us, we were sitting here, just as we are now, and our Dutch bachelor friends were with us then, too. That was something we might never experience again. The Christmas tree stood in the same spot in the corner. Only little Dick, now in his crib upstairs, had not yet arrived.

"Well, now they will have already started the second Christmas Day in Holland," one of the bachelors remarked, breaking the silence we had all drifted into.

"You were also thinking about Holland and home," I said.

"Yes, boys, we get cheated on that extra holiday," one of our friends remarked. "In Canada we only celebrate for one day at Christmas and for one day at Easter. Easter Monday is not celebrated here. In Holland there is also the two-day Whitsuntide, but no one in Canada has ever heard of that. It will be work for us again tomorrow."

This observation jolted them all into realizing that tomorrow would start early with a trip to the mountains to haul wood. "We had better harness the horses again and leave for home." When we heard the *sleigh bells jingling in the frosty air outside on the wide white road we said to each other, "Nice that we have a bit of our old country over here, too."*

Influenza Reverses Our Roles

February 1932

After the traditional gunshot which Bob blasts into the sky every New Year's Eve, we turned another page in our book of life. What will the future bring? Everybody asks this question because every day we hear about the troubles in China and Japan. In our peaceful surroundings it all seems so unreal.

We have a lot of snow and more is added every day. The roads are impassable by car, which makes us more isolated. Practically all the farmers have started their wood hauling now. We hear the merry jingling of sleigh bells early in the morning when they leave for the mountains, and again at night when they return.

That is about all the traffic we see on the road. Once in a while a snowmobile passes our place, making a lot of noise. It looks like a car, but instead of wheels it has sleigh runners in front. In the back it has a double set of wheels connected by caterpillar tracks. The snowmobile is owned by a garage in town and is used mainly by the doctors. When it passes our place we ask ourselves who might be sick. We were lucky this year not to have been honoured with a call.

Sickness is unpleasant anywhere, but here it is doubly so. The first thing that pops into your head is, "Who will do my work? My neighbours are busy enough as it is, and I do not want to bother them unless it is absolutely necessary."

Bob got up one morning with a sore throat, headache and fever. I strongly advised him to stay in bed and let me try to manage in the barn. But, as I had expected, he would not hear of it and went out himself. After two days he was forced to give in because he had become a lot worse. As a result we faced a lot of trouble.

I am sorry to confess that I am rather useless around the barn. Many women are able to replace their husbands completely, if needed, but this is far from the truth on our farm. Until I came to this country I had never been near a cow — I only saw them grazing peacefully in the meadows when I passed by on my bicycle.

As I said earlier, I lived alone with my baby son in a log cabin in the

61

bush shortly after our arrival in Canada. Naturally I needed milk for him, but since you could not go to a store, and since the nearest farm was too far away, the only solution was to get a cow and learn to milk her. Mr. Durston, Bob's former boss and owner of our place, was kind enough to lend us a cow, and one evening Bob arrived home with her. I shuddered to think about the next morning when I had to tackle her alone.

Well, I might as well tell you that I never achieved much. I sat as far away from the cow as I could and still be able to reach her. She kept moving around, kicking and trying to push me against the wall. I did manage to squeeze a few cups of milk out of her and that was all I was after. I wonder if other cows behaved like this, too, or if she knew special tricks.

The result of this experience was that I dislike milking cows and never made much progress. Moreover, with a growing young family, I had enough work to do in the house. But now with Bob sick I was up against it. To climb into the loft and throw down hay and sheaves was not too bad. But there was so much more to do. Cleaning the barn, feeding all those animals, and then pumping water for them all.

That was one of the worst jobs. The river was frozen to the bottom. In other years it flowed over the ice because it is a spring-fed river, but this winter it froze solid. Normally horses can lick snow, but ours are spoiled by the river and insist on water. At regular times they would arrive at the barn and wait for their water. Naturally the cows and pigs had to have water, too. I had realized it before, but now I found out how much unpleasant work a man has to do. After I had pumped thirty pails I felt as if my arms were paralyzed.

We decided to ask a neighbour if he would be willing to milk the cows. The rest I would have to manage myself. Housekeeping had been relegated to second place for right now. I would be able to catch up on that as soon as Bob was better.

But that's not the way it worked. After four days our roles were reversed. I was too sick to get out of bed and Bob had to do my work as well as his own. I installed myself on the couch in the living room so that I could keep an eye on things and watch the children while he was busy in the barn. This proved to be the right decision because he stayed in the barn for the greater part of the morning, which did not surprise me since he must have found a lot of his work left undone. When the clock chimed one I began to wonder when he would return to do the cooking. I felt too miserable even to attempt it. The boys pressed their noses against the window and tried to blow a peephole in the crust of ice that covered it. I presume that it was hunger that eventually drove him home.

"We better eat something that is prepared quickly," he said. "It's too late to peel and cook potatoes. So you boys better get a loaf of bread out of the breadbox." But the breadbox was empty — I hadn't been able to do any baking while doing both Bob's work and my own. "Well, if we see a sleigh passing I'll ask them to help us out and buy some bread in town," Bob said. "We better eat pancakes now."

The children thought that was just great. Loud cheers came from the kitchen, but from my couch I couldn't tell what all the cheering was about. A plop in the pan and sometimes a louder plop on the floor made me realize that the pancakes were thrown into the air with the necessary flip to be caught again, but sometimes they didn't land in the pan. There was a lot of shouting to call the cats and the dogs who were pressed into service to clean up the mess.

For the next three days not much was eaten besides pancakes, potatoes and oatmeal porridge. In the morning they swept the whole house, and Wim assured me with a big grin that "what we can't get into the dustpan we sweep under a cupboard or under a rug." I was lying carefree on the couch, trying to convince myself that I'd better enjoy it. Often on a busy morning I had thrown longing glances at this same couch and the bookcase beside it thinking, "If only I could crawl onto the couch for a while with a nice book — when will that ever happen?" Well, it was happening now, but my headache kept me from doing much reading.

I looked around at my surroundings. Mercilessly the bright winter light touched everything: a floor that screamed for a paint brush, curtains that had faded, and a carpet that had lost quite a bit of its original lustre. The furniture looked shabby, too.

When we first moved to the farm we decided to wait for a while before buying better furniture. There was so much we needed for the farm first, like horses, cows, machinery and tools. Home furnishings had lower priority. Besides, we must have had some pioneering spirit since we had visions of making some nice things ourselves. In expectation of that we bought on sale a rickety table, a few wobbly chairs, a few stoves, a wardrobe, and rugs, curtains and drapes. Knicknacks brought from Holland had to do the rest. If only we had brought our furniture along. Bob had asked me to leave it behind because he was still unsure whether Manitoba was the place where he wanted to settle.

In seven years the only furniture we had made was a wardrobe in the little hallway. Its only saving grace was its size. It was ugly and neither mouse-proof nor moth-proof, as we found out soon enough.

In the living room you can find our second artistic effort. It is a homemade easy chair, which looks nice and is comfortable to sit in, provided you lean it against a wall. It turned out to be top-heavy, as a few of our visitors found out.

So it was with very little satisfaction that I now looked around my living room and visualized all I would change if only farm conditions were not so poor.

When evening came and Bob settled in front of the fire with books and papers I asked him, "If you open your eyes wide and look around you, what do you see?"

"A cozy room," he said promptly with a very satisfied nod.

"Well, you better take a second look," I countered. "We are used to it now, but it really looks shabby and ugly. I had the chance to observe it thoroughly these last few days, and I can see nothing but all the things that are wrong, even by lamplight in the evening. If the prices go up we should do something about it."

"Well," he remarked, "I would not figure too much on better prices. The future still looks gloomy. But if you want to paint the floor and buy some new furniture, you better get busy and write articles for the newspaper while you have all the time in the world for it."

I followed his advice, but the only trouble was that I could not find very much to write about. That is why I have started to tell you about my plans in the hope that inspiration will follow.

Butchering the Pigs

February 1932

Winter has not yet released its grip. This year the snowfall has been light and as a result the roads are very poor for sleighing. This has delayed wood hauling, which ordinarily starts in the fall or early winter.

Each member of our household has been a victim of the flu, with the attendant coughing and sneezing still with us. Hence Bob decided it would not be wise to expose himself too soon to the icy blasts. Moreover, we have quite a supply of wood left over from last year, and since it is only February, there will be time enough for getting our summer supply later on in March, when Bob should feel better and the weather will be milder.

A neighbour was of the same opinion but, since both men's consciences did not allow them to take life too easy, they decided to butcher a few hogs together. That is a job which has to be done anyway before the spring work starts. We decided this would be an opportune time.

On the designated morning we built a fire under the huge iron cooking pot which stands outside beside the granary. Three pigs were selected to be butchered — one for the neighbour and two for ourselves. On the farm in Holland a professional butcher would be called in to do this job, but on the Canadian farm the farmer combines this specialty with his varied skills and makes little fuss about the job.

First the animal is shot, then its throat is slit and the animal is hoisted up over the pot of boiling water for the scalding which makes it easier to scrape off the bristles. If it is a large hog the front and hind quarters are lowered alternately into the pot of hot water as rapidly as possible. The scraping is done, and in about half an hour the carcass is hoisted again, cut open and cleaned inside, and that's that.

Though I had not experienced it myself, I do recall stories my mother used to tell about "butchering days" in Holland when she was a little girl. Mother was a good storyteller and perhaps that accounts for the homey and delectable visions I had conjured up about those butchering days. Mother did not even live in the country, but her family used to buy a pig, from which all kinds of wonderful delicacies were concocted: juicy hams, headcheese, liver paste, sausages, and so on.

However, that is not the kind of butchering we do here. When it takes place in the late fall, the whole pig is cut up into pieces or chunks and these are frozen solid. Many farmers never bother to use the heads at all, and a few meals of fried liver is all they want from that organ. If the butchering takes place in the spring, in nine cases out of ten a large portion of the carcass is immersed in a barrel of salt brine, and salt pork becomes regular fare on the farm menu.

Perhaps a taste for salt pork can be developed, but we have tried it faithfully for several years and still do not like it. Probably because of this dislike for a steady diet of salt pork Bob suggested that we try the old-fashioned way of using the pig.

"We are more or less tied to the house during this cold weather anyway," he said. "I could give you a hand, and then I would not feel so guilty not being on the road with a load of wood."

So the next morning we went into action. Hams and sides of bacon were cut, which were salted and sugared according to the cookbook and put in crocks for a few weeks, to be smoked later. Lots of head cheese was brought to the basement, and for days on end we were busy stuffing liver sausage and other kinds of sausages.

"I certainly feel old-fashioned now," I told Bob. "This work does not even belong to the generation of our parents, but of our grandparents."

✳

A Trip Into Town

February 1932

As a climax to the greasy labour of slaughtering the pigs I decided when we were finished that a holiday would be in order. Most farmers go to town every Saturday, wife and family included. For nearly two months I had not been off our own farm, and I felt it would indeed be a welcome change to see new faces and a few stores.

Bob reminded me, and justly so, that the decision to go to town was my own responsibility. The distance, together with severe winter and primitive transportation, had kept me home while he had always gone alone to sell our produce and buy the groceries.

As is so often the case here, the next Saturday was a day of brilliant sunshine. The winters may be long and cold, but we get sunshine in abundance. We were up and around early in the morning because it takes some planning and work before we can close the barn and house doors behind us with a feeling of safety.

By ten o'clock Bob had finished his many chores around the barn and came back to the house, his arms full of wood. As we have no furnace but only a cookstove and heaters, the house cools off rapidly, and nothing is worse after a long, cold sleigh ride than to return to an icy cold house. Then, too, there is the danger of frozen vegetables in the basement and frozen house plants in the rooms. So the stoves must be full of wood, with dampers in exactly the right position, not too tightly closed or the stove will smoke or the fire might go out, but not too open, either, lest the fire burn itself out too quickly. It must be just right.

After I tidied up the house, washed the breakfast dishes and the cream separator, I gathered together the children's clothes and coats and dressed them. Fortunately the two oldest can more or less look after themselves now. Self-reliance comes early here.

66

"Will you please find a good box to put the baby in?" I asked Bob, who was busy heating rocks in the oven for foot warmers. One sweater, another sweater, and then I put on his cozy woolen coat, then a knitted toque, and a scarf tied across his forehead and around his neck. He sat rigid as a poker and looked like he couldn't move hand or foot. But when I turned my back to help Wim with his scarf, in those few seconds the baby seized the opportunity to squirm out of his mitts, scarf and toque again.

Now my patience wore thin and my nerves were on edge. I thought in despair, "How do those other women manage who have to go through this every Saturday?" I told Bobby, "You watch Dick so that he does not wiggle out of his coat and sweater." I decided to get myself ready first and attend to the baby at the last minute. Outside I could see Bob putting the sleigh (a grain box placed on runners) in order. He put straw and sheepskins on the floor, and boxes to serve as seats.

"How are things coming along? Can I put the stones into the sleigh and harness the team?" a voice shouted from the gate.

I placed a soft woolen blanket in the big cardboard box. The baby and I went into round two of struggling with shawls and mittens, scarf and toque. When he was finally bundled to my satisfaction, I put him into the box with a hot water bottle at his feet and blankets tucked in at all sides.

"All right, you can go ahead, all of you," Bob said. "I'll take the baby and lock the doors." With blankets over our arms we ran to the sleigh.

"No unnecessary shouting," I warned the two rascals with me. "You sit down where I tell you to. If you make too much noise you will frighten the horses and we'll have a runaway."

"My feet are not under the blanket," one shouted. "I don't have one of the hot bricks at my feet," yelled out the other. I placed the stones and bricks into place and tucked the blankets in as best I could. Daddy arrived with the box and the baby.

After one mile we left the main road to follow a trail which cuts through a wild quarter section. Wide expanses of white snow were dotted with low shrubbery as far as the eye can see, giving the illusion that we were travelling through a quiet park.

"Look over there, boys. Doesn't that look like a wolf?" Bob shouted. Like startled jackrabbits we all scrambled up. Far away, on a little knoll in the field, an animal closely resembling a farm dog stood stock-still, looking in our direction. At our feet, in his cardboard box, the baby slept in blissful serenity. Three and a half miles were behind us, but we were only halfway there.

"Daddy, we have cold feet. Can we run behind the sleigh for awhile?" the boys asked. "All right, but be careful." This is fun, running, letting themselves be dragged, tumbling down and running to catch up to the sleigh. After a mile they had enough and climbed into the back.

After another mile we came to a halt. On the last mile a caravan of fourteen sleighs piled with cordwood blocked our path. The third sleigh from the front had tipped over in one of the many deep pitch holes in the road. There was nothing to do but wait as patiently as we could. On this road it was impossible to pass another sleigh because the snow on both sides was much too deep. Ahead we could see men unhitching horses from their sleighs and leading them back to the scene of the accident. With the additional horsepower they tried to bring the sleigh that was stuck back onto the road. Some men were busy shovelling snow in front while others unloaded the wood which hung dangerously on one side.

At last everything was ready, and with much ado the sleigh was pulled out of the hole. While the wood was reloaded we could only watch and wait. But by then I had no feeling left in my feet, and looks from Bob and the two boys told me they suffered from the same problem.

"If only the others can get through that bad spot now," I began to worry. There were eleven teams ahead of us and many more holes like that one. The last long mile of the road was truly long. But no other accident occurred, so our progress was steady if slow.

At last we reached the edge of town and I heaved a sigh of relief as we turned onto the main street. We were almost too cold and stiff to jump out of the sleigh, and our feet seemed like foreign bodies. Only the baby, who suddenly woke up, stayed warm under his woolen blankets, and he now scrambled out of his box.

Spring Chickens and Spring Frost

April-June 1932

"One day lost in the spring might mean hundreds of dollars lost in the fall," was one of the many lessons Bob's former boss, Mr. Durston, taught him.

When the second week of April arrived with warm sunny days, Bob made an inspection trip over our fields. "Tomorrow morning I can start with harrowing on the highest places," was his verdict. "If only the weather stays like this for a while, we will get our wheat in really early."

Suddenly we found ourselves in the midst of spring activities again. In the mornings we rose early because meals had to be served on time. Every evening the men were busy, treating against smut the seed grain they would plant the next day. Quite a few other farmers had started their seeding operations, too, but others said, "Why be in such a hurry? There is still lots of time."

A week after we finished seeding our wheat we had rain, which is quite unusual for this time of year. When we went to town one morning we found the roads to be unbelievably muddy. We could barely manage to get through. The river started to rise rapidly and flooded into the bush. Our ducks and geese took the opportunity to swim downstream and disappeared. Two days later they were sighted in town and we had to take the car to bring them home again.

The time had come for us to get a chicken coop. This was intended for the fluffy yellow baby chicks. Someone had told me that if we wanted to make chickens pay off we needed to fix things up right and spend some money first. We decided to follow this advice and invest in a chicken coop. When it was ready I was very pleased with it. It looked a bit like a housetrailer without wheels, and it sported a glass door and a wide window, which could be shoved open. It was bright and lightweight, built on skids so that it could easily be moved around. The children were delighted with it.

We own one incubator to hatch chickens in, and we borrowed two more from a neighbour. I felt it would be more worthwhile to set about 560 eggs at once. But where would I find a good spot for those three incubators? It was still too cool outside to put them in the new chicken coop and, moreover, it would be hard to watch them regularly at night. We decided that the best thing would be to use the boys' room, which had enough space. We lugged the boys' cots outside into the new chicken coop so that our future chickens could be housed in the boys' room.

It worked out very well, and even proved to be educational. The boys were playing "bachelor" and wanted to look after things themselves, which meant that the beds were neatly straightened every morning and the floor was regularly swept. All that was missing was that they did not make their own meals. However, a second rainy spell brought an end to it all. It was getting too damp in the coop, as we had not yet installed the heater we would need for the baby chicks. The boys had to come back to the house and we had to find temporary places where they could sleep.

If I look back after eight weeks, the chicks brought many good things but also a number of disappointments. They were supposed to hatch during the first week of May. My expectations were very high. All those weeks we had kept the temperature absolutely steady, quite a feat if you consider that the source of heat was a coal oil lamp. We used special hatching eggs. A hen could not have done better than we did. So I was rather crestfallen when only 300 chicks emerged from the 560 eggs. Another eighty had become full grown but had died in the shell. The balance proved to be infertile eggs.

When I found out that all but one of our neighbours had not fared any better, I soon overcame my disappointment and, after a few days, even convinced myself that I had a nice bunch left. But I had never realized how much time these little critters demand. Day and night a stove had to be kept going in the chicken coop. We had not wanted to go to the extra expense of a regular brooder stove, as we found them far too expensive. We felt that we could manage with our small wood heater, which was not easy to regulate but had the advantage of burning our own wood. But it was not too pleasant leaving your bed every night to fill the stove up.

If all had gone well after this, I guess I could have taken these inconveniences in stride. But suddenly, for no obvious reason, the chickens started dying. Every morning I would find ten or more dead. All the literature I could lay my hands on did not give us the reason. After about one hundred died the epidemic suddenly stopped and I breathed freer again. I still had two hundred chickens left and they had already grown a lot. In the nice weather we let them outside and they looked quite healthy.

But things did not go right even now. One night when we were convinced that everything was looked after perfectly (as we had done every night until then) the stove went out. The next morning we found thirty more dead chickens. A few nights later the opposite occurred, the stove got too hot and some of the chickens had choked to death, seventy-five in all. I cannot describe how low and disappointed I felt. All those long weeks of watching day and night, not to mention all the expense. Only one hundred chickens were left. "This spoils the whole spring," I lamented to Bob.

But there was even more disappointment to come. One night a

severe frost focussed our attention on something else. One night the lovely field of wheat changed from fresh green to drab brown. The young vegetables in the garden suffered the same fate. The frost proved to be very localized. A neighbour on the other side of the road was not hurt at all, but farmers on the left and right of us were no better off than we were. We are not sure whether it will damage the grain permanently. Some farmers tell us that wheat can survive at least three bad frosts. They even claim that it will stool out better afterwards.

But naturally the development of the wheat is set back, and if we do not get rain soon we can't expect too much. We hope for the best but can do nothing but be patient. We are worried more about these frosts because our oats are coming up and they cannot withstand frost at all. Both the wild and cultivated fruit trees in the garden have taken a beating as well. You see now that besides poetry you also have a lot of disappointment on a farm in the spring.

The Joys of a Summer Preacher

Late July 1932

The weather has been very favourable lately and even if it came a bit too late to help our frozen grain fields, it has been exactly right — warm sun and rain. The grass is lusher than we have ever seen it. Wheat, barley and oats all look promising. Only the potatoes suffered from a beetle infestation, but we treated them for it.

The sheep gave us some trouble this year. Big flies (probably on account of the abundant rain) laid their eggs in the lambs' woolly coats, and by the time we became aware of it, they had hatched and the poor animals were being literally eaten alive. Their hind quarters had become one living mass of larvae. Even baths in a strong solution of creoline did not help sufficiently. Every evening after the field work and the milking we spent hours trying to rid the lambs of this curse, but still we lost quite a few.

In one way this summer differs from the other summers we have had. We have a paying summer guest, a young minister named Frank who is working in our district this summer.

I have suddenly realized that I have never dealt with the subject of church in Canada. Religious practice here is very different from what we are used to in Holland. You will find only the odd country church here. The farms are spread too far apart and would not be able to

71

support a regular church. Not everybody lives close enough to town to attend services there.

For that reason in the spring most districts will apply for the services of a student minister in conjunction with an established church in town, which in our district is the United Church. These student ministers are young men who study theology at the university and, like many other students, want to earn a few extra dollars to support themselves when they go back to university. Classes are from October to May, so they can spend quite a few months in the field and acquire good experience.

Services are held in a schoolhouse or in a community hall, as is the case in our own district. The boys usually have room and board on a farm. They are expected to visit all the members of their congregation once or twice during the summer. They also have to attend most community gatherings and meetings and assume a leading role in them, be it in sports, education or amusement.

Naturally these young men do not impress us in the same way as a young minister in Holland would. I will always remember my own first encounter with one on a sizzling hot day in May a few years ago. On my way to town I had some trouble with the car, and was sitting rather forlornly on a lonesome stretch of road when, to my great joy, another car came rattling towards me. It was one of the most ancient Fords I had ever seen, without fenders, just like an open box on wheels. In it I saw a strapping young man in a loud sweater who certainly looked capable of getting a car started again.

Soon he was lying on his back under my car, explaining to me in all kinds of technical terms what was wrong. After that he took some tools out of his own car and got busy. He asked me if I lived in Dauphin and I told him that I lived in the country on a farm in the Mayflower district. I took the liberty of asking if he had a job in a garage in Dauphin. A face with a few black smears grinned at me from underneath the car and said, "Well, I worked in a garage last summer, but this summer I am going to be your minister. I am just on my way there now. One more year and I will be ordained."

Later he became quite a good friend of ours and then we found out more about the two-fold purpose of his summer job. If a district would like the services of a minister it can get one for a minimum expense. The student minister likely has to finance himself through college. So both parties benefit financially. Our own district, in cooperation with two other nearby districts, hired one student minister. On Sundays he preaches in the morning, the afternoon and the evening, once in each of these districts, and together they need to raise his salary.

In our district, for example, we have a ladies' club which is responsible for fund raising. At present they are busy making a patchwork quilt. Anyone who wants his name embroidered on the back of this quilt pays 5¢, which helps to raise the minister's salary. When the quilt is finished, tickets are sold to raffle it off. Picnics are organized to raise money as well. Everybody brings their own lunch and later the lunches are gathered together and sold. The afternoon is spent on sports. There will be a booth where soft drinks, ice cream, fruit, lemonade, cigarettes and chocolate bars are sold, with the district ladies as vendors.

Fowl suppers are also very popular. All the farm ladies donate a few chickens, turkeys, geese or ducks, all beautifully prepared at home. In addition, they bring large bowls with boiled and mashed potatoes, vegetables, pickles, bread and buns, jellied salads and pies. The food is kept warm on a large kitchen range. Everybody in the town and from the district and surrounding areas can come and have a very festive meal for 25¢ a person.

This summer our student minister in the district is a few years older than his predecessors and closer to our own generation. After a formal call and a few chance meetings, Frank started to drop in quite regularly. He told us that he was engaged to be married to a girl in Winnipeg. She was a nurse who had been working in Labrador, where he met her when he was a student minister there one summer. He asked us if she could come to Dauphin and stay with us for a while. She would be a paying guest. But I felt that I would be too busy to look after a guest, and moreover a city girl would likely find life too primitive on a farm.

But Frank had an answer to all my objections. He was convinced that we would get along very well. To a certain extent she was used to living in the country because she and her parents spent their summers at a cottage which was a bit primitive, too. She would not cause extra work, Frank insisted, because no doubt she would be pleased to give me a hand and we would end up having a grand old time together.

Well, that settled it. A few days later Isobel arrived and right away we felt at ease with each other. We shared daily chores, and this became the first summer that we found time for reading, walking and swimming. Frank, who boarded on a farm in the neighbourhood, spent a lot of time with us, of course, and sometimes gave Bob a hand *in the field. We often climbed into our car together to go for a picnic or a swim.*

The extra hands did make the work easier. Gathering the vegetables for canning was a lot more pleasant with someone to talk to. Frank helped Bob with the haying and even with treating the lambs with creoline. But when he eventually tried to milk a cow he discovered that our son Bobby could easily beat him at it.

The Preacher Leaves, and Not Much is Left

September 1932

It has been such a lovely summer. Now a long winter is ahead of us again. How little is left of all those lovely flowers. True, the trees still sport their fall colours, but the present grey, wet days make everything look drab. Behind the barn, like soldiers in a row, I see the haystacks, soaking wet and ragged. I remember the days when Bob and Frank were making them while Isobel, the children and I brought them lunch in the field and rode back on the sweet-smelling hay wagon. On several days we picked wild fruit (of which there was an abundance this year) in the bush. We had many picnics and swimming parties this summer. I watched all the jolly, sunburned faces around our dining room table, realizing that Isobel had to go back to Winnipeg by the middle of August and Frank would go back to university a bit later. I would think how wonderful it would be if we could only keep these nice friends in our neighbourhood.

But the day came when Isobel had gone, leaving a big emptiness behind. Frank also gathered up all his possessions and announced that he had better go back to his boardinghouse and do some studying. It was all over now. The best thing for us to do was to go back to work and keep ourselves occupied.

Not many days later, after a busy day, we were stretched out on the lawn in front of the house and Bob sighed, "I don't know if I can manage it all by myself this fall."

"Somebody coming on horseback," I remarked a few minutes later. "He is turning in at our gate. Who can that be, so late in the evening?"

"Hallo, you two," a well-known voice shouted. "Do you have a bed for a lonely man tonight?"

"Of course," we shouted back to Frank. "Put your horse in the barn." And a few minutes later Frank had joined us on the lawn.

"I studied a lot these last few days," he remarked, "and now I need a change. Can you put up with me for a while?"

"Sure can," said Bob, and suddenly he found himself with an assistant again.

During the weeks that followed Bob and the minister did a lot of work. Quite a bit of the grain had to be stooked yet, and after that a lot of fall plowing had to be done. Also the green feed had to be put in the barn.

"I'd like to spend the days with you when the threshing machine is on your farm," our new helper offered. "You better count on me to help you with shovelling the grain."

But before we could get started on that it rained again, and during those rainy days the men fixed fences and gates. They made trips on horseback to gather up the young calves which had spent all summer on the flats. The engine of our car had to be overhauled, and the radio needed to be repaired. In the evenings around a crackling fire (the evenings have started to get cool) we sorted books and magazines which we plan to read during the winter. Frank put a lot of his own literature in our bookcase and said, "If at all possible I will come over at Christmas to get them and bring you a new supply." Together we looked at the pictures we had taken during the summer and relived those happy days.

When at last the sky cleared and the sheaves were dry once more, the threshing machine came with all its accompanying fuss and bustle. We were unfortunate this year because the machine broke down four times, which means hours of delay and extra meals for me to prepare. But at last we were finished.

The crop was fairly good in our district, and we too could be satisfied. But the prices are so unbelievably low that the future looks darker than ever. Wheat brings 34¢ a bushel, barley 12½¢ and oats 10½¢. We had more oats than anything else this year. Threshing expenses were 5¢, 4¢ and 4¢ a bushel respectively, so there is very little left for the farmer. We lost quite a few chickens during the summer due to tuberculosis, and the ones that were left, together with the pigs, did a lot of damage to our garden.

How small the circle around the dining room table seems now that the threshers are gone. Frank's chair is empty, too. This morning at dawn we took him to the train station in Dauphin to catch the train to Winnipeg. Since the train was delayed in leaving, we went with him to his compartment and talked for a while. It was a strange sensation being in a train once again after seven years. Suddenly a great desire to go somewhere for a change hit me. The thought of leaving all the work and worries behind us for a while seemed so good. Wishful thinking.

On the way back to the farm we were thinking how different the times must have been when farmers received good prices for their produce. In those years, when the threshing machine had left, the farmer looked at his full bins of grain knowing that they represented a lot of money. He knew that he had not worked in vain. We thought, "If we had not grown a kernel of grain, only some feed for the animals, we would be just as far ahead as we are now."

"I guess we have to be satisfied if we have enough to eat and a decent place to live, so that we stay warm," Bob remarked. "I'll start to fix the house up tomorrow and put up the storm windows again. The first nice dry day you can give me a hand harvesting the potatoes. We have not had our Indian summer yet, and you remember other years with blue sky, warm sunshine and lovely fall colours. So cheer up."

"I can't see any poetry in that right now," I said. "All I see is a farmer with his wife crawling on hands and knees digging potatoes, and a screaming baby who is bored to death."

"I see that our sheep have broken down the fence and I will have to stand in the mud for the rest of the morning to fix it again," Bob responded. "And another sixty acres need to be plowed before freeze-up."

A Bleak Fall Season

November 1932

This fall we did not get one single beautiful day, quite different from other years when fall is generally the most beautiful time. The farmers shivered on their plows, and even their heavy winter coats did not protect them much against the icy west wind. "If only we would get some snow," people said. Generally the Indian summer comes after we have had some taste of winter.

Each day the sky looked more dark and ominous, and in the evenings the radio screamed and shrieked from static. "A sure sign of snow," Bob remarked. "Listen to this. Neepawa, six inches of snow this morning. Brandon, heavy snowfall today."

The United Farmers of Manitoba (UFM) were having a convention in Dauphin for which delegates came from Saskatchewan and Alberta *as well as from Manitoba. We, too, went to town and attended the convention. However, I am not well enough acquainted with the UFM to be able to write extensively about it.*

I do know that the UFM has been in existence for quite a few years, but it is not supported by all of the farmers. At this convention resolutions covering a variety of issues were presented and voted on, issues like the new Hudson Bay harbour, immigration, the gold standard, federal government credit systems, debt adjustment proposals, taxes on gasoline, education, etc.

In addition to the UFM there is also an organization for women called United Farm Women of Manitoba. This organization has been in existence for about thirty years, and I made up my mind to learn more about their work.

After the convention we had a snowstorm which lasted for two full days. Bob had to take and fetch the children from school daily on the big sleigh, which was very time-consuming and added to his heavy workload. We realized that somehow we had to make or buy a sleigh which the boys would be able to handle themselves.

One afternoon the children came home from school very quietly. Wim looked frightened. "Mamma," he whispered, "Alfred is dead." I could hardly believe I had heard him right. What had happened? Bob came in and told the sad, sad story. Alfred had fallen from his horse because of a broken saddle strap, and landed on the hard, frozen ground. When his father found him an hour and a half later, he was barely alive, and he died on the way to the hospital.

"There is no school on Thursday," Bobby said. "Alfred will be buried that afternoon." Thursday all the farm families from the district went to the funeral on their sleighs. What a sad sight, seeing the young boys carry his casket.

"I will never have a quiet moment any more, sending our boys to school on horseback," I said to a neighbour of ours who was also sitting in our sleigh. I kept thinking of my two little boys on that long cold road.

From our sympathy with this family our thoughts turned to other disheartening matters. Just this week I saw a long list of farms in the paper that were put up for tax sale. If an owner has not paid his taxes for three consecutive years his farm is put up for sale. In our district the taxes on a quarter section vary from $50 to $150 a year.

The farmers were really not the worst off even at that. At least they have a roof over their heads and enough to eat. That is not true for dismissed farm helpers and those who were laid off by the railway and other companies. Many can still find work in lumber camps, but just as many stand on street corners asking for handouts.

The town will only help heads of households. Bachelors are expected to fend for themselves. In town some people were going around with lists, asking for donations and clothes for needy families. Our own district wanted to do something to alleviate the hardship. Each farm wife was asked to make a cushion from scraps of material and ribbon she would likely find in her sewing basket. A party was organized in the school, and after we all played games, the cushions were auctioned off. The proceeds really surprised me. There were quite a few bachelors present, not used to much luxury, who drove up the bidding. After all, the bachelors could afford it the best. We considered the venture a success.

1933

A Long Winter is Brightened by a House Guest

February 1933

It will soon be March again, but we are still up to our ears in ice and snow. We had to buy a toboggan, pulled by a nice, frisky pony, to take the children to school.

Christmas and New Year's have passed again very much as in other years. However, we had one more guest than I had expected, a young Dutch fellow who has been helping Bob with the chores. Through the years we have met quite a few of our countrymen, mostly working class gardeners, carpenters, farmers and bricklayers. If a Dutchman lands in Dauphin, there is a big chance that he will be brought to our place. "Must be nice to speak to somebody from your own country again," they all say. Most of them find it difficult to get a start here in Canada during the Depression.

Our current house guest came from the same background as ours. He had spent a few unsuccessful years at a Dutch university. I guess his father lost patience with him and financed his trip to Canada, but by the time the young man met us he had no money left and was unemployed. He had been roaming around the country for the last four years and had tried his hand at many things — clerk, dishwasher, newspaper vendor, furnace man and lumberman. The Depression had driven him out of the city to the countryside.

One day he arrived in Dauphin on top of a boxcar, the usual means of transportation for the unemployed. That is illegal, of course, but I knew that the authorities do not look too closely. One day Bob ran into him and brought him home. We needed a man for the wood hauling. As he was willing to take the job, we gave him a chance and he turned out very well.

We have no spare bedroom so the living room couch has to serve as his bed. We have found out that the average hired man starts to yawn at nine o'clock, just when Bob and I start to enjoy our evenings. They usually do not care to read but only glance through the local paper. We even discovered that some frown on reading altogether. But Louis, our new friend, liked long evenings with lots to read, just as we do, and we often stayed up late discussing what we had read, or reminiscing about Holland.

Two brothers in our district live in a rather shabby shanty. We had seen them working their land in overalls, like the typical farmer, but when they went to town or attended meetings in our community hall, they wore decent suits with immaculate white shirts and ties. When we saw them for the first time we asked our neighbours who these two gentlemen were. To our surprise they pulled up their shoulders and answered with obvious disdain, "They read." After that we asked ourselves if maybe we too were labelled the same way, considering our well-stocked bookcases.

The year 1933 looks darker than ever for agriculture. Between Christmas and New Year the price of wheat dropped to 21¢ a bushel. I found out that this is about one-sixth of the price the farmers in Holland get for their wheat, because it is subsidized. The freight charges to ship a carload of barley to market would be higher than the amount of money the farmers would receive for their grain. It is the same with cattle prices. Everybody wonders how long conditions like this will last. We attended some meetings in our community hall where subjects like leaving the gold standard and using a grain standard instead were discussed. Much of what they were talking about went over my head, but Bob and I made up our minds to read up on the issues.

There was another matter which alarmed us. Very early in the new year a meeting was called by our school trustees. All parents were urged to attend. They told us that they had not been able to pay the teacher and that they owed her about $100. As there was not the slightest chance that any money would come in, there was no other alternative than to close the school for the time being.

We could hardly believe our ears. This should be the last thing a country would want to economize on. I am glad to report that our school was closed for only one week. The school inspector contacted the teacher and urged her to continue, even if she would only receive room and board for the time being. As soon as money became available she would receive her salary. But if farm conditions stay as poor as they are now, I wonder where this money will come from. The inevitable will only be delayed.

At this time of the year the main activity for the farmers consists of hauling wood from the mountains. As the snow came early this year we are ahead of schedule, because good snow makes hauling wood possible. We already have more wood than we need for our own use. The rest is stacked in the yard to be sold in town next year when it has dried out. The price of cordwood has gone down, too, so the profit is small.

The past few days were very stormy and the roads were blocked again, making trips to the mountains very hazardous. So Bob decided to start another job, getting in summer ice. Blocks of ice, about three-quarters of a yard thick, are cut from the ice on the river and pulled to the ice house, a little wooden building in our yard. The ice is piled up inside and sawdust is thrown over it all until it is covered with a thick layer. In the summer we keep our milk and cream cool there, and every other day Bob will break off a big chunk with an axe and put it in the kitchen icebox. Keeping ourselves and our possessions cool in the summer and warm in the winter seem to be our main concerns here.

A Quilting Bee in a Very Cold Winter

March 1933

Winter was different this year. We are used to having a few very cold days, maybe four or five, but after that a mild spell will come to revive us and balance things out. But this year the severe cold stayed week after week. We saw our large wood supply dwindle and discovered that over a period of two and a half months we had consumed ten cords of wood. Fifteen cords would keep a large, well-built house warm for a whole year.

The school was closed during the cold spell because the trips to and from school became impossible. Nobody went out unless absolutely necessary. We were virtually isolated from the outside world. Even the mailman stopped coming, and that is very unusual. We could see nothing but swirling clouds of very fine snow. It looked like those very foggy days we knew so well in Holland. Our fields were transformed into an undulating ocean with snow whipped and frozen into waves.

To be packed together in a rather small house for such a length of time made children noisier and naughtier by the day. They wanted to play the wildest games. There was no end to the fighting and squabbling. How was it possible that on broiling hot summer days visions of winter had sometimes looked good to me!

But now that is all behind us again, and the storms, both inside and outside, have calmed down. The children have gone back to school and the house suddenly looks a lot roomier. Bob and Louis take turns going to the mountains for wood.

I regained my equilibrium by taking some time off and leaving the household chores to the men. One of my excursions was to go with

Bob to the mountains on the wood sleigh. We made tea in a honey pail over a fire and had our sandwiches sitting on a log. It was a glorious day.

My second outing was to the home of one of our neighbours for a quilting bee. A group of people come together to make a quilt cooperatively. This quilting bee was organized by the same ladies' club that had made the cushions I wrote about a bit ago. This quilt will be auctioned off and the proceeds used to help the needy.

With my closest neighbour, Mabel Timm, I hit the road at half past eight on a bright, sunny morning in our toboggan. I sat in front, driving the horse, and Mabel sat in the back, keeping an eye on the things we were carrying. It had been agreed that each of the ladies would contribute one item for a potluck dinner. We soon saw sleighs coming from different directions on the lonesome, sparsely travelled country roads. One would have a loaf of bread, another butter or a bowl of applesauce, another vegetables, and so on. We looked forward to a regular feast.

The work on the quilt was divided up among the various ladies. A few started to pin the quilt blocks together. Another sewed them together on the sewing machine, and others put up the wooden frames on which the quilt had to be stretched. Several women went into the kitchen to prepare dinner, which was most festive.

After the dinner a layer of cotton batting was stretched over the quilt lining on which the neatly stitched blocks were stretched. Then a design was drawn by hand, which we had to follow with neat little stitches. Those without work on the quilt entertained us on the piano and sang songs. All of us who were stitching joined in the singing. The coal oil lamps were lit, and I felt as though we had gone back a hundred years to an earlier time in history.

When it was all over and we had made the cold trip home through the starry night, I found the boys in bed and the men reading books and newspapers around the fire. I walked over to the bookcase, took the shabby edition of Hildebrand's Camera Obscura from the shelf, and toasting my feet at the fire soon became engrossed in a well-known Dutch story.

Reflections from the Hospital

April 1933

For a week I have been contemplating the world from a different corner. Instead of the wide, white farm fields I am gazing from a hospital bed at the back sides of city houses with untidy gardens and the muddy mess that melting snow leaves in its wake. An unpleasant operation which had been hanging over my head for most of the winter was finally performed. After a week, when the pain had subsided and the love of life returned, I was bored. That never happens to me at home. I read until I got a headache and had to stop. Bob came to visit me every other day.

I wondered what things would be like at home while I was gone. I sometimes started to laugh, thinking about them all. Let them muddle through for awhile and sit in a mess. It won't hurt them at all. It was a regular men's establishment now, with Bob, Louis and the three little boys.

Bob told me, "I closed the living room and hung a sign on the door which read 'No Trespassing.' I also warned the boys that they would be punished severely if I caught them near the river. The water is running over the ice at present and is getting very high. In a few days we can expect more water from the mountains. After the heavy snowfall we had this winter the river will become ferocious. It has already run through our bush and over the road, carrying away the big trees from the lowest part of our field."

"And how are the children?" I asked.

"Oh, they have lots of fun. With this nice weather I naturally can't keep them indoors. They splash through the mud puddles in their high rubber boots, and are soaking wet most of the time."

"How do you plan to get the boys to school next week?"

"On horseback, the two of them on one horse. That's the only way I can think of doing it."

"Any other news?"

"Yes, prices are going up. Farmers are getting $4.50 per hundredweight for pigs. But store prices for sugar, canned fruit and vegetables have also gone up. Let's hope that grain prices will go up when we sell our grain."

Arbor Day and Diverse Nationalities

Early May 1933

Yesterday, the second Monday in May, was Arbor Day. Originally this day was set aside for the planting of trees, and while we still do this, more and more it has become a day for cleaning up parks and gardens and raking lawns. All the schools seem to take part in it.

So on Arbor Day Bobby and Wim left home, one carrying a rake and the other a hoe. Naturally a day like this is considered a festive holiday. Most often it is a nice warm day. Alas, it was not like that this year. It is still miserably cold. But come what may, the boys still had to wear their running shoes and straw hats. They left with lunch boxes slung over their shoulders and with happy, expectant faces.

The girls had scrubbed the schoolroom floors and washed the windows, and the boys had weeded the paths, raked the grass and rebuilt the woodpile. Accompanied by their teacher, they had crossed the fields to a poplar bluff and played thieves and robbers. After that they made a bonfire, put the contents of their lunch boxes together, and had a wonderful meal.

On Easter we had a heavy snowfall. How we detest the winter at this time of year. The letters from Holland told us of tulips and crocuses in bloom, the forsythia starting to blossom and the green grass. I have never longed so much for a green blade of grass or a warm spring day. In the evenings we pored over the catalogue for garden seeds and flowers. In my imagination I was busy landscaping our garden plot. Generally in past years I planted a big vegetable garden with a few flowers, but this year my desire for flowers was so overwhelming that we decided to do something about it. We wrote a letter to our friend Frank, who seemed to have quite a bit of experience in gardening, and we received an enthusiastic letter full of advice. He also wrote that he had packed a good-sized box to send us with slips and plants gathered in the garden of the lakeside home of his future in-laws.

Now fine weather has suddenly come and every farmer is back in the field. Most of the wheat has already been sown. Farmers are in high spirits, especially those who have held on to their grain. The wheat prices have improved from 24¢ a bushel last fall to 49¢. The United States left the gold standard and that probably had an influence on it. Other years during seeding the roads are quiet, but this year grain boxes full of wheat pass by from early morning until late at night. The fact that farmers are satisfied with their transactions in town is shown by the way they pass our place at night, singing loudly and leaving empty beer bottles along the roadside.

The majority of the people that pass our place are from central and eastern Europe — Ukrainians, Poles, Galacians and Ruthenians. I would say that nearly 50 percent of the people in our district belong to *these nationalities. They seem to hang on to their own customs. The older women all wear shawls over their heads, just as they used to do before coming to Canada. At home they still speak their own language. Of course, the children learn to speak English at school, but many of the older women do not speak a word of English, even if they have lived here all their lives. Most men have learned the new language because they come into contact with English-speaking people more than the women do. It did surprise us that there is not much contact between central and eastern European settlers and the more western ones like the English, Germans, Swedes, Norwegians, Danes and Dutch.*

The French presence in Canada is a different matter, but around Dauphin we do not find many French people. Eastern Europeans have not mixed very much with the rest of the population, and when a Ukrainian girl marries a Canadian boy it is still whispered about just as if something not quite right has taken place. We Dutch people do not have this contempt for people of another race. On the contrary, a lot of Dutchmen seem to consider anything foreign interesting, and an accent is often considered smart. What divides people in Holland is their social background, not their nationality.

Eight miles west of our place is a large settlement of East Europeans. We sometimes drive past their homes, which look neat and modest. The older ones are plastered with loam, and light blue seems to be a colour they favour. In the middle of the district are two churches on opposite sides of the road. One is Roman Catholic and the other Greek Orthodox.

East Europeans are known to be hardworking and thrifty. They live soberly, do not sport new cars or new machinery, and make do with old things. In contrast, other Canadians, who in many cases have lost the money they made during the prosperous years after the war, have nice new homes but large mortgages on their farms. The majority of western Europeans come from the peasant class and have an inborn love for the land. They generally have large families and their children often contribute to the family income by taking a job at an early age.

Saturday Night in Town

May 1933

It is Sunday afternoon and a most beautiful spring day. We took our chairs outside on the lawn to sit in the sun and enjoy the balmy temperature. The grass is getting green and the trees have started to bud. Our only surviving plum tree is full of buds. All the others have been destroyed by the rabbits this winter. It is expected that the rabbits will become a regular pest this year, and maybe even next year, after which they will likely contract some kind of disease and die off again. This seems to be a cycle repeated about every seven years.

In the pasture, against the sunny river bank, the sheep nurse their new lambs which arrive every day. A few clucking hens, followed by a flock of baby chicks, scuttle over the yard. Our geese have disappeared, but I expect them to return any day now with their brood.

In between the lambs and the chickens our three sons roll in the grass, not knowing which prank to pull next out of sheer exhuberance. Bobby, who celebrated his tenth birthday a few days ago, received a box of firecrackers from a school pal and scared the wits out of us only ten minutes ago, by sneaking some under our chairs and awaiting the results from a safe distance. Who would not be tempted to pull pranks on a lovely day like this?

Cars pass by on the gravel road in front of our house throwing up clouds of dust. How fast things change here, from snow to dust. We have taken our own car out of the garage, which gives us a feeling of being back in circulation again. During the winter every whole Saturday is taken up with a trip to town to sell our produce and buy groceries. In the spring we finish our trip earlier because we can take the car again.

Farmers do not have very fancy cars. They are like old boxes on wheels, with flapping and often torn tops. They shake and rattle but get you where you want to go, and that's the main thing. If we can find somebody to look after the children we leave them at home when we go to town, but mostly, to their great delight, of course, we have to take them to town with us. When the children, fresh from their baths, have been put into clean clothes, when the cattle have been looked after, the house has been tidied and we ourselves are dressed, our little old Ford drives out of the gate to take us to town.

On the way we look from right to left. Look how high the wheat has grown already. It must be at least four inches. You can see the rows very clearly; it looks clean. But my goodness, over there is nothing but wild oats. They might just as well be plowed under. Now we come to an experimental station, just two miles from town. How neat everything looks over here, not a weed to be seen. The four wooden sign boards on which they post their crop rotation have not been put up yet.

All along the road cows with their calves graze the fresh green grass. Another two weeks and the trees and shrubs will be out in leaf and blossom.

During the week Dauphin is a rather dead little prairie town, but on Saturday evening it is quite lively. The false fronts on the stores make them look bigger than they really are. The stores stay open until eleven o'clock. The street lighting is very festive. It consists of long strings of coloured electric lights stretched over Main Street in rows like coloured beads. Main Street, the principal street in town, runs from north to south. The side streets run perpendicular to it and, in contrast, are very quiet and dark.

If you are lucky enough to get a parking place on Main Street, you can take part in the chief amusement in town — to sit in your car and watch the world go by. You see your friends, shout to them and shake hands. You sit there and admire or criticize, you make a game of guessing the nationalities of the passersby. It is easy to recognize the Natives and the Métis, and the Ukrainian women with their head shawls. The pinnacle of entertainment is to get a place in front of the drugstore where a gramophone or radio blasts music in your ears all evening. With a little imagination I can visualize myself again behind the window of a big restaurant in Amsterdam or in a cozy corner patio on a Parisian sidewalk with the crowds passing by.

If you get tired of sitting in the car, or if you are not lucky enough to get a parking spot, you can join the parade of people. If you have your ears open you realize how many nationalities populate Canada. In front of the big grocery store a group of women with dark or coloured head shawls talk as much with their hands as with their lips. I can't make out a word because it is likely Ukrainian, or perhaps Russian or Polish. Among this group you'll also find young girls with hats fashionably worn at an angle, makeup on their faces, and smart Eaton's catalogue dresses. The young East European generation does not want to wear the head shawls of their elders.

In front of the post office is another group, also speaking in a foreign language and gesticulating a lot. But it sounds more familiar because it is French. I suppose we could understand it if only they did not talk so fast.

The Germans and Scandinavians are in a minority here. Of course, you can hear English in different dialects, from the unmusical "knauw knauw" of the Americans to the unadulterated English of a Cockney, the distinctive brogue of the Scots and the musical whimsy of the Irish. Suddenly we hear our own mother tongue and we are joined by the

Bos brothers, our own countrymen, dressed in their Sunday best. We shake hands and slap each other on the back. "How about it, Bob, shouldn't we go for a beer?" The invitation doesn't include me.

In contrast with the Prohibition on alcohol that now exists in the United States, Canada has never been totally "dry." All kinds of alcoholic beverages are sold, but to buy any you first need to buy a license for a dollar. Alcohol cannot be bought by the bottle in a grocery store or in a hotel. You need to buy it in a government liquor store. Bottles are sealed and the seal has to remain intact until you reach your own premises. So you had better not take a little nip on the way home because a broken seal means a good fine.

About six years ago a more lenient policy came into effect which brought us the so-called beer parlours, where you can drink only beer but do not need a license. From what I hear about them, they are quite different from the cafés we were used to in Europe. Women and children are not allowed to enter, nor can you look in and see the men sitting in front of a window enjoying their drink. It all takes place behind closed doors and drawn curtains. The result of all this secrecy is that the men act as if they were going to do something naughty. Most women are practically teetotallers and are dead set against drinking.

The crowd in these beer parlours is socially very mixed, I'm told. Farmers and hired men, clerks and shopkeepers, policemen and lawyers, teachers and office workers all sit together as equals and in most cases are on a first-name basis. Nothing other than beer is served and not in a very sophisticated way, I am told. As soon as the glasses are empty, the waiter snatches them from the table, thumbs in the glasses, and inquires if more is wanted. Serving beer after eleven o'clock is not allowed, so around that time many order two or three glasses at once, leaving the tables just loaded. In the meantime the women sit patiently in the car outside waiting until hubby has had enough.

We women do have a place we can go to, but nothing is offered to eat or drink. This is the so-called Ladies Rest Room. If I am not mistaken, the Ladies Rest Room in Dauphin is organized by the United Farm Women of Manitoba and is not really a very attractive place. It is situated in a basement and the only view you have is that of the feet of the passersby. The furniture is very simple, nothing but a few chairs and one large table. Yet it is a very convenient place, especially in the winter. A lady supervises the room so your purchases can be left in her care, the children's dirty hands can be washed, feet warmed again on a cold day, and an appointment can be made to meet someone. This rest room is often used for meetings, and twice a week a health nurse is present during the afternoon to examine the children and give instructions on baby care.

The most popular places of assembly in town, however, are the street corners for the men and the grocery stores for the women. The T. Eaton Company stores, which are to be found in all Canadian cities and towns, are especially popular as meeting places. They not only sell groceries but also clothes, tools, furnishings, etc.

One of the things that struck me as unusual and funny at first was the jovial way the public and the store clerks mingle. I remember the first time I went to town with Mrs. Durston. She took me to a big store and together we made the rounds of all the departments, in each of which I was introduced to the manager and the staff. After that they always greeted me like one of the family. They would inquire after my husband and children, discuss the roads and the gardens, and always ask how I liked Canada.

Business is carried on partly on an exchange basis. We trade our dairy produce for groceries, but since our products are priced lower than theirs, we have to supplement the price with money. What struck me as very odd in the beginning was the large quantities people purchased — a hundred pounds of flour, a hundred pounds of sugar, fifty pounds of salt, and forty pounds of rolled oats — which seemed outrageous to me. The farmers are used to this type of buying and the advantage is that there is no danger of running out. The price is also a bit lower if you buy in large quantities.

The amusements in town include a picture show for 35¢. If you want to be amused in style you must pay 50¢, which entitles you to sit in a cane easy chair instead of an ordinary folding chair. A few years ago we could only see silent films, during which a woman played an organ. She imitated galloping horses and murmuring brooks to perfection, and Bob always liked the music better than the show. Since the talkies were introduced, good up-to-date films are shown in Dauphin. I guess if farm conditions were better we would go to a show more often, but for the time being it remains a special treat.

Besides this there are also a few dance halls where the so-called jitney dances are held. I have only watched the fun from a distance and have had no desire to take part in it. The halls look bare with benches all along the sides, on which the girls sit. The men crowd into the doorway leading to the street, and after buying a ticket at a little table close to the door, enter the hall to make their choice from all these beauties. When the music stops and the dance is finished, the girls go back to the benches and the men go back to the door. Only through this doorway can you get a glimpse of the action because, just as in the beer parlours, all the windows are frosted glass.

All that is left to describe now are the Chinese cafés where meals, soft drinks and ice cream — but no beer or alcoholic beverages, of course — are served at all times of the day until late at night. A few of the hotels in Dauphin also have dining rooms, but it seems to me that the Chinese restaurants are more popular and are likely cheaper, too. They are very simple but neat places where you can sit in what are called box stalls. As is usual here, you cannot look out of a window onto the street, something we are so used to in Europe. Neither is there music to liven things up. But the food, Chinese as well as ordinary, is good. For 35¢ you get soup, a lot of meat, vegetables and potatoes, as much bread and butter as you want, and a choice of different pies for dessert, with coffee or tea. If you are very hungry you can ask for second helpings, but mostly I find that you can barely finish the very liberal portions which they serve.

At eleven o'clock the fun is over. The stores are closing and it gets a lot darker on the street. The women are looking around for their husbands, hoping to spot them in one of the groups of men talking and gesticulating on the street corners. Bags with flour or sugar are carried to the car and put on the back seat between our sleeping youngsters. We try to find a spot for ourselves between coal oil cans, machine oil and bags of groceries. North and south, east and west the carts, buggies and cars speed out of the town on their way home again over the quiet country roads.

We Build a Tennis Court

July 1933

Last winter we were complaining about the cold, and now in the summer we complain about the heat. Canada is a country of contrasts. At the end of May and the beginning of June we had a heat wave and thought we would die. We would flee to the house to be sheltered from the burning sun. But with no breeze the house was like an oven. We were forced to stay inside because outside the mosquitoes nearly ate us alive. A big thunderstorm brought us relief, and the fields and garden benefitted as much as the people and animals.

After the roads had dried up and were passable once again, we set out on an inspection tour and came home very satisfied. All along the road the wild roses were blooming, and in the grass the orange tiger lilies were playing hide and seek with the wild sunflowers. The grain had not suffered too much from the heat and looked very healthy indeed. In the garden the peas, beans and carrots were doing just as well as the weeds.

While Bob was cutting the alfalfa the rest of us, Annie, the boys and I, hoed in the potato field and in the garden. Now that it is finished, I look back with great satisfaction at the results, especially since my dreams of a flower garden have started to materialize. Zinnias, delphiniums, daisies and nasturtiums have all begun to blossom. I am so glad that many of the flowers we had in the Netherlands grow here, too.

Another dream has been realized, too, something we had hoped for and talked about a lot, but which was not as easy to achieve.

It began last year. On a beautiful summer evening we sat on the lawn in front of our house with a few friends, all young people. We were discussing the limitations of living on a farm. You have to travel quite a few miles to get to a lake for swimming. Sure, we have the river in our backyard, but in the spring it is too dangerous for a good swim and in the summer it is too shallow. We don't have a golf course or tennis courts close by.

Suddenly Bob said, "Remember all the tennis we used to play in Holland? Right after school we'd all go to the tennis courts and play until dinnertime. Why couldn't we build a tennis court here? Maybe it would cost too much to build one." And with this observation he thought that the subject was closed.

But I couldn't get the idea out of my head. A few days later we attended a young people's meeting in our community hall, which included young married couples also. Frank, the young minister who became our friend, was also present. In fact, he was in charge of the meeting. He talked to us about community spirit and cooperation, and pointed out that farmers were isolated on their own farms and should cooperate with each other. What we could not achieve individually we might be able to achieve if we joined together. "Have your regular meetings," he said. "Form a little theatre group, or a music group, or whatever appeals to you most. But have recreational contact with each other."

Suddenly I had an inspiration. I poked Bob in the ribs and whispered, "What about that tennis court? I am going to discuss it with Frank. They would sooner listen to the minister than to me."

After the meeting we met with him and right away he was in favour of it. We made up a list of people we thought would be interested, and after the church service the next Sunday he announced that a meeting would be held at our home to which everybody was invited who was interested in starting a tennis club.

To our surprise his proposal was received with great enthusiasm and a large crowd turned out for the meeting, older farmers as well as young people. Other people in the district laughed at the project, saying that tennis was no game for farmers. They even made silly jokes about bringing shovels instead of rackets, because they could handle those better. But we were not discouraged, and that same evening it was decided that as soon as the time could be found between seeding and haying, about twenty men would start work on the court. It would be built on our farm because we were most centrally located. We would raise the money ourselves by organizing dances or other parties.

One morning not much later the volunteers were phoning around to tell everybody to be present early the next morning to start work on the court. The crew selected a flat piece of pasture in front of our barn. The grass had never grown there very well because the cows and horses had trampled it so much. After plowing the area the sod was removed by big scrapers pulled by two horses. Next the surface was levelled and rolled. Then loads of sand and fine gravel were hauled from a nearby gravel pit, and it was all rolled, sprayed with water and rolled again, until it started to look like cement.

Building this tennis court naturally took longer than one day. Every spare moment was used to work on the project, and it was not until the middle of August that we could play tennis on it. One of our members, who used to live in the city and had had a tennis court in his yard, gave us an old net. The marking was done with chalk lines. Naturally it was still a rather primitive court, but the enthusiasm to play was enormous. Every Sunday afternoon and evening, and sometimes also during the week, a lot of interested people turned up.

We needed to raise money to buy rackets, balls, fencing for the backstops, and whatever else might be needed. We decided to hold a barn dance. It was held in the loft of the barn of our Dutch bachelor neighbours. The entrance fee was 25¢ a person. We hired a band and served refreshments. The first two dances cleared $20 each, and the third time we made $10. With the $50 we bought four rackets, six balls and the wire fencing for the backstops. We had hoped to enclose the whole court, but the funds ran out so we have to wait.

A few weeks later when farm work was slack a number of the young men hammered poles deep into the ground and put up the wire netting. By this time we had acquired linen tape lines to use for markings instead of chalk, and that was a big improvement. The women came along and as usual each brought their own contributions towards dinner. One even brought a can of fresh cream and an ice machine to make ice cream for dessert. We had a lovely day, and towards evening the court was completed.

Every car that has passed our farm since then has stopped to take a good look. It is quite a novelty to see a tennis court on a farm. Another curiosity is the virtual absence of white flannel pants on this court. Most players come in overalls or work pants, which may account for the curious looks of the passersby. But they can laugh as much as they like — we have achieved our goal and quite a few of those participants in overalls promise to become good players.

An Exciting Week's Holiday in the Mountains

August 1933

A camping holiday this year was quite an event for me, especially since I left my husband and children at home. It has been eight years since I have had a regular holiday. This year I took a whole week off before the summer rush and the harvest started again.

It happened that this spring the young people of the district formed a theatre group and were planning to produce a play. They asked if I would be willing to help with the production during the summer. I would work on it with a teacher and the new student minister. We had regular rehearsals and got to know each other fairly well.

One day the teacher made a proposal. A friend of hers had a tent and they were making plans for a camping holiday at Clear Lake. Would I like to come along? To pitch a tent in the tourist camp would only cost a dollar, and we could take most of our food along, so the main expense would be gas for the car.

There was room for six in the tent. We left on a lovely Saturday afternoon. Three of our group had left the day before and would spend the first night in the tent of another friend. So our travelling party consisted of four, including Bob, who would take us there in our own car.

We strapped the tent and the sleeping mattresses on top of the car, stuffed food and suitcases inside and in the trunk, tucked pots and pans wherever we could find a spot. In the end it was doubtful that there would be room left for ourselves. In fact we couldn't open the doors after the car was packed so we had to crawl in through the windows.

Once we were underway we saw the Riding Mountains come closer and closer. Instead of the grey-blue ridge we always look upon, we now saw little spruce trees on top of the mountains like those you find in a toy box. Before we realized it, we had climbed the first rise and were suddenly surrounded by forest.

We followed a winding trail for about twenty-five miles through dense poplar bush, a very scenic route with hills, valleys and lakes. From the road we saw six-foot ferns intermixed with yellow sunflowers, goldenrods and red fireweed. There was no sign of wildlife. Still, we knew that many wild animals live here. The sun had begun to set, and as we continued our trip we saw the beautiful silhouette of a very large moose on a hill, totally immobile, like a statue etched against the rose-tinted evening sky. It was an unforgettable sight.

Then we caught our first glimpse of the lake, our final destination. The spruce trees grew close to the shoreline and there seemed to be a nice sandy beach. Among the spruces we had a glimpse of about a dozen cottages. We could hear the strumming of a guitar coming from one of the cottages, and it gave me the impression of a very peaceful holiday spot for an overwrought housewife. We reached the south shore of the lake, and found ourselves in a tourist town which reminded me of the wooded country around Arnhem and Nijmegen in the Netherlands, but with the lake added.

But as I had already feared, no idyllic rest could be expected. Crowds milled in the street, casually dressed. Girls in skirts were a curiosity. Everyone wore bathing suits, pants, shorts or beach pyjamas, but no skirts.

The men were not dressed any better. None wore the smart white flannel pants and blazers you would expect in a European resort. Instead men wore jeans and overalls. A couple of gents who stood in front of a restaurant were most outlandishly dressed up in bathing suits, high black boots without socks, felt hats and pipes. I don't know if things have changed a lot in Europe during the last ten years, but personally I had never seen such unconventional dress behaviour.

The campground was as crowded and noisy as a fair. It was built like a village with main streets and side streets crossing each other, but with tents instead of houses. We searched for the other half of our

Bob and Jane Aberson, 1979

Sunday morning at the Dawson Place log cabin, 1926

The Aberson farm, 1927

The tobaggan to school

The tennis court serves as a hockey rink in winter

Log cabin in the Riding Mountains — cutting wood for the winter

The Aberson family, 1977 (left to right: Bob Jr., Wim, Jane, Bob Sr., Dirk)

party but couldn't find them. Soon it would be getting dark. Then Bob spotted an open place on one of the side roads from which we could have a view of the lake. The two girls looked a bit doubtful, but at last they agreed to set up the tent right there.

I must say that the people in the camp were most helpful. From all sides men turned up to give Bob a hand. Together they hoisted the poles and stretched the ropes. After we finished unloading the car, the other three girls arrived with a lot of noise and excitement.

"Oh, what a dull place you have picked," they complained. "Come with us, we have found a far better spot right on the main street and close to everything. Is it much trouble to take the tent down again? Sorry we were not here an hour earlier. It is getting dark already, but you will find that everybody is willing to give you a hand."

Well, Bob looked doubtful but amused at the same time, and he could not assert himself against a group of excited women. He dutifully pulled up the stakes and loaded up the car again. It was impossible to get everything stowed back in the car as tightly as we had it before, so we decided to make a few extra trips back and forth.

The new camping spot certainly could not be called dull. Practically everybody who entered or left the campground had to pass by our campsite. Bob took me aside and whispered, "The beach is very close, and that is where you will spend most of your time anyway, so don't worry too much."

When at last the tent was pitched and our belongings stowed away, we decided to have something to eat. Fortunately the other three girls had prepared dinner already. I must say, as far as conveniences were concerned the camp had its advantages. Each block of twenty tents had its own cookhouse — a roof built on poles, open on all sides, with two big stoves made of cement, and huge fire boxes capable of burning logs two feet long. Park attendants supplied, free of charge, big piles of wood stacked by each cookhouse. On both sides of the stoves were long picnic tables with seats attached. Containers for garbage, connected with drainage pipes, functioned as waste disposal systems. Water pumps were located at each cook-house and the water was beautifully clear.

Icehouses contained big blocks of ice piled in the centre, around which were built lockers to keep your food reasonably cool. The huge ice blocks are all packed in sawdust, the same way we do it on the farm. These lockers were supplied with padlocks, and each camper had access to his own numbered locker. I must say that all these features are very convenient, but they take away from the idea of camping. I had visualized having a campfire in the forest to cook our meals on; but open campfires are not allowed anymore in the Riding Mountains because of the danger of bush fires.

One of our girls told us that there was going to be a dance tonight. We decided to go, but the only person from our group who had a really good time was Bob. Since we had not come to know anybody so far, the six of us women were decorating the side benches for most of the evening. Bob distributed his favours equally among the six of us, and when we had each danced twice with him, it was time to go back to camp.

That night we were crowded into the tent because Bob had to be squeezed in, too. We found our mattresses thin and lumpy and were awake most of the night, except for Bob, who slept like a log. Many of our neighbours headed for the lake in their bathing suits first thing in the morning, which struck us as a very good idea. The morning dip became a regular event for us.

The beach was rather narrow, but the water was beautifully clear. After our swim we went on a sightseeing expedition, and one of the things that attracted us most was a group of eight beautiful free tennis courts. The town had a few sports stores, a bakery, drugstore, post office, and quite a few restaurants.

Bob had to leave in the afternoon. He promised me that he would come back on Sunday and bring the children. By that time I would be ready to go back home.

During the day we spent our time swimming, playing tennis, walking and reading. In the evenings most campers gathered under a big roof where a campfire was lit and the benches were filled to overflowing with summer guests. Many were sitting on the ground, too. We sang community songs, and performances on piano, violin and guitar were given by the guests.

I found it to be a welcome change to be able to spend most of the day in idleness, to eat meals I had not prepared myself, and to read or sleep or play tennis when I felt like it. I was not very eager to go home again.

Saturday morning, the day before we had to leave, we were startled by the tinkling of raindrops on the tent roof. While we were sitting around the table for breakfast in the cookhouse it started to pour. We all rushed to the tent, hoping to find a dry refuge there, but to our consternation the tent was not very waterproof. We all put on our bathing suits and huddled together. We hung our blankets on the washline in the rain. The mattresses were soaked through. Little children had a great old time, spashing knee-deep in the water around our tent while all six of us sat morosely in the mud watching their fun.

Then we heard that there would be a free concert in town that evening. At once we decided to attend, if for no other reason than to have a dry roof over our heads again. But it took us so long to get ready that when we finally arrived the hall was packed and the door closed. On the way back, after much stumbling over roots and splashing through mud puddles, our group got separated and only two of us found our way to our cookhouse, where a group of young girls offered to squeeze us into their tent for the night. They didn't need to ask us twice. Though a bit damp, their tent was heaven compared to our own.

We must have dozed for about an hour when suddenly a heavy clap of thunder woke us all up. That was followed by a massive cloudburst. It was one of the worst electrical storms I have ever seen. We held our breath in terror as the water streamed in torrents from the tent roof, and every moment we expected to see it come through and soak us. That didn't happen, but suddenly one of the girls screamed, "The mattress is getting wet." Water had seeped in from underneath, and in a few minutes everything was soaked.

At two o'clock in the morning the seven of us were sitting on a mound of shoes and boxes, covered with a few soaked blankets. At five o'clock, wet to the skin, shivering and nodding our heads from tiredness, we were still sitting there. Then suddenly the rain stopped and the sun came through.

This was the Sunday morning I expected my husband and children. I never took my eyes from the main road, watching every car as it turned into the camp. At eleven o'clock, just as I had begun to give up hope, our car, hardly recognizable because of the mud, skidded around the corner.

All my worries were over. The boys put on their bathing suits in no time and joined the other youngsters splashing around our tent. Bob had to listen to all our adventures of the past night. The rest of our party had not been able to find a dry spot to sleep, but had thought of the fireplace in the community hall. They lit a fire, and even if the ground was hard to sleep on and there were no blankets to cover them, they had dried out a bit and had kept reasonably warm.

Around four o'clock the sky became overcast again, so we quickly packed our belongings and got into the car. We left Clear Lake in a heavy downpour.

We had a rough time going home over very slippery roads. Twice we had to stop, once for a flat tire and once for an electrical short-circuit. Around midnight we turned into our farm gate. I cannot begin to tell you how glad I was to have a roof over my head again and a bed to sleep in.

Everything looked fresh and green the next morning. The flowers were at their very best, and the grass looked as green as an emerald. Everything seemed so quiet and peaceful. I had a wonderful week, but I was not lonesome for the tourist camp. Home is best, after all.

Reminiscing on the Big Move, Eight Years Later

September 1933

Bob is hunched over the table by the window, and on each side of his dark head of hair are two smaller heads lighter in colour. They are studying our new world atlas. They have found the small land we call Holland, and even its northern province of Groningen where these articles are sent and published.

"Now lets look at Canada again," says Bobby. "It sure seems bigger than Holland!"

"It's 240 times as big," agrees Bob. "Manitoba alone is eighteen times as big as the whole country of Holland."

Lying stretched out on the couch I think back to the train trip I took across Canada with my two-year-old son, a trip that took three days and four nights. Eight years ago already! Bob had come a year earlier to learn something about farming. What a gamble that had been for us! No wonder our family in Holland thought we were crazy to consider the move from a comfortable life among family and friends to the risks and hard work of the Manitoba prairie.

We have lasted this long because we were young and were able to look upon our new life as a great adventure. I could write a whole book about our first two years living in a log cabin on a small farm out in the bush. It was beautiful, and it was lonesome. In that isolated log cabin our second son Wim was born. I lined a laundry basket with golden yellow satin and lovely handmade lace we brought from India. That was where he first lived in Canada. The yellow satin matched his golden hair and his sunny disposition.

After two years in the log cabin we bought a 160-acre farm and have lived there ever since. We are situated on a secondary road and *have a beautiful view of the Riding Mountains to the south. We are sheltered on the north and west by the trees of the bush, but to the east we have rolling grain fields as far as the eye can see.*

It is a great feeling of satisfaction to see the crops grow every year, and to see our animals and birds mature. We have never had a real crop failure, but constant low prices for what we grow do discourage us sometimes.

But now the boys must go to bed. After they are tucked away, Bob suggests, "Let take a walk before we go to bed. It's such a lovely night." The stubble fields are golden in the moonlight, while the bush is dark and mysterious on our side.

We do feel very much at home now in Canada, our adopted land.

In Praise of Indian Summer

October 1933

After the first killing frost, when the flowers die and the leaves change colour and fall, we can expect a few weeks of brilliant sunshine and summer temperatures. We've not yet had frosty nights so our fall flowers are still in bloom in our garden. Vases full of them — sweet peas, zinnias, chrysanthemums, daisies and asters — brighten the house.

The colours of the leaves on the trees are now at their most beautiful with reds, golds and yellows against the green. Our pride and joy is a wild vine which grows against the house and around the windows. We found it in the bush two years ago and brought it home, where now it lends some colourful charm to our otherwise austere house. There is very little wind now, and we bask in the brilliant sunshine that warms the land.

This year's spring calves and foals are now grazing on our stubble fields after having spent the summer on the open prairies and along the roads. But every day their domain shrinks because Bob's plow turns the ground over in broad strips. The garden and fruit trees are empty of their vegetables and fruits, which will feed us through the winter. Six haystacks are lined up along edge of the forest, and the granary is piled high with grain.

The year's good produce gives us a feeling of great satisfaction. That must even more be the case when the prices are reasonably good. Bob made me climb in the hayloft to inspect the full barn, go with him to the granary, and after that we walked around the haystacks. Then I took him to my cellar and showed him my summer's work stored up for the future. We said to each other, "At least we have plenty to eat for ourselves and our animals. We can even give away quite a bit to the people in other parts of Manitoba and Saskatchewan where the drought and the grasshoppers have cleaned them out." Strong appeals for such help have been made in the papers and on the radio. We feel very prosperous compared with them.

That feeling of prosperity disappeared when we saw what was happening to grain prices. Wheat has been selling for 53¢ a bushel, barley 35¢ and oats 25¢. Even if that is rather low, it is better than last year. But now the prices have fallen, with wheat going down by 4¢, 7¢ and even 11¢. Satisfaction gives way to disgust. We should have hired trucks to take the grain to the elevator when the price was higher. Or wait, as those who can afford it advise, until prices rise in the spring.

In most countries agriculture is subsidized. But the financial position of Canada is so poor that the government cannot seem to do anything about subsidizing farmers. We do export large quantities of grain to other countries because Canada grows the best wheat in the world.

One effect of the depression of prices is that a new political party has come into being. It is called the Co-operative Commonwealth Federation, or CCF. This party has proposed some drastic changes in policy, such as the nationalization of banks and natural resources like mines, forests and hydro power. Farms would not be nationalized because the farmers do not see themselves as capitalists but as an exploited class. The CCF will likely get quite a few seats in Parliament in the next election because it has considerable support from labourers and farmers.

The news we get from Holland tells us that everything is much cheaper there now. That may be good for those who buy food at the stores, but it is not good for the farmers. Other commodities like woolen yarn, materials, machinery and even many foods are mostly imported. I learned at a lecture here last week that we need to pay very high duty on all these products. Take wool, for example. When we sell it from our own sheep we only get 3¢ a pound. But when you buy wool yarn or woolen blankets you have to pay very high prices because there is a duty of 90 percent! The same is true of machinery.

But it's very doubtful that even if the CCF wins the election, or whoever does win, much can be changed. Change is needed, though, without a doubt. At that same lecture we heard that if conditions do not change, in seven years the interest on the national debt will be several million dollars more than the national revenue!

Help on the Farm Makes a Holiday Possible

Late October 1933

We just came back from a three-day holiday, and have prospects for another holiday of five days! Our hired girl promised to stay until the end of the month. And now we have a reliable young man working for us, too.

A few weeks ago a young Galician fellow named Andy walked in and said, "I have no work until freeze-up and am quite willing to work for you for just room and board until then. After that I'm going to the bush to cut wood."

We have known this young man for a few years. Andy had walked barefoot into our yard about four years ago. He had come from Galicia and had been working for a few months in a community of other East Europeans settlers. He did not speak a word of English and had thought it better to stay with people whose language he understood. But his own countrymen took advantage of him and treated him shabbily. He owned nothing but the clothes on his back, and we had some difficulty finding out what he wanted. But at last we understood that he wanted work, and as we could use some help, we hired him on the spot.

We have never had better help and a friendlier worker. He helped with milking the cows (which you needn't even ask a Canadian hired man to do), with working the land, hauling water, and even dressing and feeding our boys. Every evening he retired to a corner and studied English. It was with deep regret that we saw him leave, but he found work up north in construction. He worked hard there, too, and soon climbed the social ladder.

When Andy suddenly turned up again, two years later, we hardly recognized him. Instead of the poor Galician boy with bare feet and shaggy hair, we saw a very nice looking young man. He was very well-dressed, groomed and confident, and he spoke fluent English. He was as energetic as ever. He now had money in the bank and a job for the winter. "But," he said, "if you can use help, I'll work for you until freeze-up, just for room and board." We could use him very well indeed. In no time he was on the plow in the field, so Bob could do other jobs that needed to be done before winter set in.

Then, unexpectedly, Frank and Isobel turned up. Frank had been preaching about 120 miles from here during the summer and they were able to pay us a visit. Naturally we were delighted!

"Times seem to have picked up around here," they both remarked. "Help in the field and help in the kitchen! Why don't you make use of it and pay us a visit in Winnipeg? You have been in Canada for nine years, and it is time to see more of the country. It will do you good!"

They stayed with us for a few days, during which we made preliminary arrangements for a visit. Toward the end of September a letter arrived in which Frank said, "My church in Carberry is having a big fowl supper to raise money for my salary. And the duck hunting season is opening. So I'm expecting you both (with guns) next Saturday. After the weekend I'll drive you to Winnipeg."

Well, it didn't take us long to make up our minds. Bob is very fond of duck hunting and had already heard that there were many ponds around Carberry which would attract ducks. The prospect of a delicious fowl supper in church looked pretty good to us, too. We left our farm and the boys in Andy's care and set out on our first vacation in this land.

A Duck-Hunting Vacation

October 1933

We left home on a bright morning and started our trip to Carberry going south on the beautiful highway which goes straight to Winnipeg. The Riding Mountains were on our right and the autumn colours of the trees were glorious, going from green to yellow to deep bronze and red, with the bright blue sky above us. We stopped for lunch in the small prairie town of Neepawa, already about ninety miles from home. But there we had to leave the beautiful highway.

Now the country we travelled through was quite different from our own. Around Dauphin we have pretty good land generally, but our buildings are a bit neglected and often in dire need of paint. We don't have much by way of landscaping around the homes, either.

But here we found the soil to be rather light, even sandy in some places. But the buildings were first-class, in contrast to our own. There were well-built barns with windmills for pumping water for the cattle. The big, prosperous-looking homes with nicely kept grounds reminded me strongly of the nice farms you find in the northern Dutch province of Groningen, which was my home before we immigrated. But the farms were much larger than in our district, where the average farm is a quarter section, 160 acres, though some farmers own three or four quarter sections. Here each farm was a half section or larger. We wondered how it was possible that on rather poor farm land the buildings looked so prosperous.

We heard the answer from the farmer with whom Frank was boarding this year. These people were kind enough to invite us to stay at their place, the kind of hospitality you will find all over Canada. Their farm was half a section with nice barns and a comfortable big house.

"Did you have a good crop this year?" Bob asked our host.

"Yes, we are quite satisfied," was his reply. "Our wheat yielded nearly twenty-five bushels an acre this year!"

This surprised us because our own wheat came in at twenty-five bushels an acre, and we were not too pleased because quite a few of our neighbours got thirty-five and even forty bushels.

"We have had our good times here in previous years," our host told us. "About forty or fifty years ago the Carberry Plains was considered one of the best districts in Manitoba. The Dauphin district did not even exist at that time — when the first settlers pulled into Dauphin around the turn of the century, we already had an established community here in Carberry. It was more than sixty years ago that the covered wagons, drawn by oxen, pulled into this district and people settled here. Most of them came from Ontario. My mother-in-law tells us about the long trek over the prairies, hills, and through forests and swamps, all uninhabited and wild then. The land proved to be very fertile around here, and the first crops gave very high yields. The settlers who struggled with all the hardships of pioneer life were thrifty and hard-working. Many of the settlers came from old Ontario families which originated in Great Britain. The district's population was homogeneous, not made up of all the different kinds of nationalities and races you will find in many other parts of Canada. They built their homes and barns after they acquired the money for it, along the old Ontario lines. But they took too much out of the soil, every year harvesting big crops without returning anything to the land. By now all the decayed vegetation, the humus, has gone out of the land and the soil has become dry and powdery. Every windy day the soil starts to drift, causing great dust storms and exposing the soil underneath the surface. This year we had very little rain and we didn't have enough hay for the cattle. So we feel lucky that we still got over twenty bushels of wheat to the acre."

The next day Frank had to preach in three different places, so we were left to our own resources. Bob had a look at the stock and I helped pick strawberries. After seeing their beautiful patch of plump berries I decided right away to try to grow some in our own garden.

"If you want to go duck hunting with us tomorrow, you have to get up early in the morning," Bob told me. But a strong wind and very chilly air in the morning dampened their enthusiasm a bit, too. However, we were on the road by seven o'clock, shivering — in spite of our heavy sweaters — as we drove through the swampy meadows. We soon discovered that there were hundreds of ducks, but whether we'd be lucky enough to bag some was another question. The wind was far too strong for good hunting. Slogging through the soggy fields was not my idea of vacation excitement. So after a few hours I had enough of it and went back to the car to read a good book until they returned. A few shots in the distance told me that they were still at it, and they would likely stay a while if they had any luck.

I was quite surprised to see them not even half an hour later, running full speed toward the car with a few ducks hanging from their shoulders.

"What is the matter with you?" I asked Frank as soon as he reached the car. "You look positively blue in the face!"

"Here, quick in the car," said Bob. "We better drive home in a hurry so Frank won't catch pneumonia. I thought I was a fanatic duck hunter, but do you know what this fool did? After we shot these measly ducks, they happened to come down on the other side of the pond. Frank stripped in a hurry and waded up to his shoulders in that icy water to retrieve them! Not for twenty fat ducks would I have done such a thing!"

"Tomorrow," said Frank, his teeth rattling from the cold, "we'll go back again and take a water spaniel with us. One of our neighbours has one." I was dumbfounded at such perseverance.

That evening we went to the lovely fowl supper in the church basement. There was a great variety of meats, fowl, vegetables, salads and fruit, and of course dozens of pies for dessert. Just a week earlier I had helped with a fowl supper in our own district, so I knew only too well how much work and organizing skill is needed for such a huge dinner. I must confess that they really outdid us. About 380 people attended the supper and a fair amount of money was raised for the church, which naturally pleased Frank very much because it would go toward his salary.

The next day our hunt went better than the day before. The wind had died down and it was not half as cold. The spaniel was with us as we watched the ducks settle on the lake. He was a good retriever and after each round of shots he would hit the water and return in a few minutes with a duck in his mouth which he neatly deposited at our feet.

We were sorry when it was time to go back home to Dauphin. But Frank said, "I have another proposition, and I don't want to hear any objections. I need to go back to the university, of course, but the church has hired me to come back every weekend for the Sunday services. So I want the two of you to come here on Sunday afternoon, the second week in October. You'll stay here overnight and then go with me to Winnipeg the next day. The Flemings, the parents of my fiancée, have invited you to stay at their home. The next Saturday morning I'll drive you back to Carberry, where you can pick up your car. And don't forget to bring your rifles!"

A Week in Winnipeg!

November 1933

Our week in Winnipeg was fantastic, like a dream. It was beautiful right from the start. We decided to take the route to the south that goes over the Riding Mountains because the trees still had lots of their fall colours. The lakes, like mirrors, reflected the gold and green and yellow foliage of the trees. The resort town of Wasagaming, on the shores of Clear Lake, was deserted. Not a single person could be found on the streets, which we had only seen in the summer when crowded with tourists.

Leaving the national park behind us, we entered into farming country again. It was a delightful pleasure to drive along the roads and see farmers working with their horses in the fields and women carrying water pails to the henhouse. How often passing tourists had watched us doing our daily chores. Now the roles were reversed!

Our old 1926 Ford sedan just purred along beautifully. We had worried about taking it on such a long trip. With the bad roads in the farm country the cars wear out pretty fast, especially when they need to carry the heavy loads we put in them. But we arrived in Carberry around three o'clock.

We learned that there was to be a supper and a concert in the church that night. We already felt pretty much at home during the evening because we had met many of the people during our earlier visit.

We left the church around midnight and found ourselves under a beautiful starry sky. Suddenly Frank said, "How about leaving for Winnipeg right now? It is such a beautiful clear night, and so quiet on the highway. If we leave in the morning we will have the sun in our face all the way."

Bob agreed, and I did too, since it didn't matter to me whether I slept in a bed or in the car.

I was sleeping soundly around three o'clock when I heard a voice, "Behold the bright city lights after eight years of isolation!" Suddenly my heart started to beat faster. Back in the city again! I cannot describe the strange sensation it gave me. We came to a nice quiet street and stopped in front of a pleasant brown villa.

All of a sudden it hit me what a crazy stunt it was to arrive at a stranger's house in the middle of the night! I whispered to Frank, "I hope you will explain to your future in-laws that it was entirely your idea to arrive at this hour!"

He answered with a broad grin and pushed us into the library. "I will have a look upstairs and find out which room is prepared for you," he whispered.

Here we were, sitting by ourselves in this strange house. "Goodness," I whispered to Bob, "what did we get into? After living on the farm for eight years I feel positively countrified." I had a glimpse of the hall, with an oriental rug on the polished floor, and through the hall an open door through which I saw a nicely furnished drawingroom.

A moment later Frank came down the stairs again and whispered, "All is well. Just follow me."

We slipped upstairs as quietly as we could, but then we heard voices from a room and a voice called, "Is that you, Frank?" An elderly gentleman in a robe emerged and all my trepidations disappeared. Such a very kind face! He welcomed us with such a genuine friendliness that all my doubts disappeared.

A moment later his wife appeared, smiles all over her face. Before long the whole household woke up, because our hostess was very deaf but wanted to know everything. We took turns shouting into her ear and apologizing for coming at such an ungodly hour. She kept nodding and laughing and obviously took it in good spirits.

When at last we entered our bright bedroom I whispered to Bob, "I know I will sleep like a log, and I am sure we will have a whale of a time in this house."

And so it turned out to be. Part of each day we were left to our own

106

resources because Frank had rooms a few streets away and had to attend classes at the college every morning. Isobel and his sister Margaret both had jobs and so were also gone most of the day.

Our host, a philosophy professor at the University of Winnipeg, was the only one who had breakfast with us. It was very different from breakfast under similar circumstances in Holland. Here there were no servants to dish it up. We all went into the kitchen and helped ourselves to porridge, bacon and eggs or ham, which our hostess had put in a warming tray. After we loaded up we went back to the dining room where we helped ourselves to tea or coffee.

Our hostess was in and out, busy with various household duties. Never have I seen a person who took severe deafness so cheerfully. Instead of being withdrawn she was the life of the party. Sometimes she would unknowingly butt into a conversation and one of the family members would shout in her ear, "Be quiet, mother." Instead of feeling hurt, she would smile cheerfully.

Some mornings Isobel or Margaret would bring us breakfast in bed, but that luxury worried Bob because it would make it too hard for me to go back to the farm.

We could even talk about Holland with the professor. After getting his degree in Edinburgh about thirty years ago, he studied half a year at the University of Leiden. To our surprise he remembered quite a bit of the Dutch language, and we found books of the Dutch writers Vondel and De Genested, along with Hildebrand's Camera Obscura, in his library.

How wonderful to have electricity again! Electricity is very cheap in Winnipeg because it is generated from waterfalls. So they use it for everything here — lights, toasters, vacuum cleaners, refrigerators, washing machines, radios and cookstoves. To have hot and cold running water was a real luxury again! My mother was probably right when she wrote me that a visit back home would be no kindness to me because I would have to get adjusted all over again to our primitive way of life on the farm. But I loved it now, and was cheerfully willing to take my chances on the future. One thing I kept thinking — how simple housekeeping seems with all these conveniences!

Then there was the sensation of going downtown. The crowded streets and all the cars overwhelmed me. The traffic lights and the rules of the road confused me and made me scared to cross the street by myself. But Bob knew quite a bit about Winnipeg because he had studied there before I came to Canada, and he was a good guide for me.

Once I got used to the bustling city again I recognized a lot of the small prairie town in Winnipeg. Downtown has two very large main streets with imposing tall buildings, but the side streets are modest and not so very different from those in our own town. The residential quarters are beautiful with large elm trees and flowers and gardens in front of large and imposing homes. Especially along the river the homes are gorgeous. Bob said that they were built with capital that originated from the farms. They were owned by people who gambled on the grain exchange with our grain and had made fortunes from it. What a great contrast with the homes of the people like us who actually grew the grain!

For me a special attraction was the two very large department stores, The Hudson's Bay and the Eaton Company. You could buy practically anything you could think of! Far different from buying from the Eaton's catalogue, called "the farmer's Bible," or from the modest versions of these stores out in the country. You could have a quick snack in the cafeteria or could dine in style in the dining room on the top floor which gave a beautiful view over the city. Life was new and exciting again after eight long years out in the country.

Bob would have gone to the movies three times a day if we had let him. In the morning the cost was only 15¢. In the afternoon and evening the price was 25¢. There were some very good films, and with our friends we saw several of them.

Beyond the movies Winnipeg does not seem to have much by way of entertainment. You can't find a cabaret or café featuring music and a floor show while you drink tea or coffee or something stronger. Once in a while a play is given in the Auditorium, a nice big concert hall, but the performers are travelling artists from other places.

Of all the buildings we saw it was the provincial legislative building that made the greatest impression on me. The whole building is made of limestone which looks like marble. Its floors and hallways are made of the same material, and they are so vast you can get lost in them. But when I look at such costly buildings I wonder how they can be paid for! We have such a sparsely populated country to provide these palatial buildings.

We also enjoyed visiting the agricultural college where Bob spent his first winter in Canada. They have big, imposing buildings, too, complete with gyms, swimming pools, cafeterias and dance halls. Surrounding the buildings were experimental plots, but there was not much growing at this time of the year. We saw beautiful model barns, henhouses and piggeries, much different from what you find on the average farm.

108

A special treat for us was visiting a few Dutch families whom we have known for years and who have visited us once in a while at our farm. They are connected with the Dutch consulate in Winnipeg, and some of them had been friends of my parents, too. There was a special charm to finding ourselves back in genteel Dutch surroundings and hearing about mutual acquaintances in the old country. It was a good thing that we had three little boys waiting for us back on the farm, because otherwise we would not have left the city for our rather primitive lifestyle in a very cheerful mood.

How the Winter Wears Us Down

December 24, 1933

It's Christmas Eve! The snow outside is a metre high and the thermometer stands at minus 37°F. When we walked from the barn to the house after chores we heard sounds like someone firing shots in the bush. We always hear that on the coldest nights. And when we opened the door of the house we were hit in the face with a white fog, like smoke.

We can hardly keep the house warm during the day, and at night it becomes unbearably cold. In the fall we discovered that we needed a new kitchen range — the old one had simply worn out. Our new one was highly recommended. It has a large firebox to take big chunks of wood. It has turned out to be a perfect stove so long as the temperature outside is not lower than ten degrees below zero. But when it got colder than that we simply could not keep the kitchen warm, no matter how much wood we piled in it. So we had to buy an additional stove. That is a pain because it makes our kitchen much smaller.

I can't write about this past month very cheerfully. The ice on our windows is at least an inch thick, and I'm not exaggerating. It is a slanting sheet, thickest on the bottom. When we wake up in the morning the prospect of going downstairs, where it is much colder, does not attract us. The icy winds seem to blow right through the walls.

The ordeal begins each morning when Bob lights both stoves and I sweep together the snow which has blown into the hallway. I put a boiler of snow on the stove to heat water for the pump. When Bob comes back inside after taking out a few pails of hot water to thaw out the pump, he looks pretty pinched and blue in the face. No heat comes from the stove yet, unless you stand very close to it. With fingers frozen to the bone I start making breakfast, working with frozen butter, frozen bread and frozen meat. As Bob puts on his numerous sweaters and leather vests and disappears into the barn with his milk pails, I wonder if he misses the soft office job he used to have.

Upstairs a voice hollers, "Is it warm yet? Can we come downstairs now?"

I look at the clock. It's quarter to eight. At half past eight they need to get ready for school, which starts at half past nine during the winter months. So I shout, "Better wait fifteen minutes."

Now I need to make the sandwiches. I had sliced the bread last night because it thaws faster that way. In a bowl near the stove a hard lump of butter swims around in its molten fluid. I can't spread it on the bread so I just pour the butter on. A good thing I sliced some ham and cheese last night. Even if it is frozen, that is better than trying to cut it in the morning.

My patience is now wearing thin. What kind of climate is this, anyhow! Suddenly I remembered a friend in Winnipeg saying, "I really do not find this climate too bad at all. It has never bothered me too much." No wonder, in a house with central heating that never gets cold at night, and wearing a warm fur coat and taking a heated car or streetcar to a warm office! I fervently wish him a week on the farm in the dead of winter. That would show him!

Now the boys come downstairs, each with a bundle of clothes under his arm. Shivering they crowd around the stove. "Hurry up!" I shout. "Out of your pyjamas. You only have half an hour left." They start to dawdle. "My hands are so cold I can't manage these buttons." "My moccasins are hard as a board." "What do I have to wear now? One of my buttons is missing."

I am losing my patience, which is easy to do on a cold winter morning. I feel like shaking them up a bit, but there isn't even time for that. I grab a needle and thread. "Why didn't you tell me that last night? Now hurry up and eat your porridge and sandwiches."

While I am packing lunches for the two oldest, Bob comes into the house with full milk pails. Big chunks of snow, mixed with manure, stick to his rubber boots and start to melt over the floor. I look at it with venom. All the same I know that it is practically impossible to scrape off all that frozen stuff outside. However it does not improve my temper. What's the use trying to keep the floor decently clean?

At half past eight Bobby and Wim leave for the barn to give their horse a drink of water and harness it to the toboggan. I make a hole in the ice on the window to watch them. They have taken off their mittens and are blowing on their fingers, stamping their feet as they walk around the horse trying to fasten the buckles with their frozen fingers.

After the horse has been harnessed they come back to the house to pick up their school bags, lunchboxes, blankets and hot stones. "Poor things!" I am thinking as I see them turn out at the farm gate. "They sure get their education the hard way." I hope they do not tip over like they did yesterday when the horse shied at that high snowdrift on the road.

Later in the day as I tidied up the house I faced the fact that Christmas is already upon us and I do not have any Christmas surprise treat prepared as we always have for each other. Bob and I had promised ourselves a new loudspeaker for our radio. The old one had fallen down and broken one night when the storm wind had blown our door open and blew through the house.

But that was no surprise anymore. We have kept the Dutch custom of making little handcrafted personal gifts for each other at Christmas. We always get a lot of satisfaction from that. But here with all the work and extra inconveniences of the winter it's hard to find time for anything extra at all.

My mood, which had been improving a bit as the house gradually warmed up, took another dive. Now I faced a stack of newspapers and magazines without any place to put them. Maybe I should put them in a box and take them to the barn to use for lighting the stove.

Suddenly I remembered that a few days ago Bob said, "Don't throw this magazine away. There is such a cute picture in it. It reminds me of things in the past."

I had been busy at the time and had no chance to look at it. Which magazine could it have been? I started to rifle through the pile, and sure enough I soon spotted the picture. There was a big heather field, all purple, with a purple sky stretching over it. In the distance was the figure of a young girl in a red skirt and white blouse sitting in the midst of all those colourful blossoms.

That picture pulled me right back into the past, about fifteen years ago when I was a high school girl bicycling over the heather trails with my school friend. We were city children but were both very fond of the country and the wide open fields. Sometimes we would go to the fields in the early morning to hunt kievit eggs. After school we would play tennis or bicycle over the country roads, picking bouquets of wild-

flowers. On a free Saturday afternoon we could venture farther afield, even up to Paterwolde to go sailing on the lake! Never to be forgotten were those warm, sun-drenched days when the fragrant heather was in blossom. We would lie on our backs, stretched out on the spongy mass underneath, soaking in all the beauty around us and dream our lovely dreams. No cares of the world to wear us down!

As I stood there in my farm kitchen staring at that picture and thinking about all those wonderful dreams, I realized that I was now standing in the room I was once dreaming about. Well, it was not the kind of home I had visualized then, and it was a lot colder than I had ever imagined it could be. But the afternoon sun was now hitting the frozen windowpanes and the room was becoming nice and cosy again. There were no bright flowers today, but the sun gently warmed the cat stretched lazily in front of the fire, and warmed little Dick as he built a castle on the floor with his blocks. From the direction of the barn came a cheerful whistling, the same whistling I gladly listened to fifteen years ago.

"This picture reminds me of former years," Bob had said. Then I suddenly knew exactly what my Christmas surprise would be. I would keep that memory alive by hanging the picture right in front of our noses from now on. When Bob went to town to shop, I busied myself with glue and cardboard and glass. The result was quite satisfying. Framed with some tape and with "Lest we forget" neatly printed on the back, it made a very presentable gift. Wrapped in tissue paper and tied with a red ribbon, it is now among our other Christmas gifts. Working on this surprise made me a bit more cheerful.

This evening I feel really sentimental, which is something that does not often happen to me. In a corner glistens the little Christmas tree, under which are the presents for the children. Will they have fun when they come down in the morning! In the afternoon our Dutch friends, the Bos bachelors, will be with us for Christmas dinner again. Two of them, though, have gone to the old country and will be celebrating with their friends and family there. In their place I have invited a couple who will be working for them this winter. The man is Dutch and his wife is Scottish. So we will need to talk English this year for her sake. But the fact that for once I will not be the only woman in the group more than makes up for that.

1934

A Winter To Remember

February 1934

When I lived in the Netherlands I used to read unbelievable stories about the climate in Canada, about snow metres and metres high, of people who froze to death in blizzards, and wolves and bears wandering around. I was disappointed to find out that things here are not that dramatic. Yes, we have lots of snow here, but not metres high. Except for this year.

The fences and the shrubs, like the lilacs and raspberries, have all disappeared under the snow. Our mailbox, which reaches to our shoulders, is now level with the ground. The mailman needs to get out of his sleigh and get down on his hands and knees for our mail. He says we will need to dig the snow away from the mailbox or he won't deliver our mail any longer.

But even if the snow piles up a metre or two high, you don't sink down into it as you might expect. Wind and frost pack the snow together and form a hard crust on the top. You can generally walk on top of it quite easily, especially with snowshoes. It's only when the spring tha sets in that the troubles start. The snow starts to "rot" and anyone walking on it, and especially horses, will break through it.

We consider ourselves fortunate because we are protected from the west and also somewhat from the north. But even so, this year our buildings are surrounded by high snow hills. We visited a farm yesterday where we could walk on the snow right over the barn roof! When you get water from the pump you are surrounded by a high wall of snow and feel like you are entering a volcanic crater.

This winter we are having very unexpected snowstorms. The morning can start out bright and crisp with brilliant sunshine. Then suddenly it clouds over, the wind starts to howl and snow whirls up from the ground. New snow starts to fall and the wind increases to a screech. We can no longer see objects a few feet in front of us. Sometimes this will last hours at a time, and sometimes only five minutes.

Three weeks ago a storm like that broke out on a bitterly cold night. We went to bed early but woke up when the whole house shuddered and creaked frightfully. We later learned that on that night a family had visited a neighbour and on their way home the storm suddenly broke out. Most likely the horses got frightened and broke something on the harness and ran away to their farm. The neighbours started searching and found the sleigh buried deep in a snowbank. The child was in the sleigh, wrapped in a blanket, frozen to death. A little distance away, partly covered by snowdrifts, were the husband and wife frozen to death. They had obviously tried to gather wood for a fire without success.

Another winter hazard is fires. We constantly hear about fires caused by overheated stoves in wood houses. Too often whole families find their death in flames in the freezing weather.

Feed for the animals is a special problem in a hard winter. Usually the dry cows, sheep and horses stay outside much of the winter and forage for food around the straw piles in the field. This year it is so cold they are in the barn at night and often during the day. Because many of the animals stay outdoors all year around, the barn is now so crowded that sometimes there is not even enough space for the animals to lie down. Our boys, the rascals, have a great time running from one end of the barn to the other over the backs of all those close-packed animals.

Because the winter started so early this year, and then became so severe, farmers had to start using their winter supply of feed early. In addition to hay the animals are fed straw, which is not very nutritious but is needed to stretch the hay through the winter. Usually farmers have an abundance of straw, but this year we lost all our new straw in a fire started by a spark from the threshing engine. We were lucky that the fire did not destroy any buildings, but at the time we didn't realize the problem we'd have this winter. We need to haul the straw more than three miles over rough roads. The straw piles are covered over with snow which first takes some hours to shovel aside, and often the wind blows during the night so the snow removal needs to be done again the next day.

This is the first winter we have had to forfeit our cozy evenings with our books and magazines and papers. The enjoyment of reading and listening to music and news of the outer world on the radio is not only very enjoyable, but has become for us a symbol of our former life, as well as a great way to forget the constant demands of farm chores. But this year the extra winter work has made that impossible, though we compromise by leaving the door open between the kitchen and living room so that we can at least hear the radio. We console ourselves with the thought that most of the winter is behind us, and that this is a really exceptional winter.

✳

An Overnight Treat for Bobby

February 1934

Bobby had a nice treat last week. We don't socialize very much with people in town because the distance is too great, especially during the winter. But we have gotten to know a family in town who have children the same ages as our boys. One day they invited Bobby to stay with them over a weekend, from Friday night to Sunday night.

I had thought he might be somewhat shy, since he has never been away from home alone. But he was not, and if anybody was a bit worried it was me. Social customs in Canada are quite different from what we grew up with. We were brought up with rather formal social relations, but here in the country things go quite easy. When I tell my boys they are supposed to take off their caps when they enter a building, they ask, "Why do we have to do that? A lot of other people don't do it, either."

With little hints at the table it goes the same way. Sometimes they try to embarrass me by playing the enfant terrible. They will say to a guest, "Daddy says you are not supposed to eat with your knife." Or, "You are not supposed to make noises when you eat your soup, says Mamma." Teaching the boys the rudiments of social behaviour without making snobs out of them takes considerable diplomacy. So we talk of "Dutch manners" and say that we could never take them for a visit to Holland if they don't learn the customs of that country. This helped with the problem of visitors, because nobody would expect Canadians to have Dutch manners. But Bobby seems to have seen through the charade because before he left for his overnight outing he said, "I guess I better act Dutch over there."

Even if social differences are not as tightly drawn in Canada as in Holland, there are certain social distinctions here, too. In Canada we have our clubs and societies, too, though there is a difference. You will see a doctor, a lawyer, a blacksmith and a grocer play golf together in the same country club. You will find a bank manager take a drink of beer in the company of his clerks, a plumber, a farmer, or a teacher. I have seen a lawyer joking away with the clerks in a grocery store and then walk away with a head of cauliflower under his arm. It all seems more free and easy than we knew at home. I assume there are certain distinctions here that we don't know so much about, but Canadians seem to be more influenced by the possession of money than by origin of birth.

I could hardly wait to see how Bobby would make out on his weekend. Bob and I were invited for tea on the Sunday afternoon when we picked him up. I felt proud when I saw him there, calm and collected among the other children, but very excited about everything he had seen and done. With shining eyes he told us about the ice hockey game they went to on Friday evening. And on Saturday he had skated on the rink himself.

"Oh, Daddy, you should have seen how interested everybody was in my Dutch wooden skates! After a while a big man came and chased the curious kids away and said, 'Give the lad a chance now to skate on them.' "

On the way home he never stopped talking. "Now Bill and Jack can stay with us on the farm some day, too, can't they? I promised I'd teach them to ride horseback. They said they wouldn't mind living on a farm if it had a river running through it like we have. I'm so glad that I can now visit some place, too, just like other boys, even if I don't have any uncles or aunts in this country."

Later on, in their bedroom upstairs, the boy's high voice still kept talking away to his duly impressed younger brothers. I said to Bob, "Maybe the boys feel more than we knew the lack of relatives in this country. We better encourage them to mix more with others."

Moods During a Long Winter

April 1934

It's the second week of April and we take it more or less for granted that spring is just around the corner. But March stung us with temperatures thirty degrees below zero. I feel downright miserable when I think of the first violets and blossoms on bushes that Hollanders see in March. But even lifelong Canadians start to grumble about stinging cold weather in March. "The longest winter I have ever seen" is the standard comment of practically every old-timer I'~e seen in the past few weeks. But to be quite honest we hear that all the time: the hottest summer, the driest spring, the coldest spring, the wettest fall. I start to think that their memories are not any too long.

Even so, I will say with hand on heart that this is the most miserable winter during the nine years we have been in Canada. Everybody seems to get on edge. It wouldn't be so bad if you could really give way to bright fantasies about the coming growing season, but bitter experience has taught us that often the most modest expectations have proved to be too optimistic in the end.

"What are you going to grow this year?" I asked Bob one evening as an introduction to our mutual planning for the season ahead. Usually he will grab pencil and paper with enthusiasm and we plant and sow all evening, visualizing it all in our minds. But now his impassive face looked up from the paper and in a rather bored voice he said, "Nothing unusual, I guess. Forty acres of wheat, forty of oats and forty of barley. Nothing to get excited and make plans about. And if it doesn't turn out well, I'll mow it down for feed and summer fallow the land."

A few nights later when I was sitting with a pencil and paper and a frown, a voice from behind the newspaper asked, "What are you doing? Making plans for the garden? Are you going to try something new?"

Now it was my turn to scowl and say, "Goodness no! I was just figuring out if it really pays to plant a garden at all. For some reason a lot of my sealers spoiled this winter, and considering the time and seed, and all those hours of canning during the hottest days of the year, I wonder if it was worth it. If I only knew what went wrong. What's the use of seeding lots of vegetables, and crawling through the mud on hands and knees most of the summer to keep out the weeds, if you just end up with failure?"

Bob had no answer for that, of course. I knew that we both felt the same way — ho miserable you are when you don't feel like making plans any more. Will it ever change? Will things look rosy and happy again some day? Everybody you talk with these days seems gloomy, too. We certainly live in depressing times.

Even a sudden thaw on the first of April didn't lift our mood. "What a godforsaken mud puddle," I thought, looking out on the barn yard that looked more like a junk yard. Sticks of wood, tin cans, mounds of straw everywhere. And mud and more mud. Even though we had gotten sick and tired of the snow, at least it had mercifully covered all that mess. It would take days of grubby work to clean it all up, once the yard was dry enough.

"At least you can find satisfaction in your work," I said to Bob one afternoon when I was keeping him company for a few minutes while he was splitting wood. "After you've worked a while you can see the split wood pile up. But keeping house you don't have that satisfaction, because as soon as I've cleaned a bit you boys muck it all up again with your filthy boots. When I cook a good meal it disappears in no time at all."

"Well, we can't do without food," said Bob, "but cleaning the house all the time while it's muddy doesn't make sense. Leave the floors alone and go take a walk. Maybe that will cheer you up."

That made sense. So when the dinner dishes were done, I started to prepare for my walk. In my closet hung a smart little suit my mother had sent in my Christmas parcel, and I had been dying to show myself off in it. Today for the first time since Christmas it seemed warm enough to wear it. I'd take a coat along just in case it was too chilly.

I confess that it gave me great satisfaction to dress up in this finery and admire the result in the big mirror upstairs. High rubber boots and a leather belt gave a sporty look to the outfit, I concluded. I felt like a city girl again, out for an afternoon of sports, not like a farm woman with no place to go.

As I left Bob was at his wood-splitting again, whistling happily. Blessed is the man who does not need walks and nice clothes to keep his emotional balance, I thought. He gave me a yell as I pranced out of the gate, whether admiring me or teasing, I don't know.

I didn't have much choice of where to walk, with the roads all muddy. I could walk in the slushy mud in the ruts or on the packed snow mixed with horse manure which formed a ridge or berm in the centre. There was a bit of company on the road, a couple of year-old calves bumming around in their shaggy coats, plastered with mud from top to toe. The odd rabbit would jump out and sprint over the road ahead, looking conspicuous now in his white winter fur. Those and some shrieking crows were all the life there was to be seen or heard as far as my eyes could see.

If only a few people lived a bit closer so that I could visit them and talk. About a mile and a half straight ahead I saw smoke coming out of a chimney, the home of an old bachelor who was deaf and lived alone. I doubt if he wants visitors. Once I was hunting for our cows and wanted to ask if he had seen them, but he just slammed his door on me.

Two miles away lived the Nicholsons. They have three children, but they've had scarlet fever most of the winter. But I remembered that they would be out of quarantine any day now. I wasn't crazy about going inside the house, because of the illness, but maybe we could have a talk over the fence. It would be a diversion for them, too, having been isolated for a big part of the winter.

I had just made that decision when I heard wheels splashing and harnesses jingling behind me. I looked back and saw a sleigh pulled by two horses. It was Mr. Johnston, our neighbour, riding on a pig crate. There was a pig in the crate who looked me up and down through the slats with its squinty little eyes.

"Ha, ha, ha!" shouted Johnston. "All dressed up and no place to go. Come up and have a ride with me," he said as he moved to one side of the pig crate.

"No, thank you," I said politely. "I'm really out for a walk."

His face clouded over at once. I realized right away that he didn't believe a word of it. Who would ever refuse a ride when one was offered? Here in the country nobody ever walks on a road unless really necessary.

"Where are you headed?" I asked, trying to show that I didn't mean to offend him.

"Only a few miles further, to the McDonald farm," was his reply. "I have to bring this pig over there."

"Maybe I'll have a ride back with you," I said. "I just want to walk over to the Nicholsons to find out how they are doing."

A half hour later, when I turned in at the Nicholson's lane, the ride back didn't look too bad to me. The distance was longer than I had expected.

As soon as the dogs started to bark the jolly faces of the whole Nicholson clan appeared at the windows. The paper with the scarlet fever warning had disappeared.

"Come in! Come in!" shouted Mrs. Nicholson. But I called back that I was really a coward and would rather stay outside. I know the slack enforcement of the health service here only too well.

We had a nice visit, with them all crowded in front of the window and me outside the gate.

"How did you disinfect it all?" I asked.

"Oh, I washed everything very thoroughly, and after that we burned formalin for a few days," was the reply. "But I'm not yet finished upstairs. I'll wait with that until I start housecleaning." I made up my mind then and there to stay a safe distance from the family for awhile.

"Aren't they sending out an inspector to see if you have done it all safely?" I asked.

"No, no," was the reply. "The doctor just told us what to do, and when we had done it we took the scarlet fever sign off the door and burned it in the stove. The children will go back to school the day after tomorrow."

Well, they can't do much damage at school, I thought. It seems like all the children had scarlet fever this winter, and the school had even been closed for two and a half months. It is amazing how widespread these epidemics of scarlet fever — and diptheria, too — are here in the country. There are rules and regulations to control the diseases, but they do not seem to be enforced. I have seen cases where families had these diseases but, even when the quarantine sign was on the door, members of the family who were not sick would go to town and stand next to you in the store making their purchases. I even saw it once where a member of a quarantined family was in the store selling their eggs, cream and butter!

"My, you are wearing a smart suit today," somebody shouted through the window. So after all I had the satisfaction of being admired from top to bottom, even if from a distance.

After that we started to gossip about all the district news, and soon got into discussion about the poor farming prospects. "Grain stayed very much the same the whole winter, didn't it! Wheat is only 55¢ or 55¢ cents a bushel, not even better than last year. Cows are very low. Only pig prices have gone up. We sold one for $7.50 a hundredweight. Yes, we sold one for that, too. Too bad we didn't have very many of them this winter. What are you getting for your eggs? 10¢ a dozen — it is really dreadful. Hardly worth gathering them up. And to think I was so excited when my hens started to lay!"

"Well, I guess I better start for home," I said. "Bill Johnston was bringing a pig to the McDonald farm and he'll pick me up at your gate. Look after yourselves!"

Half an hour later I was sitting on the pig crate next to Johnston, listening to his stories. He is a veteran of the big war and had been in the thick of the fighting. He was shellshocked, he told me, and he claims that sometimes pieces of shrapnel still come out of his head! Sometimes I think he's a bit mixed up. He seems to be a man of moods, and his wife likely does not have a very easy time with him. But she knows how to handle him perfectly.

Chewing tobacco and spitting left and right he suddenly said to me with great emphasis, "You know what, Mrs. Aberson? The only thing that will fix prices for the farmers is another war." Even shellshock doesn't seem enough to scare people off! Is he right?

✳

Communal Spring Cleaning

May 1934

We have been without snow for quite a while already, but the air stays raw and chilly. Huddled in sweaters and heavy winter coats the farmers ride their plows, cultivators and seeders. The low hanging clouds give us the feeling of sombre fall days. The Riding Mountains look like a dark threatening mass against the gray horizon. From morning till night a sharp east wind carries the icy cold from the still-frozen lakes.

But the farmers say, "We shouldn't complain too much. At least we could get on the land early this year. They say that in Saskatchewan the wheat is up already!"

A week later, though, none of our farmers wanted to change places with Saskatchewan farmers. The winds, instead of dying down, got much stronger and started to blow the now-drying topsoil high into the air. The sun in a clear sky was blotted out by the dust and came through as a lurid red haze. Saskatchewan topsoil blew all around us and into our homes. Their crop was totally ruined. In some places it was so dark during the day that people had to burn their lamps all day long. Along our fences drifts of topsoil two feet high have replaced the snowdrifts.

But now the wind has calmed down and we can see rows of young wheat coming up. The grass is green again, the bushes have started to sprout and in place of bare branches the trees show a green haziness. Big flocks of wild geese fly overhead, and robins and some small yellow birds are seen on the lawn. We are outside now from morning to night.

It is unbelievable how much rubbish lies under the snow in the winter! Old tin cans, pieces of paper and broken pottery stare us in the face. My helper Annie and I spend hours raking the straw that has blown all over the lawn and my flower beds. Bob picks up the rubbish with the horse-drawn cart, and even little Dick is busy picking up dead sticks and paper with his own little cart.

In the evening when the big boys come home from school the real fun starts. We make big piles of all this rubbish and then burn it. The boys shout and dance around the flames, keeping the fire burning by throwing more sticks and rubbish on it. Without the fire they would have hated the cleaning job, but now it seems like a party.

Now our farm starts to look very different. The black earth of the garden and field contrast nicely with my fresh green lawns. The raspberry bushes which Bob has cleaned out stand like soldiers in a row. Here and there the first asparagus shoots are peeping through, and my perennial plants are now visible. In a sheltered spot I've placed my flats of vegetables. Cabbage, cauliflower and tomatoes all look healthy, having been started indoors in front of a sunny window. The sun and outside air will do them good, but they need to be carried indoors again at night because we can still expect frost.

People have become more active again. Sports and dances and the odd concert have been organized. The older generation grumbles that these late evenings after hard work in the fields tire them out too much, but they always come at night anyway. It seems that we shake off the feeling of winter with all this stir and activity. Forgotten are the long distances over blocked roads. Now cars are on the roads again. The feeling of isolation has disappeared and we feel like members of one close community again.

One day the word went around that everyone was expected to help clean the Community Hall. In a few weeks the new student minister will be coming, and everything has to be fixed and cleaned before he comes. The Community Hall serves as a meeting place and dance hall, as well as a church. As always the cleanup is made into a party. The men clean the yard and split wood for the kitchen stove. They also need to bring in trees to be sawn into blocks for next winter's heating.

Indoors the women are busy as bees. One washes the windows, another scrubs the tables and benches, and three others are on their hands and knees scrubbing the wooden floor. Someone has been nice enough to take the curtains home and wash and iron them so they will be ready to be hung.

By five o'clock the hall was fresh and clean. A big pot of coffee was made, and everyone brought out their sandwiches, cookies and cake. The men talked about the crops and the women talked about their young chickens and their gardens. The misunderstandings and squabbles of the winter months were forgotten and there was only a spirit of good will. People left calling out, "See you in church!"

The Peace of Summer

Late June 1934

How is it possible that our world can change so much in a month's time? I now see the trees along the river in full leaf, with the river itself at such a low level that we see broad gravelled beaches. The trees are *clearly reflected in the nearly stagnant water, and our geese with their young brood silently glide past. The water is so clear we can plainly see the gravel bottom. Minnows and water bugs dart to and fro in the sun-speckled water.*

The left bank of the river is pretty steep and is overgrown with scrub growth and ferns as high as your head. Little white anemones and yellow daisies peep above the green ground cover.

The right bank has a more gentle slope which is very convenient for us because it is a natural watering place for our cattle and horses. In the summertime we never have to pump water for them, and as soon as the barn doors are opened in the morning they all push to get out at the same time, crowding and shoving to make a beeline to the river. In the trees overhead the birds chirp and twitter. We identify them more by their bright plumage than by their song. Only the whippoorwill has a distinctive, charming call. Wherever we might find ourselves in the future, the call of the whippoorwill will at once bring back visions of wide grain field(under a vast expanse of sky, a silent summer evening, a river shadowed by trees, the tinkle of a cowbell, the neighing of a horse, the bleating of a lost lamb. . . .

That place on the river is really the most charming spot on our farm. Rinsing the laundry, ordinarily prosaic, becomes a romantic adventure. It is even something I look forward to, especially if I put on a bathing suit for the occasion to spash around and take a dip when the job is done.

Bob and the boys followed my example a few days later when they brought the car down the river bank and put it up to the axles in water to wash it. With much splashing and shouting the car eventually emerged much cleaner that it generally is.

The grain has just been shooting up, now at least a foot and a half high. We don't really expect it to grow very tall this year because of the lack of moisture. But we can't complain, because quite a few local showers have saved us from total drought.

It is surprising to me how much rain you really need here to give the soil a thorough soaking. Very likely the reason is that we have had many dry years behind us. Neighbouring areas are less fortunate that we are. The southern parts of Manitoba, Saskatchewan and Alberta, and parts of the northern United States are totally dried out. And what did grow was ruined by grasshoppers. Grasshoppers often appear during prolonged dry spells.

I am truly sorry for the people there because they have had quite a few bad years in a row. The government is giving them help if they want to move to better areas. Through our own district we have seen caravans of people who have left their lands and homes and are hunting for greener pastures. From their stories and their envious looks at our own green fields we realize how fortunate we really are.

Smelling the Roses

Early July 1934

Looking after the garden is my responsibility. Since the garden is close to the road, people who pass by naturally look at it and comment on it. Sometimes someone will stop and give me a compliment. Bob tells me that an old farmer from Keld once told him, "You have a darn good woman, always busy in that garden!"

Most of the people who pass our place are East Europeans. They come from Russia, Austria, Galicia, Romania or Poland, but they are generally referred to as Ukrainians, Galicians or Ruthenians. Seated high on their grain wagons, they come from Keld, a settlement solely populated by these races. They talk loud and fast in their own language, so I can't understand what they say.

The busy spring activities are behind us now. The summer fallow has been plowed and in a few weeks they will start haying. This gives us a chance to catch our breath. We often stop a little earlier at night to play a game of tennis or to go for a dip in the river. The tennis court, fixed up again by the community, is quite popular lately. Our neighbours seem to have acquired a taste for the game!

The other day I read an article in the paper about the growing interest of people here in Canada in music, theatre and sports. This is not only a good counterbalance for hard manual labour, but also for the abnormal, depressing conditions we have been experiencing these years.

It is true that more and more amateur groups are coming up which give quite good performances. In the case of theatre, we have a good example right here in our own district. There have been amateur groups in the cities for some time, but lately the smaller towns have started forming "little theatres." Groups of people will meet regularly to study a suitable play, often a one-act play. New actors and actresses are given the chance to try out their abilities. By the end of the year the group will know what talent the community has. Then local competitions are held, and the winners go on to the provincial competitions. National competitions are then held in Ottawa.

The town of Dauphin has taken part for several years already, but until now we had never done anything out here in the country. But this spring our district took the plunge and produced two one-act plays. I took part in the directing, and naturally was very nervous the night we produced our play in Dauphin.

You can understand our joy when we won second place! The town of Dauphin itself won third place, so we were tickled to upstage them. The judges were from Winnipeg, and they gave us a lot of encouragement to keep at it. Who knows, maybe our simple country group might even get the chance to compete in Winnipeg some day! For me personally an extra advantage was to meet a whole new set of people I would most likely never have come to know otherwise.

Retreat to the Mountain Lake

Late July 1934

It's hard to believe — we've taken a holiday! To tell you the truth, we fled the farm.

The summer started out with such promise of a good crop, but has turned out to be very disappointing. For weeks on end we didn't get a drop of rain. Every morning the sun rose brilliantly in a cloudless blue sky. Toward noon the termperature was often over 90˚. Even 100˚ in the shade has become quite common.

We see great numbers of cars stream past our farm every day, often loaded high with camping gear. People are escaping the towns to cool off at one of the lakes. Often they stop at our river to replenish their water supply and we will have a friendly chat with them. Soon they will say, "Well, we better get going again. It should be nice at the lake today. We hope you will get rain soon, so long as it stays dry at the lake."

With envy we'd see them leave and disappear around the bend in the road. We'd then drag ourselves back to work. Our wheat field, once so promising, was deteriorating more every day. Maybe there wouldn't even be anything left to harvest.

Now was our slack time. The hay was put up and the summer fallow plowed. So we had plenty of time to give ourselves over to gloomy thoughts.

Then one evening, after another murderous day, we looked at each other and said, "Why don't we start to enjoy the sun for a change? On the farm the sun gives us nothing but grief. What would prevent us from going to the mountains, too, and camping there for a week or so?" Andy, our hired man for the summer, is totally reliable. Bob hasn't been working so hard anyway because he's been bothered with a muscle infection and needs to give his arm as much rest as possible. So it was decided.

I started by spending two whole days at the kitchen range, baking a dozen loaves of bread, a big box of cookies and a very large cake. We filled a big hamper with a few sealers of fruit, with jars of jam, a lot of vegetables and potatoes from the garden, and ten dozen eggs. Our only expense would be a few quarts of milk each day and a piece of meat once in a while.

So we left on a bright sunny morning with mattresses, blankets and a tent on top of the car, and pots and pans and pails rattling away at the sides. Our destination was Clear Lake in the Riding Mountains, the place where I had been a year ago.

We've been camping now for ten days, and we feel reborn! For the first time this summer we look at the sun with benevolent eyes and get ourselves a deep brown tan. Of course we do hope it is raining on the farm, but we don't give the sun worried looks all day. We've just become fatalistic and stop worrying because we can't do anything about it anyway. We might as well enjoy the sun here.

There are about 3,000 people in this tourist camp right now. We were lucky to find a nice rustic spot for our tent, where we are not bothered by a lot of traffic. The group of people with whom we share the kitchen, washroom and ice house are very nice, and we already feel like part of a very large family. In the morning we women are together washing our breakfast dishes and doing a bit of laundry. The men sit together reading the morning papers, which are delivered each day. We can see them sitting together wagging their heads over the political situation in Europe, which does not look very good.

If only people all over the world could live together in harmony as we are doing here in this camp! When I opened the tent flap this morning and looked around, it was clear that people here trust each other completely. Maybe that is one of the secrets of good mutual understanding. Clothes and towels were hanging on the washlines everywhere. Food was standing in boxes outside of the tents, and in the kitchens our sad irons, pots and pans and kettles were standing right out in the open. Nobody ever misses anything! In Holland a place like this would be crowded with police to keep order. But here you hardly see police at all. Once a day a Mountie in his scarlet jacket and black pants with yello stripes rides by on a horse, but as far as I can make out, it is only a sort of ritual. Nothing disorderly has ever happened as far as I know.

The camp certainly gives good value for your money! The only cost is one dollar a week for the right to have a tent here. For that we can use as much firewood as we want, piled high right by the kitchen where we need it. We can swim, play tennis or golf to our hearts content. There is also a big shuffleboard, with disks as big as dinner plates. Instead of playing the game sitting at a table like we do in Holland, they walk around with big sticks to move the disks.

There is a new museum without an entrance fee, which is very attractive and rustic. Evening lectures are given in this building dealing with wildlife and plants found in the Riding Mountains. There are beautiful photographs of elk, moose and bears. Even though the films are changed only once a week, our boys faithfully attend every night!

For children this camp is really like a paradise. They have made friends with other children and are delighted they can see and do so much without charge. They spend much of the day in the crystal clear water of the lake, and our two oldest have learned to swim pretty well already.

One morning Bob and I strolled on the pier and heard a lot of laughing and clapping of hands. A woman said to us, "There is a little blond boy there who is showing the bigger boys how to dive. Look, there he is again."

To our great surprise we saw our eight-year-old son Wim climbing on the diving tower. He spotted us, and was in such a hurry to show us what he could do that he didn't look to see if the coast was clear and he landed right on the back of a fat gentleman! Fortunately nobody was hurt. We are very happy that lifeguards are on duty here all day.

We spotted our oldest son Bob one afternoon in an equally amusing situation. In the morning he had been begging us to rent a bicycle. There were quite a few boys with bikes in the camp who had planned to ride to a famous wishing well. Since coming here he has already learned to ride a bike. The rented bike would only cost 25¢ an hour. Please, please, would we let him go? Well, we gave in, and they left with lots of shouting and bell ringing.

A few hours later Bob and I were coming back from the tennis courts after a game when, to our great surprise, we saw Bobby through the plate glass window of a bicycle shop polishing bikes. Full of curiosity, we stopped to watch him. He was working very hard, red-faced, with his tongue out in determination. Finally Bob tapped against the window. Bobby looked up embarrassed when he recognized us, but he kept on with vigorous polishing.

Then we saw a woman sitting behind a desk who smiled, tapped his shoulder and said, "All right, Bobby, that will do." He came outside to join us and we heard his story. They had a wonderful time on the bike hike. There was a zoo and cold spring water that came right out of the ground. But when they got back they found they had taken more than an hour, and the lady in the store said, "Now you owe me another 25¢. You have only paid for one hour." Well, Bobby didn't have more money. So they struck a deal that Bobby would pay the extra amount by working, cleaning the bikes that had been rented out that day.

Bobby added, "Tomorrow I'm going to the bike rental store again and will ask if I can clean the bikes again. Maybe she'll let me ride in exchange for my work." But so far it hasn't worked.

We have four more days here before we go back to the farm. We've heard that there has been no rain at all in our district, and that a lot of grain has been plowed under because it is just a total loss. But after these two glorious weeks we feel that we can put up with the disappointment.

Five Years of Drought

September 1934

We threshed our grain already on August 16. Unbelievable! The first years on the farm we threshed in October, and more recently in September. But this is a whole month earlier.

There had been no rain for many weeks, and the grain fields were no longer green. There was no grass left, and the corn didn't reach a third of its usual height. The oats and barley have all been plowed under. That's what happens when no rain at all falls during the entire growing season. Only the wheat planted on last year's summer fallow land did not look too bad. The summer fallow holds the moisture to a certain extent.

When we were coming home from our holiday, about three miles from home the boys in the back seat shouted, "Pappa, just look! There are our cows. There's Angus, with the bell on."

Sure enough, there were our four milk cows, trying to find something to eat on the dried-out berm. Later we heard from Andy that each evening he had to walk three or four miles to find them. There is no feed close to the farm anymore, and the meadows had dried out completely.

So it was not a joyful homecoming. But considering it all, we were glad we hadn't been there to see the slow deterioration of our crop.

Two days after coming home, Bob started harvesting what there was to harvest. He rode the binder and the boys helped him setting up the sheaves. Like the grown men, they wanted to wear leather gloves for the job because the thistles hurt their fingers. Bobby is beginning to work like a grown man already, and especially now that Bob has promised them wages. Bobby hopes to buy a bike some day in the future.

We looked at the sky with different eyes, now hoping for a change that it won't rain right away. Quite a few times we saw very dark clouds, and sometimes a few drops fell, but nothing came of it. The threshing gang came and finished the job without any rain falling. But we had no crop of barley or oats, not even seed grain for next year.

It is ironic that now prices have gone up a bit. Wheat was selling for 80¢ a bushel, but now it's down to 66¢. Last year we got only 49¢, so there is some increase.

After the harvest Bob and I went for our usual ride on horseback to gather up our dry cows and their calves. There were about twenty of them, and we spotted them quite soon. Five of them looked ready for market, but we'll not sell them now. A neighbour sold ten head, but after deducting the freight expense he found himself richer by only $55 for the whole ten head. That is less than we used to get for one!

But the prices have to go up. In the west where practically everything dried out, the farmers were forced to sell their herds. Naturally the market became glutted and the prices went down. At present we buy our beef for 5¢ a pound, with the choice cuts selling for 8¢. That is good for the consumer but bad for the producer.

So the cows were herded together and are now grazing on the stubble from our wheat field, where they may be able to find a bit to eat. But their grazing domain is shrinking each day as Bob plows more and more of it under. The animals will have a hard winter ahead because straw is scarce this year. The government is buying straw for $5 a ton to send to the areas that have totally dried out. This is the first time I have ever heard of getting money for straw. But it doesn't do us any good because we don't even have enough for our own cattle.

Suddenly the town is full of people. Unemployed tramps and hobos are drifting around and standing in groups on the streetcorners. Quite often you are stopped and asked for the price of a meal. They also ask for harvest work. When the long grain trains come into the station you see them jump out of the freight cars, or come down from the buffers or the roofs. It isn't legal, but the police do not stop them, and men can be seen on every train going from one end of Canada to the other in search of work and food.

I heard this amusing story about a newly married couple living near our district. The groom wanted to introduce his bride to his relatives in Winnipeg, but could hardly afford the trip. They could afford one train ticket, but not two. So the bride rode sedately in the train while the bridegroom made the trip hanging between two freight cars. I wonder how they will manage to set up housekeeping.

The number of unemployed grows daily. The government comes up with new programs all the time to try to provide jobs. Last Sunday we took a look at the new road which crosses right over the Riding Mountains to Clear Lake. It is being built by a few hundred unemployed men who are paid $5 a month plus room and board. This new road will bring Clear Lake much closer to us because the old road is fifty-six miles and the new one will be only thirty-six miles.

The government does as much as it can for people in areas totally dried out. But because the drought has now lasted for over five years, some of the lands are starting to look like deserts. The people that owned the land have lost all their money and now have nothing but debt on their useless lands. The government, in cooperation with the railroads, gives free transportation to them and their goods to better areas. They also get free seed for the first three years, and many other forms of help to get started from the bottom up again.

After temperatures of 102° it suddenly got so cold I had to get our winter clothes out without time to air them properly. When we were getting ready for church on Sunday Bob said, "We are hardly fit to come into the company of others. We're smelling too much like moth balls!" When we got to church the person sitting next to me poked me in the side and whispered, "I see you've been raiding your camphor box, too!"

❋

Of Friends and Faraway Places

October 1934

On an early winter day we were pleasantly surprised by a visit from our friends Frank and Isobel. They were taking a week's holiday and we were flattered that they included a visit with us in their plans.

I suddenly realized that the rather isolated life we lead also has its compensations. In the larger civilized world you can also form solid friendships, but there are so many other things that compete for your attention. Here in our new country we have made many friends with whom we share many things of deep interest to us, like the hopes and disappointments of a harvest, problems with children, conditions of the roads, and so on. But the majority of people here do not have very much interest in life outside of their small community.

Few of these people know anything about the life we led before we came to this country, nor do they know much at all about Holland. When we tell them about living in Holland or Indonesia or India, they listen politely but I doubt if they are much interested. We soon find ourselves discussing farm topics again.

Frank and Isobel, on the other hand, have interesting backgrounds themselves. They are both of Scottish origins, but they grew up in Canada. They met in an isolated spot on the barren coast of Labrador. Frank had his first assignment there as a student minister, and Isobel was a nurse in one of Dr. Grenfell's famous hospitals. Their stories about the isolation and the very severe winters there, how they travelled by dog team or fishing boat to isolated spots to serve the community were of just as much interest to us as our stories about Holland or the Orient were to them.

"Now we can visualize better how you spend your winters," they remarked as we were sitting together in front of the bright fire. "We have only known this farm on hot summer days, and we have often talked about you and your nice country life here, with the grain fields all around you and the river with the bush to the left. But this cozy room in the midst of wide white fields has its own charm. You really are to be envied, and I hope you realize it!"

With a lump in my throat I thought that very often I had not realized it at all!

Their visit, short as it was, was a kind of elixir for us in the days ahead. We talked together about all kinds of new plans and possibilities to cope with the hard times we were having. Whether they will be realized in the end is another question, but at least they stimulated our minds and opened new possible horizons and dreams which were pleasant to think about. It's better to do that than dwell too much on the present harsh conditions.

After our guests left I had a rather uneasy week. I could only blame myself for it. In July someone from an organization in town had asked me to give a talk about the educational system in Holland. How I ever had the nerve to accept, I cannot understand. But they told me this meeting of the Council of Women would not take place until September, which seemed a long way off. They assured me that usually not many people came to the meetings, and since I was brought up in the Netherlands I would at least know more about the subject than the other people.

So I wrote to some well-informed friends in Holland for information, and to some friends with the Dutch consular service in Winnipeg. They were all very helpful. So I was not stuck for material. The problem was to condense and organize it in the best way.

Never in my life did I study as hard at school as I now did for this talk! I had the feeling that I was studying for an exam. Never before had I known so much about the educational system in Holland as I do now. I even got so interested that I found myself reading about education in other countries, too, and started making some comparisons.

The talk turned out a lot better than I had dared to hope. There were quite a few men in the audience, too, because several teachers turned up. My heart was in my throat when I started because I was afraid that, thinking so much about Dutch things, I would forget all my English and start talking Dutch! But fortunately that did not happen. I felt proud that I could point out that everyone in Holland who goes to high school has to learn English, French and German, as well as their own language, and if you take a classical education to prepare for university, you need Greek and Latin as well.

Bob was a big help because he drew up on a large sheet of paper a fine diagram of all the educational systems in the country that we could think of. With this in front of my nose I didn't need to worry about forgetting anything. But the whole evening I had the strange feeling that it was somebody else who was doing the talking.

Later on I was asked to give the same talk for a different club, so I took that as a compliment. It was good that people sent me so much good material from Holland and Winnipeg. "Fortune seems to favour the bold," said Bob, and I guess he was right.

※

Remembrance Day

November 1934

We are having the most beautiful fall weather you can imagine! The grass is still green, and the sun has such power we can still sit outside without a coat.

Never before have we gone to the Remembrance Day celebrations because in other years the roads have always been snowed in by this time. It is too hard for us to get to town by eleven o'clock by sleigh, after doing all the chores.

This year Remembrance Day was not only on a Sunday but it was a glorious warm Indian Summer day besides. So we decided to attend this year. By now we've gotten to know the families here more personally. In many homes we have seen the pictures of young sons in uniform, some who have returned and some who have not. Knowing what Remembrance Day means to these families gives it more meaning for us, too.

Remembrance Day is celebrated throughought the British Empire on the 11th of November, the eleventh day of the eleventh month and the eleventh hour. In all the cities, towns and villages throughout Canada you will find cenotaphs and monuments built to honour and remember the fallen soldiers. In Dauphin the monument lists the names of eighty-four young men who gave their lives and are buried on the other side of the ocean. On this day the churches have special early services.

At quarter after ten we could hear the muffled drone of many feet on Main Street, heralding the coming of the veterans of the Great War, marching in rows of four. It gave us a strange sensation in a land which has practically no military parades. The ceremony must bring back poignant memories in those who remember the troops marching away some twenty years ago to defend home and country. They were young men then, some practically children who had managed to enlist at age seventeen. We now see their greying hair, and some of the bounce has left their step.

This year the Anglican church held the special service. Each year a different church is chosen. Naturally the sermon is in line with the occasion. After the church service the veterans march to the cenotaph, where people from other churches and other people have assembled.

After the singing of a hymn and reciting of the Lord's Prayer, the different corps, various organizations and also some individual persons place wreaths of flowers at the foot of the monument. Then suddenly church bells and factory sirens pierce the silence. After the sounds of the eleventh hour have died away, everyone joins with people all over the world to bow their heads and observe a two-minute silence to remember the men who gave their lives for their country.

Suddenly this intense silence is broken by a trumpet which sounds the "Last Post," the signal for going to rest. The old warriors stand at attention, and their minds are no doubt flooded by memories of eventide in Belgium and other places of battle. After the turbulence of a day of battle, the "Last Post" would be sounded as a sign that they could now rest because their duties for the day had ended.

After a short benediction for their fallen comrades, the reveille is sounded as a reminder to those present that on them lie responsibilities for the wounded, the widows and orphans. It is a deeply moving moment.

Two rather young veterans hold up a third comrade who lost his leg. A little further a blind veteran faces the sky which he has not seen for twenty years. A few steps away from me stands an old lady whom I know well who remembers her son who stayed behind on Vimy Ridge. Her other son returned a wounded man who died from his injuries just last summer. A bit further away a widow wipes the tears from her eyes, and the eighteen-year-old boy at her side is looking straight ahead, no doubt thinking about the father he has never known.

Then suddenly the national anthem is played and the soldiers stand at attention again. After the last salute in front of the cenotaph the ceremony ends.

In the evening quite a few touching speeches were given in the town hall. After an emotion-filled day like this, we go home and read the many articles that appear in the newspaper every day about rearmament, insurrections, riots and political turmoil which can easily lead to new wars. You can't help wonder if all this sacrifice might be in vain. Probably not many of the veterans would like to take part in another war, and the papers tell us that about 60,000 of them are unemployed. It would not be surprising if after years of forced idleness and no hope for much change in the near future, they would start to glorify their war years. That was the time when they were badly needed, when something was asked of them! They left as heroes, got their three meals a day, and returned as heroes. But now they may start to feel a burden to themselves and to their country.

For the new generation, alas, it is just as bad. There is no work for the young people, either. They stand on the street corners from *morning to evening. They don't remember the anxiety and pain of the war years, so it is easy for them to glamorize the war. What else can you expect of young people who can't find work and have little else to keep them occupied?*

A party was given for the veterans the next day in the Legion Hall. During the war years Bob lived in neutral Holland, but he was called up for military duty in case of national need. So he became a member of the Canadian Legion and he went to the party. In the basement of the hall a bar was set up where beer was served (it is not legal to sell stronger alcoholic beverages). Around the piano they sang the old war songs like "It's a long way to Tipperary," "Keep the home fires burning," and "There's a long, long trail a-winding."

Old memories from the trenches were recalled, and beer was foaming in the glasses — "just as good as over in France, remember?" A few young fellows who slipped in were listening with eyes gleaming and said, "Gee, you must have had a swell time over there!"

But all through the country you will find the cenotaphs. . . Will it ever happen again?

Speaking of Indonesia, and Expecting Immigrants from There

Late November, 1934

I have such exciting news that I can hardly settle down to write about it! I have been flying high for the past two days. There are two reasons for that. The first reason may be a bit of vanity, but the second is a coming event which may make our life here considerably more pleasant!

Ordinary household chores are too dull for me these days! I make the beds with a lick and a promise, straighten the rooms, and make as little work of the meals as my conscience will allow me. Out of restlessness I will walk outside again, telling myself to help Bob, but in reality I'm more of a burden to him. If he hadn't held me back, I probably would be shouting our big news to people on every wagon and car that comes past our house. So now, to let off steam, I'll write about what I'm not supposed to tell our neighbours.

Here's where it starts. Three days ago I had to give a talk for a group in town, the second time I've been invited to speak. This time it was to a ladies' club which invites speakers during the winter months. It is all done on a voluntary unpaid basis, not like in Holland where you are paid if you are invited to speak.

They asked me quite a few weeks ago, and I agreed without giving it much thought. But when the date was only a week away, I suddenly panicked! It always seems like I wait too long to prepare myself. The days seemed too short for all the work that still needed to be done. At night, sleepy and tired, I pestered Bob to give me a few suggestions or anecdotes.

Bob just laughed. "It's just your vanity that you got yourself caught in this," he said. "You don't earn anything from it, and you have more than enough to do with your household duties and your writing. I told you so at the time, but you wouldn't listen. Now you better manage on your own." Not much comfort.

Well, I could hardly blame him. I had decided to tell them something about life in the Dutch East Indies, or Indonesia as it's now called. Most of them would likely know very little about that country.

I rummaged among our old letters and hunted up a few curiosities like batik sarongs, Indian brass, and so forth, and read up a bit in my old geography book. I awaited the evening with some anxiety.

On the afternoon of the day I had to give my talk, my new friend Eleanor, who lives in town, dropped in for a visit. We had a pleasant afternoon, mending socks and drinking tea. As she left she said, "Do you want me to get some groceries for you today, which you can pick up from me tonight? By the time you get to town for your eight o'clock speech the stores will be closed."

I said I didn't need any groceries, but it would be nice if she could pick up my mail at the post office, since it would be two days yet before the mailman would be delivering to our farm.

I got to Eleanor's house at quarter to eight, and she had two letters for me. They were both from Indonesia! What a coincidence, getting two letters from Indonesia fifteen minutes before I was going to speak about life there! Maybe the letters would give me some fresh ideas for my speech.

I tore open one of the envelopes and gave a shout of surprise! "Dear People, we have also decided to move to Canada and start farming there. Our ship leaves November 4" (today was the sixth, so they were already at sea!). "We sail by way of Japan and land in Vancouver on December 10. About four days later we hope to meet you in Dauphin!"

In the second letter they were asking us to rent a house for them in Dauphin and buy for them whatever they would need to get started.

This news did not come as a total surprise, of course. The husband is a second cousin of Bob, and when we lived there we had visited them in Java, where he was the manager of a rubber estate. They had written us a few letters earlier about unsettled conditions in southeast Asia, and had mentioned that they had thoughts of emigrating. We had not taken that too seriously. Many more people had asked us about prospects in Canada and shared with us their plans to emigrate, but that led to nothing so often that we never got very excited about it anymore.

Eleanor called me back to reality by saying, "Our meeting starts in three minutes. We better hurry or we'll be late."

Well, I surely wasn't in the mood for a lecture anymore. I was so full of the news of these letters that I couldn't think about anything else. I ran with Eleanor to the meeting place, only a short distance away. I calmed down a bit when we entered the meeting hall and saw rows of ladies turn their heads to see us when we entered.

It felt like I was in a dream world as I heard the president open the meeting, listened to the minutes of the latest meeting, and the financial report.

Then suddenly I heard my own name! My head felt totally empty. Let me see, what is it I am supposed to talk about? Oh, yes, Indonesia, the Dutch East Indies, the country from which seven people had just left, heading for Canada, for Dauphin!

Suddenly I seemed to forget the whole meeting. I was back in Indonesia, it was New Year's Eve and we were the guests of these people who were now coming to Dauphin. I described the tropical night on the rubber plantation, full of strange sounds. The continuous sharp chirping of the "anting tonahs," the cry of a bird, the slow call of the "tokeh-tokeh." We were sitting outside under the tall trees. Impressive and exotic, the high palms were silhouetted against the sky.

The baby slept peacefully in a wicker basket under mosquito netting. Noiselessly on bare feet a baboe (native nanny) came out of the house and said, "nonnie, Poekoel delapan," which is Malay for "Missy, it is eight o'clock." She took the two-year-old sister from her father's lap where she had fallen asleep.

It was like a hallucination! I felt again the warm night air, heard the well-known sounds, and smelled the scent of the East. Then, vaguely, I started to realize that I couldn't just go on reminiscing. That would not give a picture of the country to people who had never been there. I fell back on the notes I had made the day before.

But the whole evening I had in my mind that picture, how we had been sitting there together under the high palm trees that New Year's Eve. How grown-up we felt at that time, being world travellers already, and how in reality we had all been so young and inexperienced!

Would we find each other very much changed? That baby in her cradle would now be a twelve-year-old girl. I had been looking after her a bit for practice, because by this time I was expecting my own first baby. What were we talking about that night? Oh, yes, about Australia. Some friends of ours in Calcutta had left for Australia with plans to start farming there. It had seemed to us to be such a good and adventurous life that we almost followed their example right then and there. That was the first nudge to emigrate and farm, but when the time came it was not Australia that called us, but Canada. So now, twelve years later, they too decided to take that step!

I felt I had beem rambling in my lecture, but the audience must have liked it anyway. "We had the feeling that we have spent a night under the palm trees, too," a lady told me later. So I felt pretty good about it in the end. In fact, I was invited to give the same talk later for another club, but I said I couldn't because I was too busy getting ready for our friends from Indonesia. And Bob had been teasing me about getting too proud with all the attention I was getting.

We had to rent and fix up a house by the middle of next month. Quite a few friends offered to lend furniture and other things, which was good because they would have something to start with and later on they could pick out their own things. But we needed to buy such things as blankets and mattresses. Since prices here are considerably higher than in Winnipeg, and since with a cheap excursion fare you can buy a return ticket by train to Winnipeg for $3.25 instead of the usual $12, we decided to do that.

This move will be quite an undertaking for these people! They are only a few years older than we are, but we have the great advantage of having lived here for ten years already. They have four children, two girls and two boys. Her father, an active older gentleman, will also be with them. I certainly hope they will not be disappointed. When they asked our opinion about their thought of joining us in Dauphin, we didn't give them too optimistic an account. I'm glad about that now. They are expecting a life of hard work, a life where you do the work yourself and do not have coolies to do it for you! The relative loneliness of country life here will mean nothing to them, since for the past ten years they have been living in the hinterlands of the island of

Sumatra. It is a lot more lonesome there than here. But our thoughts now are about a safe arrival and good first impressions.

Welcoming Immigrants from the Far East

December 1934

Three little peep holes have been blown in the heavily frosted kitchen windows. Three children are watching our struggles to start the car in bitter cold weather. We want to drive to the train station in town to meet the new immigrants from Indonesia.

Starting the car in the dead of winter is no joke. But our roads are still pretty fair, and going to town is a major undertaking until we have more snow. We need to use thinner oil and put antifreeze in the radiator instead of water. A problem right now is that our radiator is leaking.

It has been impossible to start the car with the self-starter, and we had no better luck with the crank. So Bob hitched two horses to the car, and he sits behind the wheel and gives me instructions from there as to where and how I must drive the horses. I stomp my feet, blow on my fingers, and give the horses the signal to pull.

The horses give a powerful tug, rear up, and the car moves. Hanging on to the reins I run along and get pulled. The car follows but so far the motor hasn't started, partly because the wheels do not get much grip in the snow. After two times around the tennis court I gasp for air, completely out of breath. Breathing becomes almost impossible in such cold air.

I was on the verge of giving up when the motor gave some halting coughs. The horses pricked up their ears and I hung onto the reins as best I could, having visions of Bob inside the car grabbing for all the handles and levers at the same time.

"Keep the horses straight!" Bob yells. Too late. I stumbled over a root buried under the snow, pulled in desperation on the wrong line, and the horses went the wrong way. Everything stopped.

We looked at each other in dismay. But we started around the tennis court again, and were rewarded with a few more coughs. On the next round we heard the sounds we wanted — pprrt, ppprrrt, ppprrrttt! Now it kept going, and Bob jumped out of the car, threw a blanket over the hood, and jumped back inside to adjust the levers and knobs.

It is hard to believe that this very night we will greet our friends who have been travelling for six long weeks from Indonesia, from the other side of the world! Will they find the land dreadfully bare here after being surrounded by Indonesia's luxuriant vegetation? We still have several hours of waiting, since the train is not due until quarter to one in the morning.

Our friends Eleanor and Earl, who live in Dauphin, offered to drive to the station in their own car, since our car is not big enough for the whole family. We took them to the house we had rented and checked to see that everything was ready and that the house was warm enough. We played cards, watched the clock, drank coffee, and waited and waited.

Finally it was time to drive to the train station. I thought about the time many years ago when I arrived at the same train station from Holland with our first baby, with Bob there to meet me. After a while we saw the lights of the train, and heard the whistle, sounding so different from the train whistles we knew in Holland. People were getting off the train, and suddenly we heard shrill children's voices talking Dutch! There they were, dressed in coats without fur collars, the boys wearing short pants in the bitter cold night.

A few minutes later we were all packed together in the two cars. On the porch of the house we sang out, "Welcome to all of you!"

After a glass of milk the children were put to bed. A bottle of wine mysteriously appeared. We didn't have glasses, only borrowed teacups, which we used to toast the new arrivals. We talked and talked, about politics and geography, and travel.

After a while the tiredness got to all of us. Earl and Eleanor left, the family went to their new beds, and Bob and I settled down to sleep on the couch in the living room. When all was quiet, Bob said to me, "I do hope they will never regret this step!"

1935

Christmas with International Connections

January 1935

Christmas 1934 was very different from our other Christmases in Canada. For several years it has been our custom to invite for Christmas dinner the Bos bachelors, our neighbours who also immigrated from Holland. This year it was not feasible to do that because of the recent arrival of the Volkers family, our friends from Indonesia.

Our special Christmas celebrations started on Christmas Eve, the 24th of December. On that day two big Christmas parcels arrived from New York, where my youngest brother and his wife are now living. And two other Christmas boxes came from our family in Holland. What excitement!

And then we told our boys that before the night would be over, there would be another big surprise! We hurried with the evening meal and the work in the barn. At eight o'clock we all started to decorate our Christmas tree. Bob and I kept watching the clock.

Suddenly the telephone rang! I was so nervous I said to Bob, "Here, you take it. I'm too excited!"

With studied nonchalance he took the receiver, and I stood beside him with thumping heart. The boys looked at us with startled faces.

The phone operator said, "Long distance call from New York!"

I said to the boys, "Here is our special surprise! You will hear the voice of your Uncle Dirk right from New York on the telephone! He wants to say a few words to each of you, but it will be very short. We have only three minutes altogether."

"You mean Uncle Dirk and Aunt Charlotte of the Christmas parcels?" asked Wim to be sure.

"All ready?" asked the operator. "Yes."

I heard the voice of my youngest brother, which I had not heard for ten long years. Then briefly I heard the voice of his wife, my American sister-in-law whom I had never met, whom we only knew through letters.

It seemed as if the distance fell away, as if they were right with us in the room! We said the most incoherent things, and barely remembered later what we had said. "We are busy tonight decorating the Christmas tree." "The same here." "Do you still recognize my voice?" "Merry Christmas to you all." The conversations took place mostly in English because my American sister-in-law does not understand Dutch.

Then suddenly the operator's voice broke in, "Your time is up."

Suddenly it was quiet. I stood with the receiver in my hand. The illusion of being close together had lasted for three short minutes, but now it was shattered. New York was thousands of miles away again. I suddenly burst into tears. My three young sons were frightened out of their wits.

"Why is she crying now?" they asked their father. "Uncle Dirk didn't say anything that made her cry, did he?"

A few weeks later a letter from New York said that the reaction over there was very much the same, even though a man doesn't easily burst into tears. "When it was all over," Dirk wrote me, "I felt like placing another call right away to say all the things I had forgotten to say!"

Christmas was a very cold day and we scurried to get ready for our trip to town for our Christmas celebration. We would have liked to have the Volkers come to our farm for the day, but it was out of the question to transport the seven of them, since they do not have their own transportation.

Bobby and I gave the horses and cows an extra sheaf of hay for their Christmas dinner. "What about the cats and dogs?" Bobby asked. "Do you think Aunt Tekla will give us the turkey bones to give them? Otherwise they won't even know that it's Christmas!"

The drive to town went all right, though once we got stuck in the snow. Everybody had to pile out, shovel the snow away and give the car a push. But we were prepared for that by taking two big shovels with us. "I hope it doesn't start to blow and drift on the road tonight," said Bob. "If we get stuck with these kids in the middle of the night..."

We had a very happy Christmas! A lovely Christmas tree stood in the living room, frozen in a big tub of ice. Colourful streamers of paper and tinsel were hung above our heads, and the table was set with nice china and gleaming silver.

We had a lot to talk about. After the big dinner we all sat around with the candles burning on the tree and sang Christmas songs. The

Christmas presents were opened, and there were lots of surprises. We were impressed with the lovely things their children had made. In the boarding school in Brastagi which they had attended they had learned all kinds of crafts. The girls had made lovely woven cushion tops and scarfs, and the boys made nice fret work and carton work.

"I hope our boys can learn something from these children," I said to Bob later, clearly realizing the shortcomings of our children in this regard. They had never really learned anything of this sort.

We left for home around midnight. It was a difficult trip. The wind was blowing rather hard and the temperature dropped to -35°. The windshield of the car froze up constantly and we had to stop to scrape a small hole in the ice so Bob could see where he was going. The water in the radiator froze a few times, so we had to stop for that to let the motor run a while to warm the water. We couldn't follow car tracks on the road anymore bcause the wind had filled them with powdery snow. What would happen if we got stuck here, I thought at a certain point where there were no farms for two miles in any direction. With this strong wind and low temperature we would get frostbitten in no time, and we would likely freeze to death within an hour or so. I did not say anything, but when I looked at Bob, I saw that his face was pretty grim and I knew that he was worried, too.

With intense relief we reached our farm gate at last. "This will be our last trip by car this winter," said Bob. "It is really a marvel that we made it tonight without any mishap. Never again will I take such chances."

"What would you have done if we really had gotten stuck tonight?" I asked when we were huddled by our warming stove.

"Well, of course we would make a fire," Bobby chirped in at once. "There was lots of dry wood along the road, even if it was covered by snow. I had ten matches in my pocket, just in case."

I thought, "Even if you are not much of a fretwood artist, and probably have to learn a few more table manners to match your cousins, you are a smart fellow all the same! I haven't the slightest doubt that you will get on in life all right!"

Individualism Wins Over Cooperation

Early March 1935

We are totally isolated from the outside world right now, snowbound in a blizzard. The wind screams and howls against our back door. The hallway and part of the kitchen have blown full of snow, which always penetrates through cracks around the ill-fitting doors and windows. We plan to make some long-awaited improvements to the house next summer!

The whole family is gathered in the living room. It is impossible for the boys to go to school today. It's warm and cozy in the room but we can't even look outside because ice is frozen all over the windows. It's as if we are sitting behind frosted glass.

The coffee pot simmers on the woodstove, in which a fire burns merrily. Our whole menagerie of cats and dogs have gathered with us. We hear nothing but the howling wind, which shakes the house on its foundation, and the sizzling sound of fine dry snow blowing against our windows. No sound of sleigh bells today! No one ventures outside.

I find it a nice change to have the whole family in the house together for a day. Normally the children are gone from eight in the morning until five at night, and Bob is either hauling wood from the mountains or is busy in the barn. But today the boys helped their father with his chores, and now they are all sitting around the living room table occupied with different hobbies. Bobby is busy with a fret saw. Wim is making paintings to present to us later in the day. Dick is colouring pictures and cutting them out. The head of the family is engrossed in an article about a plan for a compulsory maketing board for poultry and eggs, while at the same time turning the handle of a churn, combining useful work with pleasure. I take turns admiring what the boys are doing and learning about the marketing board all at the same time.

The marketing board plan is stirring up the farmers very much lately. Much is being written about it in the farm papers, both for and against. Until now we have had a poultry pool with membership on a voluntary basis. The same is true about the wheat pool and a co-op for cattle. But we haven't seen much by way of results from all this. Instead, the memberships have been declining.

The Cooperative Poultry Pool asked the government to develop a plan for compulsory participation, and a plan was developed. Everyone who has more than twenty-five chickens would be a member, and each producer would have one vote. A majority of producers in Saskatchewan and Alberta voted in favour of the plan, but Manitobans have voted it down!

The idea behind the plan is that by working together the producers would have a certain amount of control over the products they bring to the market. This would improve the quality of the product, establish a stable and satisfactory market, and even out some of the price fluctuations.

We ourselves voted last week, but our hopes were not very high that it would be accepted in Manitoba. At least not if the public opinion in the Dauphin district is an indication. Most of the farmers object to losing their freedom. With red excited faces they stood discussing the issue in little groups. "This is a free country!" I heard from different sides. "We want to sell our produce ourselves to whom we choose!"

"You can still sell to whomever you want," was the reply. "All you need is a permit which does not cost you a cent. That is your protection. If the consumer doesn't pay the price set by the board, you can protest to the Board of Directors, which is selected by the members themselves."

"But we live in a free country! We don't want to ask anybody's permission!"

I couldn't help but think that this so-called freedom is rather relative when farmers don't have a voice in the pricing of the products they grow and deliver themselves.

We discovered how little control farmers have when our relatives from Indonesia took steps to buy a farm. There are lots of farms for sale but the prices are pretty high. When you start to ask questions you find that most of the farms for sale have big mortgages on them. So the farmer himself does not have much say in setting the selling price of his farm and in the arrangements for the sale. The buyer deals more with the seller's mortgage company than with the farmer who is selling the farm.

But now the Volkers have bought a farm. It is only a mile and a half from town, with the land of average quality. They are in a consolidated school district, so the children will attend schools in the town. They will be transported there by a school van in good weather, and by a large covered sleigh in the winter. The drawback is that in a consolidated district the taxes are higher.

Speaking of the schools, another issue came up recently which shows how hard it is to organize farmers here for cooperative effort. There are many country schools around here with anywhere from five to forty pupils, each governed by a local school board of farmers who live in the area. Especially with the shortage of money these days, I hardly need to say that the system doesn't always work very well.

Some people decided that there is room for improvement, which could be achieved if a central school board were formed consisting of farmers delegated from all of the district school boards. This central board would appoint teachers on a uniform basis, establish salaries and handle complaints.

Two meetings on this proposal were held in town, and Bob and I attended. We were disgusted at how pig-headed people are on such a matter. In the end no one voted for the proposal! The argument was, "We would have practically nothing to say anymore about our own business."

So it came down to the same thing that prevented the marketing board proposal from passing — losing our (imaginary) freedom.

The Family Co-op

March 1935

I've been complaining about the unwillingness of farmers to cooperate in public action, but now I have a happier story about cooperation on the home front.

It all started during one of those winter storms in which we are all snowbound in the house for a few days in a row. Except for chores in the barn, Bob and the three boys and I stay together in the house all day. This sounds romantic, and it is rather nice for a while, but before long we tend to go stir-crazy. The boys get into mischief, start to play rough games, and yell and fight as you would expect. I feel like my workload has doubled.

At one point when I was cleaning up a mess caused by horseplay, Bobby said to me with a half-guilty expression on his face, "I bet you're jealous of Aunt Tekla in town, aren't you? She has two girls to help her. Both aunt and uncle have help — they have two boys and two girls."

"Yes, but you boys can help me now and then, too," I said.

"It would be nice to earn some money by helping," he replied. "I'd love to have a bicycle like a lot of other boys, but I guess that's too big a present for a birthday or Christmas. Max McCrea earned his own bike from money his Dad gave him for helping milk the cows. But I guess they are a lot richer than you, though."

I didn't say anything, but he gave me an idea I wanted to discuss with Bob.

We decided to give it a try. The pocket money they would earn from jobs wouldn't be very much, but each would earn according to his age and achievement. The money would be theirs and they could spend it as they wanted. They would learn something about how to handle money.

So we got together and the boys each made up a list. It was a bit like a school timetable, with times for doing each job, and also play time.

I must say that so far it has worked out very well. If someone would visit our house at seven o'clock in the morning, they would find the two older boys making their beds, sweeping the floor and putting away all their clothes. While I am busy separating the fresh milk, one of the boys is setting the table and the other is busy pumping water at the well outside. Even little Dick is busy filling the woodbox.

When Bobby, age eleven, leaves for the barn to comb his horse and give him water and hay, Wim, now eight years old, helps me dry the dishes. In the beginning that job was very slow business. But after much patience from both of us, he is now quite good at it.

When they come home after school they play until suppertime. When everything is put away after the meal, all three disappear to the barn with their Dad. Bobby milks two cows, Wim milks one, and Dick sits on a block of wood watching them. We never realized how much this kind of systematic help can mean to us.

One day Bob got word that the wood he had cut in the mountains last winter had been cut up and was ready for him to pick up. Hauling the wood meant making five trips, each of which would take two days. For several days and nights we would need to manage without his help.

But the boys were all excited. "Don't worry! Just go ahead. We'll manage all right by ourselves!" they told Bob.

Their exhuberance almost got to be too much for me. The first morning, while it was pitch dark, I was awakened by little pulls at my hair. There stood Wim, shivering and stuttering beside my bed. "Mamma, wake up, it's nearly daylight!" he told me. "We have to go to work!"

There really is a lot of work that needs to be done in the morning. They need to feed all the cows and horses that are kept in the barn, pump water for them, and clean the stalls. Then they need to find a place on the frozen river where they can cut a hole in the ice so the cows that are left outside can find water. Then they milk the cows, feed the pigs, feed the hens, and carry the fresh milk to the house for me to separate. When the toboggan leaves for school about quarter to nine, there is very little work left for me to do.

They must have talked at school about all their extra work at home, because their teacher phoned me to assure me that it would be all right if they came to school an hour late because of their extra work.

When Bob came home with his first load of wood after a few days, he was glad to see that everything was in good control. But on the day when he came back with his last load, we all rushed out to greet him with great relief! That evening, when three freshly scrubbed boys sat in the living room to receive their money, they were all paid double wages!

"Really Earned Money"

April 1935

Our oldest son Bobby has been strutting around like a peacock these days. The simple question, "What time is it, Bobby?" brings a blush of pride to his cheeks. He grins from ear to ear and pulls out his brand new watch from his pocket.

The watch was not a gift, but he bought it with his "really earned money." He calls it this to distinguish it from money given as a present.

Bob and I have worked out an ongoing system of paying our boys for the various chores they do around the house and barn. Every Saturday night we have a kind of ceremony. After the three have had their baths (in front of the kitchen stove in a washtub), they get into their pyjamas and come into the living room looking rosy and smelling of soap. Daddy says, "What now, boys?"

Then all three run to a certain cupboard in the corner, and with shining eyes and triumphant smiles, come back to the table and each places on it his own piggy bank. It is a moment of sheer drama when the weekly payment takes place.

It is amusing to see the different way each boy reacts to the same thing. Bobby has a piece of paper on which, in very neat figures, he has written down his accounts. He has put this, together with his little pig, in a box and locked it up with a key attached to his new watch chain. He is the tidy one, meticulous in all his ways.

Wim, the second oldest and eight years old, is the opposite in every way. For the entire week his little pig seems to have "gone to market." It has disappeared as completely as if by magic. Everybody is accused of having run off with the critter. This untidy, mischievous rascal, is the sunshine of our house, and a prime favourite of all he meets. Early in the week he sort of pretends to hunt for his pig, but when Saturday comes near he becomes serious, and the piggy turns up in some impossible corner.

Dick the youngest, is more like his oldest brother, though lacking his patience. His great ambition is to "kill" his pig right away so he can admire all his precious hoarded coins.

In their spare time the boys are often bent over the Eaton's Catalogue, often called the "farmer's Bible." You can order by mail from this catalogue anything your heart could desire.

"My gosh, things are expensive, aren't they?" sighs Bobby. "It takes an awful long time before you can buy something nice. I wish I could make some more money." The catalogue has done its work — Bobby has an incentive.

Then one day his eye fell on an ad in the paper. "Boys and girls wanted! Easy way to make some money. Write for full particulars." All kinds of desirable items were pictured as rewards for good work.

Bobby went into action that same evening. With his tongue firmly between his teeth, he composed his letter in his most beautiful handwriting.

Exactly a week later the answer arrived, congenially addressing Master Bob as "Dear Friend." A seed company wanted to sell garden seeds. You weren't tied to sell any certain amount, nor was it necessary to send money when the seeds arrived. All was done on trust.

"I'm going to try it!" Bob decided. After a few days he was in possession of four dollars worth of garden seeds. Every afternoon after school he set out on horseback, peddling his seeds at the neighbouring farms. Sales were better than he had dared to hope. It was a well-known seed firm with a good reputation.

"I'm following all their rules," Bobby confided to me after his first successes.

"What rules?" I asked.

"In this little book it says be neat in appearance, have a pleasant smile, and be polite."

"Well," Bob said later when I told him about that conversation, "This is turning out to be a pretty good educational project, isn't it?"

In two weeks time he had sold all the seeds, and then came the great day of choosing his reward. After lots and lots of weighing the choices, he decided in favour of the watch. As an added bonus he received a tie pin and also a certificate testifying that he was "an honest young man," which made him blush with pride.

"Next spring I'll do it again," he declared. "But now I'll start catching gophers."

Since gophers are destructive of crops, the municipal government pays one cent for each gopher tail brought in. So the boys set snares and traps all over the place. Even in the garden we have to walk with care to avoid being trapped ourselves. Yesterday the first twenty little gopher tails were taken to town in a grimey paper bag.

But then we had another example of the ideas boys can get into their heads. One of our neighbours had four little fox terrier puppies. Our boys visited there and came home full of stories about the puppies and their long tails. "But Mr. Nicholson took an axe and cut the tails off. He put a bit of iodine on the stumps so they wouldn't get blood poisoning. Wouldn't that hurt them to have their tails cut off?" they wanted to know.

Their Daddy reassured them that the puppies were so young they did not feel it much and would soon forget the pain. Did they remember that Daddy had done the same with the lambs last spring? They wouldn't have as much value with long tails.

A few days later when I gave the boys their baths I noticed yellow stains on their hands. "What's that?" I asked. "How did you get those stains?"

They looked at each other with some embarrassment, and decided to tell the truth. "It's iodine," they said.

"Why did you need iodine?" I asked. "You didn't hurt yourselves, did you?"

"No, but often when we catch a gopher it is not dead, and we thought that if it didn't hurt too much cutting such a little tail, maybe we could cut it off and put a little iodine on it, and maybe the gopher would grow another tail."

I looked over at Bob, and he couldn't contain himself but just burst out laughing.

"But that's cruel!" I said, trying to be stern. "Don't you understand that you are cruel?"

"But they do that with little lambs and dogs, don't they?"

That stopped me for a minute. Then I said, "But that's not honest. The government doesn't just want gopher tails. The tail is merely the proof that you killed a gopher."

They looked perplexed for a bit, but then suddenly the dimples appeared in Wim's cheeks and a smile came through. "Well, we won't do it again, Mom," he said. "You know what happened? This morning nearly all the gophers we caught in our traps didn't have tails. So it's not working anyway."

Death of a Friend

May 1935

Spring has arrived in all its beauty. Flowers are coming out all over and the trees become fuller and greener every day. But amid all this beauty around us, I need to write about the darkest days we have experienced in our ten years here. It happened so unexpectedly that we can hardly believe it is true.

Only several days ago, on a beautiful evening, Bob started the car and hollered to me, "Do you want to come along, too? I want to go to the Bos brothers because I've run out of seed and I've heard they still have some for sale."

I grabbed a sweater and rushed outside. No formalities of dress are needed when you visit each other in the country. When we got to the Bos farm we saw that the fields of our friends had fewer weeds than we see on other fields.

"What a beautiful place they have," we remarked to each other. "With four strong men you can really get things done. The house and other buildings are in such good shape. The lawn they sowed last year has come up beautifully."

Bob blew the car horn and in a minute one of the brothers came to the barn door and called, "Be with you in a minute! We've just finished here."

When they came to the house we all sat inside and asked each other about how things were going. During the busy season we don't see very much of each other.

"Did you get any news from Holland lately?" we asked each other. We all had letters, and everyone was well. It has been nine years now that we have lived near each other, and we have developed strong ties. Each of us represents for the other a little piece of Holland and our early lives. We have shared our struggles and our good times over these nine years and have helped each other in many ways. It is hard to put into words what we and the four Bos brothers, Klaas, Tokko, Dirk and Bouko, mean to each other.

A week later we were together with the four Dutch brothers, but this time in the hospital in Dauphin! We were gathered around a hospital bed where Tokko, one of the brothers, lay deathly ill. The words we had heard that afternoon, "There is no hope," rang in our ears, but we could still hardly believe them. He had been operated on earlier in the day.

Quietly we slipped out of the room and sat together on the wide hospital steps. It was a beautiful evening. There was a silence in the air, filled with anxiety. In Holland the tulips would be blooming.

A young nurse motioned for us to come back to the room. Bob and I followed the three brothers. Tokko was breathing more peacefully now. But his breathing had become more shallow. Then it stopped.

As we helped the three remaining brothers prepare for the funeral and burial we all felt keenly that we are in a foreign country. The customs in Canada are different from what we have always known.

The funeral was held in the church in a simple way. For someone who went through life so modestly and quietly, only simplicity seemed right. But friends and neighbours — the whole district came to the funeral! What spontaneous sympathy everyone was showing!

Everyone was wearing their ordinary clothes, in contrast to the Dutch custom of having everyone wear black. The casket was covered with flowers and was carried out of the church, not by hired professionals, as would be the case in Holland, but by friends and neighbours.

The casket was put into the hearse, and a procession of cars started to form behind it. A long row of cars slowly proceeded to the cemetery. We all stood around the grave as the minister spoke a few comforting words.

We silently looked out over the green fields. We could vaguely see the buildings on the Bos farm, against the blue haze of the Riding Mountains. That is where Tokko had worked for these last nine years. Always full of ambition and ready to help others, never asking a thing for himself.

Tomorrow the work will be taken up again, but without him. Oh, how he will be missed! The first member of our small colony who has gone.

✳

Violent Storms and Building Plans

July 1935

This summer is different from our ten previous summers in Canada. The weather, for one thing. We are having rain, lots and lots of rain. What a blessing rain can be! We couldn't get too much of it. During the years of severe drought the soil had turned to powder, even deep down.

After a few days of torrential rains, Bob and I put on our high rubber boots and went out to inspect the fields of young grain. We had high hopes, because from our windows the grain looked so fresh and green. We had sixty acres in wheat this year, and that would help our financial position, which was very stretched out from poor crops and low prices.

What we found to be growing so well, though, turned out not to be our grain but wild oats! It was growing like crazy, right in the rows of grain as well as between the rows. I am told that wild oats can lie dormant in the soil for many years, and will sprout under certain temperature and moisture conditions. Well, we sure had the right conditions this year! It was a sorry sight.

"The only solution I know," said Bob, "is to plow it all under and work the land again. Maybe we can still sow barley on that field. But there won't be enough time for me to do it with the horses. I'll have to hire a man with a tractor." We were both pretty glum.

What made this especially hard to take was that we were planning to build a new house. Our first thought had been to fix up our old house to make it more livable. But everyone advised against it. It would take too much money to fix it up properly, and then we'd still have an old house.

Then out of the blue we received a windfall of money from Holland. Now we could consider building a new house, even if it had to be modest. We probably couldn't have it all finished at once, but we could always do the finish work ourselves later as we had time. We would have a full basement and central heat.

When we got back from seeing our dismal grain field, I got out the house plans and with a heavy heart tried to find ways to save money on the new house. We decided not to finish the upstairs bedrooms right away, to use cheaper wood for the kitchen cabinets, and try to do as much of the work ourselves as we could.

Two days later a man with a tractor undid the biggest part of Bob's spring field work, while he followed the tractor with the seeder and planted barley. We hired Fred, a farmer who did some carpenter work in the United States as a young man, to build our house. He would do it for less money than a professional carpenter. George and Clarence, sons of nearby farmers, would help Fred during their holidays from high school.

In no time the men were tearing the old house down over our heads. We moved into the granary for the summer, and the workers would live in a tent. Naturally I had to cook for all of them, plus Ruth, a farmer's daughter who moved in with us to help me with my work.

The boys were delighted with the prospect of living in the granary for the summer. We covered it all around with mosquito netting and installed mosquito-proof doors. It was good to have a nice group of people around us for the summer. All of us looked upon the venture as if it were a summer-long picnic.

The first night in the granary we heard all kinds of unusual noises. It didn't take us long to find out that the place was crawling with mice! Well, what do you expect from a granary? So we opened the door for the cats, and that took care of the mice.

At quarter to five in the morning we woke up to hear loud scratching and gnawing sounds. Four squirrels were running back and forth on a beam that runs under the high-vaulted roof. We were to find that they did this, with accompanying noise, every morning. No alarm clock is needed this summer!

We lived like summer campers. In the morning we'd all run to the river to splash and wash ourselves. The singing and chirping of birds mixed with the children's voices. It was all very lovely.

But that only lasted a few days. One evening the sky looked ominous. Lightning flashed on all sides. The trees stood motionless as if they were waiting for something to happen. Then suddenly it came! A roaring wind threatened to blow us from the earth in one swoop. A minute later one of the heaviest thunderstorms I have ever seen broke loose. A deafening noise bombarded our roof, which started to leak in various places.

Around two o'clock in the morning I heard an awful noise that sounded like the end of the world was coming. Screaming, roaring wind, and then a terrible rattle that could only be hail! We looked aghast at each other. Water came streaming through the roof, and we kept busy emptying the pails we had set around to catch the worst of it. This terrible torrential rain kept up through all the rest of the night, and we didn't sleep another wink.

When the first grey light of morning came, the storm seemed to calm a bit. But then we heard an ominous roaring sound from the direction of the river. And we heard men's voices crying out, "Help! Help!" It was the men from the tent, each lying on his cot with the tent spread over them like a blanket. They tried to keep covered by the tent but the wind kept blowing the tent off them, so they gave up and wrapped in sheets and blankets were wading through muddy water towards us.

We all walked to the river, barefoot because by now the water stood ankle deep around the granary. The river was a mighty spectacle, a thundering wild stream. It rushed under the bridge taking with it uprooted trees which smacked into the metal structure of the bridge. The water was rising by the minute. After a quarter of an hour the water was running over the river banks already. We were standing in the middle of the road when suddenly the water rushed towards us and we had to wade through it to reach our living quarters.

We were actually in an excited, rollicking mood, not yet realizing the danger. Fortunately our buildings were on the east side, the higher side of the river, and the flood waters would not reach there. But when, towards noon, the water still kept rising, and telephone connections were broken, our mood became more sober. At the bridge cars and trucks started to gather, hoping to reach town and get food and other supplies, but that was impossible. A big part of the road had washed away, and a wild stream rushed over our field, destroying our beautiful oat crop. A train had been derailed. Quite a few bridges had washed out. Horses and cows, and even some people, had drowned.

Although the granary stood on a high cement foundation, by two o'clock the water was only ten inches from the floor. At three o'clock it was only six inches away. We were considering all sorts of plans about what to do in case the water started rushing into our living quarters.

Then suddenly — we could hardly believe it — the water seemed not to be rising any more. Then we saw that it was even beginning to go down a little. What a relief! Now there was no question about it, the water level was going down and for the time being the danger had passed. Towards evening we felt sure there was no danger any longer.

But what a mess the storm and flood had left! And yet the weather still did not settle down. After some more rainstorms, one evening towards dusk the sky became very ominous and threatening again. A strange yellow kind of light seemed to glow behind the clouds. What would it be this time, we asked each other.

Suddenly we heard a strange lowing noise. It came out of the sky, but it wasn't the kind of sound made by strong winds. We stood in the wide door of our granary home, anxiously waiting.

Then suddenly hail started to come down with a loud rattling noise! When I say hail I don't mean those tiny white balls we sometimes had in Holland. These were like chunks of ice, some the size of walnuts, many as large as eggs, and a few bigger than teacups!

We stood paralyzed with fear. The horses galloped away, scared out of their wits. A big goose was instantly killed right in front of us. The children were the only ones who sensed no danger. They saw the hail as a great adventure, excitedly pointing out ever bigger chunks of ice.

Then it became clear that we were getting only the edge of the storm, that the brunt of it would miss us. But some of our neighbours fared worse. Our carpenter Fred, whose farm is a few miles south of us, lost half of his crop. He said that his whole farm looked like a plowed field. And our Dutch friends, the Bos brothers, lost the crop on a hundred acres.

Since then the days are very hot. The sun just beats down and the air is sultry and oppressing. Mosquitoes are making our lives almost unbearable. In spite of our screens, it is impossible to keep them out of the granary. I don't need to tell you that this is the worst possible summer to be building a new house!

Building the House During Hard Times

November 1935

The summer is now past and its lessons are part of our lives. We had so many difficulties this summer, and so much occasion to despair, that I did not trust myself to write for fear that I would sound too pessimistic. But now we can have some perspective on the adversities of the summer, and we have the joy of living in our new house, even though the house is far from finished.

The summer started with the sudden death of our friend and countryman, Tokko Bos. Then we had the disappointment of the lost grain crop that had to be plowed under and resown. Then came the excitement of starting construction on our new house, and moving into the granary for the summer. After that came the flood and the hailstorm that we narrowly missed.

A problem with our house construction was that, in contrast to other years, it seemed to rain all the time. Our lumber was constantly being soaked, and then had to be dried out again. It seemed that forever we were hearing shouts from the house, "Come quick! Another rainstorm is coming, and we need a hand to move those boards inside again." The lumber had to be stored outside because otherwise Fred didn't have enough room inside to move around as he needed.

In the granary we lived in a horrible filthy mess. It was useless to try to do something about it. Everything was covered with sticky mud. When it got too bad we would take a hoe and scrape it off a bit and throw the mud outside by the bucketful. The cottons and linens got damp and started to look very spotty, but there was no place to dry them. Moths fluttered out of boxes in which blankets, winter clothes and drapes were stored. Mice made a big hole in our best rug which we had nicely rolled up and put in the garage.

I lamented, "We soon will have a new house, but if this keeps up we won't have a decent thing left to put in it."

I didn't get any sympathy from Bob. "No use whining about it," he said. "Nothing can be done. Everything seems to go wrong this summer. But be thankful that when winter comes we will have a roof over our heads in a house where we can keep warm."

Often our neighbours would drop by to see how we were getting along. When they saw the long table with all those young men sitting around it fervently discussing European politics, the troubles in Italy and Ethiopia, our boys climbing like kittens on the beams over our heads, and Ruth and I running back and forth to look after everybody, it must have looked to them like a big happy family.

"This time you won't mind the winter, Mrs. Aberson," they would say to me. "The house is starting to look nice already, and with that big basement and furnace you'll be comfortably warm."

Meanwhile I'm concerned that we've already used up a hundred pounds of flour, with all the bread our crew has eaten, and our meat bills have run very high. The milk production of our cows is way down due to the way the mosquitoes are bothering them.

Fortunately our grain doesn't look too bad. We were actually lucky

*that we plowed our wheat under and replaced it with barley, because
our neighbours are having trouble with wheat rust.*

*We even had a short break from our work. Our Dutch friend Dirk
Bos got married, and we all had a merry time, even if the cloud of
Tokko's death is still over us. Dirk's bride is a school teacher who
taught in the district this past year. The wedding was just a family
affair, with Bob and I being the only ones who were not family. For the
wedding the Bos brothers and Bob and I drove in one car to the bride's
family home on the other side of the Riding Mountains. They
honeymooned at Clear Lake, and a week later we drove there together
to bring the bridal couple home. We happened to have beautiful sunny
days for these events, which stand out in our minds as the only decent
days of the summer.*

*Our driving showed us that the crops in our district were not even
as bad as in other areas. On the other side of the mountains the
farmers even burned their crops because the grain was not worth
saving.*

*In August Fred said that he could finish the work on our house
without extra help, so Clarence went back to university and George
went home to help his father with his farm work. Although we missed
them because they had become our good friends, I was glad to have
two fewer men to feed. But Bob said, "Don't celebrate yet, because I
will need to hire two extra men next week when I cut the grain because
there is so much straw this year. I hope to find a couple of workers in
town when I go there Saturday night, and bring them home with me."*

*We had barely gotten to town on Saturday when, of all things, we
ran into Louis, a young Dutch fellow who spent a winter on the farm
with us a few years ago.*

"Where have you been these past few years?" we asked him.

*"In different relief camps, all over the country," he said. "At least
you get room and board, and some clothes, plus $5.00 a month. But
we thought we might as well try to make a few extra dollars in harvest
time, so we came here looking for work. I have a friend with me, Jim,
who also is looking for a job. Do you know of a framer who needs extra
help? We'd like to stay together if we can."*

*Bob hired them on the spot. Louis's friend, who was an office
worker and had never worked on a farm, made up in muscle and
energy what he lacked in skill. On rainy days they did not object to
hauling water and wood to the granary. They dug potatoes and
vegetables out of the muddy garden, and one day even gave Ruth and*

me a hand when we were busy canning corn. I felt that we were pretty lucky, because some hired men would refuse to do any work on a rainy day and would only show up for meals, spending the rest of the day in bed with a cigarette.

In the evenings we were entertained with stories about the relief camps, and we often ended up singing songs, with Bob accompanying on the piano. These days gave our spirits a lift.

One evening when we were singing again, a terrible thunderstorm broke loose. It seemed just like the bad storm we had in the spring. The granary roof started to leak again, splashing water all over the table and on our beds, and rivulets started to run over the floor. In the lightning flashes we saw that the granary was once again surrounded by water.

"Well, that will finish off our barley, the one crop that might have escaped disaster," said Bob quietly. The storm lasted only an hour and a half, but a great deal of damage can be done in that short time. The next morning we saw that two-thirds of the barley was broken off and lay on the ground so that it could not be harvested. The stems had been weakened by the rust.

But a few days later life went on as usual, as if nothing had happened. Jim said to me, "It's strange. I'm twenty-eight years old and have lived in Canada all my life. But this is the first time I have realized what farmers are up against. We often felt sorry for ourselves in the relief camps, without a job and without good hope for the future. Nobody really needed us. But how you and Bob can stick it out on the farm, with one disaster after another, is a riddle to me. If the harvest is good, you don't get a reasonable price for your grain. If the price is good you have a crop failure. And this year, when the prices are up and the crop was not too bad, you lose it all in the very end. But there is Bob now, romping and laughing with his boys out in the yard. Ho does he do it?"

The storm caused a lot of extra work in cutting the grain. The grain lies in all directions, flat on the field, so it is hard to pick up with the binder. You can only cut it in one direction at a time, so it was necessary to go over it all twice. The threshing bill will be higher because there is lots of straw but little grain. So this year the cost of threshing is not based on the number of bushels of grain you get but on the time they spend threshing. Otherwise it would be a losing proposition for the threshing operator.

But where could we put the threshed grain, since we were living in the granary? In desperation we decided to move our beds to the unfinished house to make room for the grain. The windows were not yet installed so there was a cool draft at night, but fortunately the mosquitoes were not too bad. I had dreamed about moving into a clean, brand new house, but here we were sleeping with sawdust, wood shavings, lumber and tools.

Soon the threshers came, twenty strong. To top it off the plasterers came the same day to plaster the downstairs of the house. So I had to cook for twenty-four extra men under unbelievable conditions. But in times of special stress your friends come through. Everybody seemed to understand our difficulties and pitched in as best they could. There was good will all around, and we survived.

After threshing it became unbearable to keep living in the granary. It started to get cold now, and often we had rain. We could barely keep warm, so the big doors that stood open all summer now had to be closed, which meant that we needed to light our lamps even in the daytime.

By now Fred had installed the windows, and the furnace had been lit. Finally one day we could stand it no longer. Chilled to the bone, armed with pots and pans, we stood in front of the startled Fred and announced that we were moving in. It was an inconvenience for Fred and slowed him down, but it had to be done.

In a way I was rather proud of our new house. We largely designed it ourselves and it turned out nicer than we had expected! Also we had worked on building as much of it as we could.

But it didn't take long for the muddy mess from outside to track in with us. The new white walls and the new floors — it made me shudder to look at it. We all started to get cranky again. What a miserable summer this had been. The harvest was a failure, so we had no income for the whole year, and we now had a mortgage on the new house besides!

I don't know how we got through the next few weeks. With all the busyness of the past weeks the gravity of our situation finally sank in. What have we really been working for, after all? What guarantee do we have that next year will be better? Year after year of disappointment. Maybe our family in Holland was right after all when they advised us not to start on this wild scheme!

For ten years we had put up with a cold drafty house, dreading the winters. Now we had a new house and didn't seem able to enjoy it. It is true, of course, that not many people had been able to afford to build a new house in these hard times.

There was still so much work to do. Bob needed to do the fall plowing, and the first coat of paint had to be put on the outside of the house. Inside painting and staining was needed to prevent the wood from drying out with the furnace on. What a contrast to life in Holland, when every spring we would sit and watch painters and plasterers come in to keep the house in first-class condition.

And the floors needed to be treated, and we needed to throw soil around the basement walls before the ground freezes. The pump needed to be installed — imagine, we won't need to get all our water from outside anymore!

Good old Louis and his friend said, "Don't worry! We'll stay to help until you are through the mess here!"

Well, we got through it all right, eventually. Naturally we have our work cut out for us this winter, with lots of finishing to do. But at least it looks like a house now! Everything has found its place. I am proud of my new built-in cupboards!

The sun streams through the big windows on all sides, and the furnace keeps a constant temperature, at night as well as during the day. How much simpler housekeeping is now! I don't need to go outside for every drop of water, and I have a sink with a drain!

Certainly things will soon change for the better. Crops may be better, and prices may rise. Who knows! If you lose courage, you lose everything. But we came pretty close this year!

Christmas Improvisations

December 1935

Today is December 26, which is called "Second Christmas Day" in Holland. It is called Boxing Day in Canada, but until now people have not taken much notice of it. We were so used to having these two Christmas days in Holland that it didn't seem right to treat the 26th as just an ordinary day. So we usually compromised by leaving all the heavy work undone and doing only the necessary things. We'd treat ourselves to a walk, play games together or skate on the river, depending on the weather and our mood. And we'd always have a nice afternoon tea.

This year I was pleasantly surprised to read in the newspaper that from now on Boxing Day will be a national holiday in Canada. Today, Boxing Day 1935, I am writing at the table in our festive living room *while father Bob and our three boys are on the river bank, where they have made a nice toboggan slide.*

Throughout the room the boys have hung decorations, and the aroma of spruce is heavy from the boughs and the Christmas tree. Our two oldest now enjoy preparing for Christmas, but for our youngest, at five years old, Christmas is still a time of enchanting mystery. His belief in Santa Claus is as simple as it is sincere.

Bob and I are only gradually making the transition from the stately bishop St. Nicholas of our childhood to the Canadian Santa Claus. We have many delightful memories of St. Nicholas Day, December 5, when the good saint was supposed to ride on his white horse over the roofs of Dutch homes, followed by his faithful servant Piet. The jolly and rather clownish old man in the red suit with white fur trim didn't seem nearly so impressive to me.

But our boys are no longer Dutch children. They are young Canadians who generally need to be reminded to answer back in the Dutch language once in a while, so they don't forget Dutch altogether. To them the jolly Santa Claus is the height of ecstasy!

This year Bob, who remembers St. Nicholas fondly, too, decided to act as Santa Claus. Since he didn't have the costume, he needed to remain invisible. So he took refuge in the Dutch custom and climbed up on the roof. But on the way up he first banged on the windows with an elk horn. Since we all had a clear view of the elk horn, this made a great impresssion on the children. After all, Santa Claus comes down the chimney from a sleigh drawn by reindeer!

The rattling of chains (that's the Dutch version) and a hollow voice through a funnel shouting down the chimney gave just the right atmosphere. We all thought it was wonderful!

The two older boys, who knew what was going on, had an air of superiority, enjoying themselves immensely, giggling and winking knowingly at me as they watched five-year-old Dick hold tight to my hand and look up with starry eyes.

Much of what Santa shouted from the roof was lost to us, though, because we had forgotten that strange noises on a quiet Canadian farm don't go unchallenged. Our dogs, ever on the alert for anything unusual, gave out with a horrible racket, and the horses, feeding at a straw pile to the rear of the farm, pricked up their ears, threw back their heads, and with manes and tails flying, came galloping into the yard.

To top it all off, a neighbour, passing by on his sleigh and hearing the commotion, decided to investigate. Being slightly inebriated from an afternoon of Christmas Eve celebrations in town, he was quite convinced that he had come in the nick of time to help us in an emergency. So there he stood, in the middle of our kitchen. Not knowing anything about the Dutch legend, the whole performance was a deep mystery to him. I tried to catch his eye and draw attention to the enchanted look on Dick's face, but it didn't penetrate his befogged brain.

"What the dickens is all the shouting on the roof for?" he demanded. "Tell the boss to come down and have a drink with me. I've got some saved!"

Santa Claus on the roof realized by now that something had gone wrong below. He shouted a hurried "Till next year!" and departing with a lot of noise and rattling of chains, hustled down.

"Please try to get rid of Jackson," I whispered to Bob as soon as he entered the house. "Our whole evening will be spoiled if he stays." I particularly resented this intrusion on Christmas Eve because we were expecting a long distance phone call again from my brother Dirk in New York, and it would be much nicer to be alone as a family for that.

But to get rid of Jackson was easier said than done. He was "feeling good," and found it to be nice and cosy in our house. Moreover, he seemed to think that he would be more than welcome because he had a bottle on him. In a hoarse whisper which was quite audible to me he asked Bob "if the Missus was very much against it."

People in Canada have a much different attitude toward alcoholic beverages than we were used to in Holland. Here the sale of alcohol is quite restricted, and only men are served at the town "beer parlours." Women generally are opposed to having the men drink.

Jackson was quite relieved when Bob produced a few liquor glasses.

"Well, I'll be darned," he said. "I never saw such funny little glasses. They won't hold much, will they! We'll have to drink quite a few." And then he finished his, bottoms up, in one gulp.

I was relieved to see that there was not much left in his bottle. But my feeling of hope was short-lived because, as they were about to drink each other's health for the second time, a knock resounded on the door. Here came Pete, a farmer who lived a few miles away, from whom Bob had bought a few cows last summer. Pete was also armed with a bottle!

I pulled Bob aside for a few seconds. "I hope you're not going to upset all our plans for this evening!" I whispered. "Tell them to come back some other time!"

"But I can't do that!" he protested. "They came here out of pure friendliness. Pete walked three miles to come here. I can't just send him home like that! Try to make the best of it. Do you think I like it so much?"

So the only thing to do was to change our program for the evening. I went to the basement and brought up a sealer with canned raspberry juice for the children. They just had to drink out of the small glasses, too!

Presently there was another knock at the door, and this time a whole family asked if they might come in for a while to get warm. They still had twenty miles to go and one of their horses seemed to be sick. The night was cold and their progress had been very slow.

Just when the house seemed to be overflowing with strangers, our eagerly expected long distance call from my brother and his wife came through. I was getting all choked up again, and deeply resented having all these people around for the three minutes in the whole year when we could hear my brother's voice.

I don't know what I said, and I can't remember what my brother said. All I remember is the extreme emotion which nearly choked me. And I was conscious of the annoyance in the background of our uninvited guests taking it all in.

"Thanks ever so much for your Christmas parcel," I heard Bob shout over the phone. "We were just going to open it."

"Yes," I thought when the connection was broken, "we can't open our Christmas presents tonight, either." It's always so nice to do that in the evening. In the morning all the chores need to be done. Doing it in the evening always reminded me of the St. Nicholas evenings in Holland, too.

"But I won't let the children suffer from this," I thought. "Tonight after our guests have left, Bob and I will hide the gifts all through the house and we'll have a kind of treasure hunt for them in the morning." Mother always used to do that with some of our presents at home, and we loved it. We'll put some presents under the Christmas tree, of course. But I had made such different plans for tonight!

It often happens that things turn out differently from what we plan. This was a disappointment tonight, but how much we have to be *thankful for this Christmas! Here we are, in our brand new, cosy warm house. Who would have dreamed of that last year? I saw our guests looking around with furtive, admiring glances. That was itself a satisfaction.*

We spent Christmas Day, as has been our custom over the years, with the Bos family, the bachelor brothers who also immigrated from Holland. But one of the brothers, Dirk, got married this year, and for a change they wanted us to have Christmas dinner at their place instead of ours. For the first time in years this former bachelor home was decorated for the season. It was quite obvious that a woman was running the house now! We had a marvellous dinner, too.

When we got home Bob and I decided that as long as we can have celebrations like that we have no right to complain. And we already have three new calves, and the hens — about three hundred of them — are starting to lay quite regularly. Eggs are 32¢ a dozen, not bad at all! After we are through with our shopping on Saturdays and bring our produce to market, there is generally a little money left over! That has not happened for a long time.

Especially in hard times there are distinct advantages to living on a farm. We have turkeys, geese, potatoes, vegetables of all kinds, fruit, milk, cream, butter and eggs — all from our own farm! In the city you need to pay a tidy sum to buy those. If only the farmers could get a little better price when we sell those things.

We look forward to the new year with hope!

1936

Illness Changes Our Schedule

February 1936

Sometimes I think back and wish I had started writing about our experiences sooner after we came to Canada in 1924. We were so excited and optimistic about our new life! It was so romantic to live in a primitive, isolated log cabin with nol hing but dense bush around us. We felt like Adam and Eve in paradise when we would run to the river for our baths, with baby Bobby crowing at the excitement. Deer and elk sometimes stood like statues watching us at the edge of the bush, and then suddenly vanished with great leaps.

I often couldn't wash the floor in our lean-to kitchen in the winter because the water would immediately freeze on the floor, turning it into a skating rink, even with a fire in the kitchen range. "Look!" I'd say, "all the nails in the ceiling have ice on them! Everything I touch seems to stick to my fingers. Do you think it will get colder than this? What will it be like then?" I'd shout for joy at the first heavy snowfall when Bob would get out the sleigh!

These things are not so fresh and exciting after almost twelve years in Canada, but we still do have our new experiences. This winter, for example, is the coldest we've had, and in fact it is said to be the coldest here since 1888, almost fifty years ago! For over six weeks there has been no let up, with temperatures of -10° to -60° constantly, with strong winds to fifty miles an hour. I don't know how we could have survived in our old house!

Two new forms of winter transportation have appeared this winter. One is the snowplane, which looks like a small airplane on ski runners with a motor and big propellor in back. It was originally developed for polar expeditions. Doctors are using this to visit outlying patients. But they are so noisy they scare our horses whenever they come by.

The other vehicle is a kind of covered sleigh. It's like an ice fishing hut on sleigh runners. It has a little woodstove and stovepipe sticking out of the top. I made a trip with a neighbour in one of these, and we never felt the cold. We even made a cup of tea on the woodstove. Farmers can use this to take their eggs to market without worrying about having them freeze on the way.

Our radio was fixed recently, and the first thing we heard on it was that George V, king of England, had died. The funeral was to be broadcast by radio all over the world. Bob said right away, "We'll want to listen to that! That is world history, and we'll stay up that night to hear it." So we sat together at the dining room table. Shivers of excitement ran up and down my spine! Here was a king being carried to his grave, and it was possible to follow it over land and sea, even on a Canadian farm isolated by winter snow. We heard the commands of the officers, the muffled steps of marching feet. In my mind I saw the new king follow with his brothers, bareheaded, arriving at Windsor Castle for the service. George V, by the grace of God, king of Great Britain, Ireland and the British dominions across the sea. . .

A few days later Bob was laid up with a severe case of influenza. After his flu was gone, Bob stayed listless and tired, and finally had to see the doctor. He came home with a worried look.

"The doctor says I have to go to bed right away and stay there for a month," he said. "He said I should really go to the hospital, but I told him I absolutely would not consider that."

"Is it only rest you need, or do you need some special treatment?" I asked uneasily.

"No, just complete rest," he said. "The doctor said I would never manage that if I stay home on the farm and see all the work that needs to be done. He thinks I'll start to worry, and that is just what I need to avoid. As far as I can make out it is not a matter of life and death, but something is wrong with my heart. It would be more serious if I were forty-six years old instead of thirty-six. He said that medicine will not help, and rest will likely cure it completely. But what will we do now?"

I felt just miserable. One thing after another. Where would it end?

But later I saw it from a different side. We were really lucky that Bob had gone now to see the doctor, so we can take preventive action right away. And it is a good thing he is not ten years older. I worried when I remembered that he had a complaint like this fourteen years ago, but it had not been too serious then. And he never had a recurrence. If rest could bring about a complete recovery, it was not as dark as I first thought.

We needed to act right away. We were lucky to find a strong and healthy young man about twenty years old, recommended to us as reliable and a good worker. We have always been very fortunate with our help. The worst part of it is that we give up our privacy. Hired help is taken in as a member of the farm household. They eat with you at the table, and sit in the living room with you in the evenings.

Our man Walter was quiet, got along well with our boys, and seemed quite capable of running the farm. "Don't you worry now," he told Bob. "With your other three hired men here, we'll do just fine!"

The faces of those other "three hired men" just shone with pride! Soon Bobby told his father, "We've divided the work, Daddy. We will be getting up at half past five, and Wim and I will do the milking while Walter feeds the horses, cows and chickens. After we go to school Walter will clean the barn and haul wood. In the afternoon Mamma can feed the cows and look after the chickens, and when we get home from school we'll do the evening chores."

"Yes, and if something goes a bit wrong once in a while, don't go running to Daddy right away," I said. "You run to me, and we'll see what we can do."

I had planned to set up Bob's sick room in the south bedroom upstairs, but he would not hear of it. He insisted that we put a bed in the front room, which also gets the sun from the south. "You could not have it better in a hospital," I said to him one morning when the sun streamed through the large windows. Everything was so bright.

The children now feel that we really need them, and they have risen to the need. Even six-year-old Dick, often passed by at the hand of his older brothers, has an important task. They have told him, "You go to the henhouse every hour and gather the eggs. And be sure to close the door behind you!"

Dick is so proud when he comes in the house with his little basket full of eggs that you'd think he laid them himself.

"Ho many already today, Mamma?" he asks.

"Fifty-two already, dear."

"Can I tell that to Daddy? That doesn't make him sick, does it?"

"No, you can tell him that. He'll be pleased."

But yesterday he came back to the house with his finger on his lips dragging a big hen inside with him. "This one was naughty," he said with a very serious face. "She was busy eating an egg! I shouldn't tell Daddy, should I? You better shave her beak now."

He looked at me in curious expectation, knowing my distaste for that kind of job. I hesitated for a minute. Should I take the hen to the front room and ask Bob to clip the beak? It really did need to be done, because there is no other way to break the hens of the nasty habit of pecking the eggs.

I cringed at the thought of actually doing it myself. But I had sternly told the boys not to bother their Daddy with all kinds of little things. So I gritted my teeth and did the job.

When the first drop of blood appeared, I said to Dick, "There you are. Now she will hurt herself if she pecks into an egg again."

The little man pressed the big bird closely to his heart and tiptoed to the living room door. "He never heard a thing," he whispered. "He's still reading his book."

✳

Medical Help in Winnipeg

April 1936

After Bob's enforced month of bed rest, he needed a doctor's examination again. The result was a disappointment for us. The doctor told Bob that he has a leaking heart valve in addition to his other heart problem. He said that it is nothing to be alarmed about, that people often grow to be quite old with this condition. "Just take it a bit easier," he told Bob. "Don't do any heavy lifting for a while. Take plenty of rest and don't worry. There is no reason you can't do a certain amount of work, but leave the heavy lifting for someone else."

That was certainly not the kind of news we had wanted to hear. Bob grumbled that the doctor should have told him about the leaking heart valve right away. Maybe we should get a second opinion.

That is not easy to do in a small place like Dauphin, so we decided that Bob should see a heart specialist in Winnipeg. Wim should see an eye specialist in Winnipeg, too, for his lazy eye, and there is no eye specialist in Dauphin at present.

By the time we left Dauphin for home we couldn't believe how much the snow had melted under the warm sun. Main Street had turned into a pool of mud. From the edge of town we saw that many of the fields were completely flooded. It was unbelievable that so much snow could melt in just one day!

Our only chance of making it was where the snow on the roads had been trampled solid all winter. We went along all right for a while, but then suddenly one of the horses fell through the softened snow nearly up to his belly. The sleigh tipped and nearly slid into the ditch. A glass crock with about a gallon of coal oil slid from the spot we thought safe and broke. At once our groceries, and we ourselves, were soaked in coal oil.

The following week Bob and Wim went to Winnipeg for their medical appointments. The report on Bob's heart is not as bad as it might be, though it basically confirms what our Dauphin doctor told us. Bob must take it easy for the rest of the summer, leaving the heaviest work to others. But the long term prospects are all right.

Little Wim walks around with a new pair of glasses, which he detests. But going to Winnipeg is the highlight of his life! Bob and Wim got back home at eight o'clock in the morning. "We didn't go to bed for the whole night, Mamma!" he said with eyes twinkling through the new glasses. "Did you ever stay up the whole night?"

"What did you like best in Winnipeg?" I asked him.

"Streetcars, escalators and elevators!" was his immediate answer.

"Taking care of Wim during the hours when I had to wait in the doctor's office was no problem," said Bob. "I would just take him to a large department store, and he'd amuse himself by riding up and down the elevators and escalators. The employees got to know him pretty soon and got a big kick out of his enthusiasm."

"And who do you think travelled with us in the train to Dauphin?" asked Bob. "Our friend Frank! He will be taking the place of the regular United Church minister, who is not well. Although Frank will be living in the manse of the church, he asks whether we will be willing to board one of the other student ministers for the summer, the one who will be summer minister in our district."

Bob and I had talked earlier about taking in a summer boarder, partly to bring in a bit of money because we'd need to hire a man to do the heavy work for Bob. I was in favour of doing it, but Bob was was not very keen on it. "If we only knew what kind of fellow we are getting, it might be all right," he said. "We aren't very regular churchgoers, and some student ministers can be pretty stuffy about that. I don't want to change my way of life for a boarder."

But I talked Bob into it. Based on the experience of the first few days, it will be all right. Our student is a quiet type who spends a lot of time studying and using his typewriter. Every day he makes his own bed and straightens out his room, so I consider myself lucky.

One day he asked me to do him the favour of saddling his horse Trisky, the small riding pony that belongs to the district for the use of the minister. He comes from Montreal and has never been in the west or in the country. Bobby is delighted to have Trisky at our farm again. One afternoon he was bold enough to ask the student minister if he could ride the horse for the afternoon. When he got the green light, Bobby jumped on the horse without saddle and quickly galloped out of the gate.

"That boy can sure ride!" said our guest. "I wonder if I'll be able to learn to ride properly." After watching Bobby disappear in the dust down the road, he went to his room and for the next few hours I could hear him exercising his typewriter.

New Neighbours Try Farming

May 1936

One mile east of us a single man moved onto a farm that had been abandoned by people who couldn't hang on through the hard times. The land is not very good there, and it belongs to a man in town who pays little attention to it. I'm sure he never made a cent from the farm.

Our new neighbour is a Russian immigrant by the name of Daniluk, who came in much like the pioneers must have come thirty years ago. He came from the west, where his land had totally dried out and consequently he lost all he had. He asked the owner of the farm if he could break up a bit of pasture land to plant a garden and maybe also grow some grain for chickens. In return he would fix up the old dilapidated buildings a bit and repair the fences which had broken down.

One morning when we were passing the place we saw Daniluk stumbling behind an old walking plow. "My goodness, that will take him ages," Bob said to me. "I still have a small plow at home which we use only once in a while. I'll offer it to him for a while."

Daniluk was very pleased, but he couldn't use the plow because it required two horses and he only had one. So Bob offered to let him use for a few days the horse the boys use to get to school. "It won't hurt them to walk to school for a few days. I'm sure they won't mind if it helps you out."

So Daniluk got his land plowed and was able to sow some grain and plant a garden. Nothing but weeds seemed to grow. Still, we saw him fixing up the buildings a bit late in the fall. Most of the summer he had slept in or under his old Ford car because the house really didn't have a roof. He managed to cook on an old range that stood outside under some scrub trees. But it rained so much he put together a sort of tent from an old canvas.

Shortly before the first heavy frost we saw Daniluk stuffing all his possessions into his old car. "I'm going west for the winter," he told us. "These buildings are too cold to spend the winter in. But if next year is drier here, I can make the house livable."

This spring Daniluk arrived on the scene again, this time with two horses. His land is looking a bit better, but it is a shame to spend so much time and effort on such poor land. He set up his tent inside the house this time, because the roof leaks badly.

We also have new neighbours on the other side of our farm, a quarter of a mile to the west. That farm had been worked by a farmer who did not live on the place, and the buildings became quite dilapidated. One day the owner was approached by an older farmer who had immigrated recently from Russia with a wife and about seven children. He had lost most of his possessions, except for a few cows and some chickens, and was looking for a place to live for the summer months.

The farmer hesitated because the district has only Anglo-Saxons except for us and a Norwegian family, who with us seem acceptable as west Europeans. Daniluk could be accepted because he was a bachelor without children. But here you have a family whose Russian children would attend our school.

The farmer asked our opinion, and we told him we couldn't care less. They seemed to be decent people. I guess we Dutch are generally a bit less prejudiced than the British can be. We saw that when we lived in Calcutta — the Dutch mixed with all kind of races but the British seemed to stay more to themselves.

In any case the Russian family moved in. Since then I have seen more of them that I had bargained for. Never in my life have I seen people borrow so much! It started the first day, which I took to be a result of the confusion of moving in. I lent them frying pans, pails, sugar, salt, and what not! Nothing was returned. Instead a messenger arrived each day at the most impossible times, suddenly standing in our kitchen, not saying a word. Bob would ask, "Well, what do you want today?"

"Nothing much," would be the reply.

Then more silence. I'm not much good at making small-talk conversation, but when I would, there was only more silence.

Then suddenly, when we nearly forgot he was there, he would ask to borrow something. I soon got enough of it. No longer did they just want groceries, but it was broody hens, a horse, and Bobby's bicycle.

It was Bobby who made the breakthrough. When they asked for his bike, I said that it belonged to Bobby and they would need to ask him for it. Bobby said, "I can't lend it to you because I still owe three dollars on it. The man who sold it to me told me not to lend it out until it was all paid for."

"How did you get the money for the bike?" the Russian boy wanted to know.

"I worked for it," Bobby said. That gave him an idea, so he added, "Why don't you work for the things you are always asking for?"

"How?" the boy asked.

"Well, there is the woodpile and here is the axe," said Bobby. Our visitor looked at the woodpile, and then back at Bobby. Then he left. We haven't seen much of him since.

Dark Days

July 1936

I very much hesitate to write this. I am a person who does not like to complain, least of all about myself. When we have gone through hard times I have always looked for the bright side. But now I can't see a bright side. Yet, if I am to continue to write about our lives in the future, I must tell you about this darkness.

The spring and summer so far have been just great. We again have George for our hired man, to do the heavy work that Bob cannot do this year. George is so pleasant and such a good worker we could not ask for more. Bob is looking healthier every day. Our student minister who is with us for the summer is quiet but friendly and often helps with one thing or another. We often see our great friend Frank, who turns up for an evening chat.

And I have been looking forward to something wonderful. My mother wrote to say that she would very much like to see me again, after twelve years, and she is giving me the gift of a trip to Holland and back, which she will pay for. Although I hesitated to leave all my work on the farm, Bob insisted that he could manage, especially with our neighbour girl Margaret helping out, which she does very well.

Imagine going home for a visit after twelve years! To visit the old places and see friends and family again is too wonderful to contemplate. I will sail from New York, after spending a week there with my younger brother and his American wife Charlotte. I only know her from letters and the Christmas phone calls. The more I thought about it, the more excited I became!

"You need a good rest, too," said Bob. He had been telling me that I haven't looked very well lately. He wanted me to see a doctor, but I refused.

The turning point came when we had a visit from Isobel, Frank's fiancee. She is a nurse, and when she saw how tired I looked, she got on the phone with our doctor. The doctor said I was to stay in bed for a whole week, and if I didn't feel better, to see him at once.

A week later Isobel was still concerned. The result was that I went to see the doctor. The doctor was not very encouraging. He told me to come to the hospital the next day for minor surgery.

A few days after the surgery the doctor said, "Tomorrow you can leave the hospital, but I have to tell you something. From the surgery we discovered something for which you will probably need to be treated in Winnipeg. I have taken a tissue sample and sent it to Winnipeg for analysis. We will have the results in a few days."

The joy of coming home from the hospital was spoiled. Everybody was so awfully nice to me. I didn't mind being pampered, but deep inside I had a very uneasy feeling.

One afternoon when I was alone at home the phone rang. When I answered it I recognized the voice of our doctor. "Is your husband home?" he asked. "I would like to speak with him right away."

"Did the report come in from Winnipeg?" I asked him.

"Yes, it came this afternoon. Please send your husband to see me as soon as you can. And keep your chin up!"

When I put the receiver back on the hook there was only one thought in my head — thank the Lord that I was alone! This I have to fight out all by myself. I have to get used to the idea that I have a serious illness. Oh, why did this have to happen to us now! Bob is not supposed to worry, on account of his heart. And suddenly I realized — this is even worse for him than for me! You are always much more worried about somebody who is near to you than you are about yourself!

What happened afterwards is confused in my mind. "Do not lose any time," the doctor told Bob. "Take her to Winnipeg tomorrow if you can manage. There is evidence of cancer that needs to be treated right away. I will phone the specialist so that she can be helped the first possible moment."

We left bright and early the next morning. It was terribly hard for me to leave.

The doctors decided not to operate but to give me a good dose of radium, and after that daily treatments of deep x-rays. The doctors were friendly and encouraging, and gradually I was able to relax and come to terms with my condition. But still in the background was the awful question — will I ever be safe again? It can come back!

I had to stay in Winnipeg for a whole month for the treatments. I was very fortunate that I could stay at the home of Isobel's parents, whom we had come to know and love from an earlier visit.

One afternoon Bob came in with an opened letter in his hand. "Guess what!" he said. "A surprise for you. You will get a visitor from New York. Your brother Dirk is coming to Winnipeg!"

How wonderful! He is coming already tomorrow! My brother is coming all the way from New York just to see me, coming by airplane!

Everything seems unreal to me! Was this really me, who had spent some time in hospitals twice very recently? I feel so much better now, but still in the background is that uneasiness. I have the feeling that something has been blunted inside me. There have been too many emotions lately!

It will be wonderful to see Dirk again, but somehow I don't seem to be as excited as I would have been a few months ago. And when this is all over, I will go to Holland. Bob sometimes sees me staring off into space. What am I feeling, and why do my feelings seem dulled? Will that ever change?

Letters from home come from the boys, who say that all is going well. They ask me when I'll be coming home. I'm not even worried about the boys, as I'm sure I would otherwise be. Is this acceptance or stupor? Where do I have to look now for the bright spots? Sometimes I think this is not fair. Why do we have to suffer all this misery? But even that feeling is not as strong as I would have felt earlier. Maybe one of the bright spots is that misery and worry do not register too much any more.

From the Prairies to Holland

August 1936

What a joy to be home on the farm again, to be welcomed by my husband and my sons with open arms! There is so much to see and get caught up on. The grain is ripe already, and we have quite a good crop. How lucky we are to live in such a good farm district — we've never had a total crop failure, even when we had no rain for a whole summer.

Very quickly I was back into the hustle and bustle of harvest time. Our own fields are bare already, since we were one of the first to be threshed. Our neighbours, the Nicholsons, are harvesting now, and I can see the hayracks loaded with sheaves going back and forth.

"You better take it a bit easy at first," the doctor in Winnipeg told me. "You are young and strong and our medical knowledge has increased a lot in the past ten years. We have had some good results with the radiation treatment we gave you, and we should see you for a checkup every three months. Don't worry. Time will eventually give you back your self-confidence."

How is it possible not to worry? I wrote to Holland to say that maybe it would be better to postpone my trip, but the answer came back immediately. My mother had contacted a doctor, a relative, who said it would be good for me to come right away.

"You don't look sick at all anymore," Bobby said to me one night. "Are you all right now?"

If only I could become convinced that all was really right! Sudden anxiety gripped me again. If I could really feel that, yes, it is all over and done with, that there are still many more beautiful years to come! Those same years ahead could be long and lonesome if one of us were suddenly taken away.

Sometimes in a sleepless night thoughts will pop into my head and I will think, "We have had our worries and disappointments all right. There is much I would like to have done differently. But I have already had a full life. If it has to end now, I still have had a lot more to life than many people have. And there is very likely a reason for everything, even if we ourselves do not fathom the reasons. Maybe we have to learn to trust that whatever happens to us is the best in the end. If only we can truly believe that if the dark days do come."

But things look brighter in the morning sun. Margaret and I bring the afternoon lunch to the threshers in the field. I've known most of the young men from earlier years when they have been on our threshing gangs. We are on easy and friendly terms, less stiff and formal than people often are in Holland. Jokes fly back and forth, but there is some awkwardness and reserve because they know that I have been seriously sick.

But then a latecomer arrives with his loaded rack, and waving his big hat he jumps from his load and stretches out his hand to me. "My, you are looking fine and dandy again, Mrs. Aberson!" he says. Suddenly the ice is broken and questions pop from all sides. "Are you going to Holland all by yourself? You must have a really good husband to let you go alone. When will you leave?"

Only ten days from now! I fly from Winnipeg to New York and stay with Dirk and his wife for a week. Then I take a boat to the Dutch coast. I will be gone for nearly six months!

Those last ten days went very fast. There was so much I had to do for my family before I could leave. There were goodbye calls to make, and visitors to receive. One afternoon I had a visit from twelve farm wives with whom I had taken a knitting course last winter. They gave me a present of a nice fountain pen and pencil set. I was deeply moved by the kindness and generosity of these women who, in the busiest time of the year, wanted to pay me a farewell visit and spend their meagre savings on me.

On August 30 Bob and our three boys took me by car to the Winnipeg airport, about 200 miles from home. I am close to tears as I think about our last moments together. As the older boys were each holding one of my arms, and little Dick was clinging to my knee I thought, "How can I ever do this, leave them for months on end with thousands of miles between us!" But there was no turning back. At last I had to pull little Dick away from my leg, to which he had clung with all his might. The last thing I saw before I left was three little faces, stained by tears but smiling bravely.

What will it be like to return to the land where I had spent my youth? Will I feel like a stranger after being gone for twelve years? How will my life — so different from life in Holland for these twelve years — have marked me? Words like "struggle for survival" are not just empty words for me. I am anxious, and I know there will be strangeness at first, but I also know that I will be received from the Canadian prairies with love.